KING STEPHEN
1135–1154

King Stephen
1135–1154

R. H. C. Davis

Longman
London and New York

Longman Group UK Limited,
Longman House, Burnt Mill, Harlow,
Essex CM20 2JE, England
and Associated Companies throughout the world.

*Published in the United States of America
by Longman Inc., New York*

First published 1967
Second (paperback) Edition 1977
Third Edition (reset) 1990
Third impression 1993

British Library Cataloguing in Publication Data
Davis, R. H. C. (Ralph Henry Carless),*1918–*
King Stephen, 1135–1154.—3rd ed.
  1. England. Stephen King of England
  I. Title
942.02′4′0924

ISBN 0-582-04000-0

Library of Congress Cataloging in Publication Data
Davis, R. H. C. (Ralph Henry Carless), 1918–
  King Stephen, 1135 – 1154/R. H. C. Davis.—3rd ed.
    p. cm.
  Includes index.
  ISBN 0-582-04000-0
  1. Stephen, King of England, 1097?–1154. 2. Great Britain—
–History—Stephen, 1135–1154. 3. Great Britain—Kings and rulers—
–Biography. I. Title.
  DA198.5,D3 1990
  942.02′4′ 092—dc 20
  [B]   89-32140
                                                                CIP

Set in Linotron 202 10/12 pt Bembo
Printed in Malaysia by TCP

Contents

DA
1985
.D3
1990
✗

List of Maps and Tables

Preface to the First Edition

J. H. Round's *Geoffrey de Mandeville* has long been recognized as the classic study of Stephen's reign, and it may seem audacious to challenge it. But in the seventy-five years which have passed since it was published, our knowledge of the period has increased considerably. We now have the final portion of the *Gesta Stephani* (from 1148 to 1154), and the texts of many charters which have since been discovered. As a result the chronology of the reign has had to be revised, and some events arranged in a new order. At times this *Life* of Stephen offers not only a new interpretation, but also a new story.

I first began to work on Stephen some twelve years ago, when Professor H. A. Cronne asked me to be his co-editor for the third volume of the *Regesta Regum Anglo-Normannorum*. That volume is now in the press and contains full texts of all the known charters of King Stephen, the Empress Matilda, and Dukes Geoffrey and Henry of Normandy, as well as a detailed discussion of the light which they throw on the government of the country. Since the *Life* and the *Regesta* are complementary to each other, I have inevitably benefited in the one from the work of my collaborator in the other. Professor Cronne has been a most unselfish colleague and friend, and I am extremely grateful to him for all his help and constructive criticism. I also wish to thank Professors M. D. Knowles, R. W. Southern, and C. Warren Hollister, who have all read this book in typescript or proof and made many valuable suggestions; and also my wife who has read it more times than I care to remember. A further debt is to my father. Though he died in 1928, he had already done much preparatory work for the third volume of the *Regesta*, and I have constantly been working through the material which he first collected, and on which he first commented. I therefore dedicate the book to his memory.

R. H. C. DAVIS
Merton College, Oxford

26 November 1966

Preface to the Third Edition

In this edition I have corrected some errors (particularly with a postscript to ch. vi), expanded the central portion of chapter viii, enlarged Appendix I and added five additional Appendices in place of the bibliographical postscript to the edition of 1977. The fifth of these Appendices (VIII) consists of additions and corrections to Regesta vols iii and iv. I have also taken the opportunity to update the footnotes so that they refer to the most recent editions and translations of the narrative sources.

R. H. C. D.

Acknowledgements

We are grateful to the following for permission to reproduce copyright material:

Burns and Oates Ltd for extracts from *The Letters of St Bernard* trans. by Bruno Scott James; J. M. Dent & Sons Ltd and E. P. Dutton & Co. Inc. for an extract from *Anglo-Saxon Chronicle* trans. by G. N. Garmonsway (Everyman's Library 953), and Thomas Nelson & Sons Ltd for extracts from *The Historia Pontificalis of John of Salisbury* by Marjorie Chibnall and *Historia Novella* and *Gesta Stephani* by K. R. Potter (Nelson's Medieval Texts).

Abbreviations

B.I.H.R.	*Bulletin of the Institute of Historical Research*
Book of Seals	*Sir Christopher Hatton's Book of Seals*, ed. Lewis C. Loyd and Doris Mary Stenton (Oxford, 1950)
C.D.F.	*Calendar of Documents preserved in France*, ed. J. H. Round (London, 1899)
Chronicles	*Chronicles of the Reigns of Stephen, Henry and Richard I*, ed. Richard Howlett, 4 vols (Rolls Series, London, 1884–9)
D.B.	Domesday Book
E.H.R.	*English Historical Review*
E.Y.C.	*Early Yorkshire Charters*, vols 1–3, ed. William Farrer, and vols 4–11 ed. C. T. Clay (Yorkshire Archaeological Soc., 1914–63)
G. de M.	J. H. Round, *Geoffrey de Mandeville* (London, 1892)
G.S.	*Gesta Stephani*, ed. and trans. K. R. Potter, revised by R. H. C. Davis (Oxford Medieval Texts, 1976)
Hist. Nov.	*The Historia Novella by William of Malmesbury*, ed. and trans. K. R. Potter (Nelson's Medieval Texts, London, 1955)
Monast.	*Monasticon Anglicanum*, ed. W. Dugdale; new and enlarged ed. by J. Caley, H. Ellis and B. Bandinel, 6 vols in 8 (London, 1817–30)
Newburgh	*William of Newburgh, The History of English Affairs, Book I*, ed. and trans. P. G. Walsh and M. J. Kennedy (Warminster, 1988)
OV	*The Ecclesiastical History of Orderic Vitalis*, ed. and trans. Marjorie Chibnall, 6 vols (Oxford Medieval Texts, 1969–80)

CHAPTER ONE
Parentage and Early Life, c. 1096–1135

We do not know the date of Stephen's birth—probably it was about 1096[1]—but we know quite a lot about his parents. His mother, Adela, was the daughter of William the Conqueror, and by all accounts a very remarkable woman. She was genuinely religious being, amongst other things, a friend of St Anselm at whose bidding she eventually became a nun, and yet, as William of Malmesbury put it, she had been a *virago* in secular life.[2] Baudri de Bourgueil, one of her literary protégés, said that if only she could have borne arms, which convention and the delicacy of her limbs forbade, she would have equalled her father in valour.[3] He wrote a long poem describing the tapestries in her bedroom. The less interesting ones depicted scenes of antiquity from Noah to Solomon, and from the age of King Saturn to the foundation of Rome, but the *pièce de résistance* which hung round the bed itself was a magnificent tapestry of the Conquest of England. It would have been the last thing she saw at night and the first thing in the morning, and would have served to remind her of the fact, which neither she nor anyone else was likely to forget, that she was the Conqueror's daughter.

Her husband was Stephen Count of Blois and Chartres. He was not Norman but French, his uncle being Count of Champagne. He had presumably been chosen as husband for Adela—they were married at Chartres in about 1081—because he was a useful ally for the Normans

---

1 Stephen's parents are thought to have married *c.* 1081. They had eight children (five sons and three daughters), of whom Stephen was the third surviving son. His father was away on crusade from September 1096 till (probably) late in 1098, and went away on crusade again in 1101, never to return. Taking these facts together with note 15 below, it would seem that the most likely date for Stephen's birth is *c.* 1096.

2 *Gesta Regum* (R.S.) ii. 333.

3 *Les Œuvres Poétiques de Baudri de Bourgueil*, ed. Phyllis Abrahams (Paris, 1926), *Carmen* xcvi, esp. lines 33–6.

against the French king, but the great opportunity to prove his worth came with the First Crusade.

He set out in September 1096 with Adela's brother, Robert Duke of Normandy and Eustace Count of Boulogne. They wintered in Southern Italy and arrived at Constantinople in mid-May, just in time to take part in the successful siege of Nicaea, after the capture of which Stephen reported progress to his wife in an ecstatic letter:

> . . . I came by God's grace to the city of Constantinople with great joy. The emperor received me worthily and most courteously, and even lovingly as though I were his son. He gave me the most magnificent and precious gifts, and in the whole of our Army of God there is not a duke or count or any other potentate whom he trusts and favours more than me. Indeed, my beloved, his Imperial Majesty has often suggested, and still does suggest, that we should commend one of our sons to him; he promises to bestow on him a fief so large and excellent that he will have no cause to envy ours. Indeed,I tell you that in these days there is not another such as he alive under the sky. He showers riches on all our leaders, relieves all our knights with gifts and refreshes all our poor with feasts. . . . Your father, my beloved, gave many and great gifts, but he was almost as nothing to this man.[4]

Everything was perfect; even the Bosphorus, alleged by some to be fierce and treacherous, was really 'safer than the Marne or the Seine'. The Turks had surrendered Nicaea, an enormous city with more than 300 towers to its walls, and the casualties suffered by the crusaders were (so he says) quite trifling. 'I tell you, beloved, that from this Nicaea we will get to Jerusalem in five weeks, unless Antioch holds us up. Farewell!'

It turned out to be four months before the crusaders reached Antioch, and it held them up for another eight. When they had been there twenty-three weeks, Stephen wrote again to his wife acknowledging a letter in which she must have asked if he needed any more money.[5]

> Know for certain, my beloved, that I now have twice as much gold and silver and other riches as you gave me, love, when I left you. For all our leaders, by the common counsel of the whole army, have appointed me, though I did not want it, to be their lord and commander-in-chief.

At this juncture it must have seemed as if Adela could have begun to design another tapestry for her bedchamber. Her husband told her the

---

4 H. Hagenmeyer, ed., *Die Kreuzzugsbriefe aus der Jahren 1088–1100* (Innsbruck, 1901), 138–40. Cf. Mary Anne Everett Green in her account of Adela in *Lives of the Princesses of England* (London, 1849), i. 49–50.
5 Hagenmeyer, *op. cit.* 149 ff.

story of the campaign cheerfully and in some detail, ending with the following note:

> But while my chaplain Alexander was writing this letter in all haste on Easter Monday (29 March, 1098), part of our army ambushed some Turks and by divine dispensation defeated them in battle. They killed sixty of them and brought all their heads back to the camp. These are but few out of many things which I am writing to you, dearest, and because I cannot fully express what is in my mind, dearest, I bid you keep well, govern your land excellently, and deal with your sons and your men honourably, as becomes you, for you will certainly see me home as quick as I possibly can. Farewell.

On 3 June the crusaders took the city (but not the citadel) of Antioch, only to be besieged in it themselves until they made their successful sortie and defeated the army of Karbogha decisively on 28 June. It was the turning point of the whole crusade, but Stephen was not there. He had fled.

The most picturesque story was that he and two companions had escaped from the city during the siege by letting themselves down from the walls on ropes, for which reason they were dubbed *funambuli* or 'rope-trick-men'.[6] Those who had best reason to know, however, gave more credence to the account given in the *Gesta Francorum* whose anonymous author was actually in the city:

> The imprudent Stephen Count of Chartres, whom all our magnates had elected commander-in-chief, pretended that he had some illness and shamefully retreated, before Antioch was taken, to another fortified town called Alexandretta. When we were besieged in the city, we awaited him daily, expecting that he would come to help us. But he, after he had heard that the army of the Turks had surrounded and was besieging us, secretly climbed up a nearby mountain in the vicinity of Antioch, saw the innumerable tents [of the Turks], was seized with mighty fear, and turned round and fled with his army. On reaching his own camp [Alexandretta], he pillaged it and turned full speed for home.[7]

When he got back to his wife at Chartres he was the laughing-stock of all Christendom. She used all her arts to revive his courage, and in 1101 sent him back with William Count of Poitiers. In the following year, having successfully completed his pilgrimage to Jerusalem, he was killed in the battle of Ramlah.[8] But what people remembered about

---

6 Anna Comnena, *Alexiad*, Bk xi, ch. vi (trans. B. Leib (Paris, 1945), iii. 27). For *funambuli*, see *OV* vi. 18.

7 Ed. Rosalind Hill, *Gesta Francorum* (Nelson's Medieval Texts, 1962), 63.

8 *Fulcheri Carnotensis Historia Hierosolymitana* (1095–1127), ed. Hagenmeyer (Heidelberg, 1913), 443, trans. Rita Ryan and Harold S. Fink (Knoxville, 1968), 169.

him was the episode at Antioch. As Fulcher of Chartres put it: 'There's no use in making a good beginning, unless you go through to the end.'[9]

While her husband was on crusade, Adela had acted as regent. When he died she continued to rule in her own name. She had borne him eight children, five sons (of whom one died young) and three daughters. The girls had to be found husbands, which does not seem to have been difficult, and the boys had to be launched on suitable careers, an exercise which required tact, determination and foresight. The first essential was to see that the right son succeeded his father as count. Normally it would have been the eldest son, William, but he was evidently considered a disappointment. It is hard to be sure whether the trouble was that he was a simpleton, or a hunchback, or in disgrace with the Church; the one thing we know for certain is that in 1103 he went into Chartres Cathedral and took a solemn oath to kill the bishop.[10] Adela married him off to the daughter of a minor baron from the Loire, and gave the paternal inheritance to her second son, Theobald. It was a delicate operation, but she carried it through with quiet efficiency. Theobald was invested with the county in 1107, and in the course of the twelve following years Adela faded out of politics gradually. Theobald made his name and in 1125 succeeded to his uncle's county of Champagne as well. He was a success.

As for the remaining sons, Stephen and Henry, they had to be put in the way of making their own fortunes. The obvious place for them to do this was in the court of their uncle King Henry. Stephen was sent there at any rate by 1113, but his younger brother, Henry of Blois, did not follow till 1126, for Adela had no intention of letting the interests of her sons conflict. While Stephen was to be a layman and warrior, Henry was to be a monk and bishop. He received his training at Cluny, the nursery of cardinals and popes, where he made a name for himself as an outstanding man of monastic affairs. In 1126 his royal uncle gave him the abbey of Glastonbury, and three years later the bishopric of Winchester as well, and as he held them in plurality he must have been the wealthiest churchman in England. This fact, together with his noble birth and Cluniac connection put him in a position of influence at both the royal and the papal court, and made him the ideal brother for a man who wanted to be a king. Adela's dispositions for her sons were thus complete. Having done her duty as a countess and a mother, she

---

9 *Ibid.* 228, 'Non prodest alicui bonum initium nisi fuerit bene consummatum.'
10 Ivo of Chartres, letter 134, in *M.P.L.* 162, col. 144. The incident was in 1103, ct. H. d'Arbois de Jubainville, *Histoire des Ducs et des Comtes de Champagne* (Paris, 1859ff.), ii. 170.

retired from the world and became a nun at the Cluniac priory of Marcigny-sur-Loire. [11]

What sort of man was Henry I, the brother to whom Adela had entrusted the fortunes of her younger sons?[12] He is rightly celebrated as a king who took an interest in the details of government and liked to make it efficient. But though the administrative and constitutional changes which he made are important, they did not impress contemporaries so much as his ruthlessness. He was the third son of William the Conqueror. To the eldest, Robert, the Conqueror left Normandy; to the next, William Rufus, he left England; and to Henry he left nothing but 5000 silver pounds. As it happened, that was enough. Henry was present when William Rufus was killed in a hunting accident—if it was an accident—in the New Forest, and without waiting for the funeral rode off to Winchester to secure the royal treasury, and to London to get himself acclaimed and crowned king (1100). Then he fought his eldest brother, Robert, in order to win Normandy, eventually defeated him at the battle of Tinchebrai (1106), and imprisoned him for life. The only mistake he made was to let Robert's son, William Clito, go free, and that was an unusual mistake for Henry who, though an undoubted 'lion of justice', had a reputation for brutality. Orderic alleges that on one occasion when he had condemned three rebels to have their eyes put out, the Count of Flanders, who was present, protested, saying that it was wrong to mutilate knights who had been captured fighting in battle for their lord; but that the king overrode him, saying:

> Sir Count, I do what is right and I will prove it to you by manifest reason. It was with the consent of their lords that Geoffrey and Odard were my lawful men. They have committed perjury of their own free will in breaking their oath of fealty to me, and therefore they have incurred the penalty of death or mutilation . . . . As for Luke, he never did me homage, but he was in arms against me, . . . and what is more, the facetious joker wrote scurrilous songs about me, and sang them in public to insult me, thus often making me the laughing-stock of my enemies. Now God has handed him over to me to be punished, in order that he may be forced to renounce his nefarious ways, and so that others who

11 For Marcigny, a double-monastery for men and women, see Jean Richard, *Le Cartulaire de Marcigny-sur-Loire (1045–1144)* (Dijon, 1957). The date of Adela's withdrawal to Marcigny is fully discussed by d'Arbois de Jubainville, *op. cit.* ii. 254 n.; it cannot have been earlier than 1122. She died on 8 March 1138 (not 1137) and was buried in the Abbaye aux Dames at Caen, Norman to the last.

12 The essential reading on Henry I is R. W. Southern, 'The place of Henry I in English History', *Proc. Brit. Acad.* 48(1962), 127–67, reprinted in modified form in his *Medieval Humanism* (Oxford, 1970), 206–33.

hear of the punishment of his rash boldness may be suitably chastened.[13]

In spite of Henry's sternness, he was faced with many rebellions and internal wars because the first twenty-eight years of his reign were occupied, first in disinheriting his elder brother Robert by the seizure of Normandy, and secondly in ensuring that Robert's son, William Clito, did not recover it. In order to do this he had to penalize those barons who had been most loyal to Robert, and though he could not mutilate them as he mutilated traitors, he could and did condemn them to forfeit their lands. As a result he created a whole class of 'disinherited' who had every inducement to join William Clito in his attempts to reconquer the duchy.[14] Henry's barons on the other hand, nervously aware that the day would come when the king must die, were sometimes tempted to make overtures to the Clito, because he was still in the line of succession and might well, with the French king's help, be Henry's successor.

That was why the loss of Henry's only legitimate son in the wreck of the White Ship (December 1120) was such a terrible disaster, for it meant that the Clito became his heir presumptive. Henry hurriedly found himself a new wife, and when she failed to produce him an heir, brought back his daughter Matilda from Germany—her husband the emperor had just died—and at Christmas 1126 forced all the notables of his kingdom to swear allegiance to her as his heir; though she was a woman, she was the only alternative to the Clito. The king of France, however, continued to assist the Clito, gave him his queen's half-sister in marriage—in reply to which Henry betrothed Matilda to the Count of Anjou—and in 1127 made him Count of Flanders. In doing this he not only recognized the Clito as the lawful heir of the Conqueror's wife Matilda, but also provided him with the ports from which an invasion of England could be launched. There could be no peace for Henry while the Clito was alive, and his relief must have been great when, on 27 July 1128, he was killed by a chance blow at the siege of Alost. His death removed the last rival to his own inheritance and made him personally secure, though, as we shall presently see, it did nothing to solve the problem of the Clito's supporters who, having been disinherited in his cause, were still prepared to assist in any war which might enable them to recover their former lands.

In spite of these family feuds and internecine wars, the Countess Adela had shown her usual sense and foresight in deciding that Henry's

13 *OV* vi. 352–4.
14 See Appendix IV below.

court was the place for Stephen. We do not know at what date she sent him there. An ambiguous sentence of Orderic's has made some historians think that it was before 1106, which would have been bold indeed, but all the indications are that it was six or seven years later.[15] We can at any rate be sure that he was there by 1113, and that he had by then already been given the lands and title of the Count of Mortain who had been captured at the battle of Tinchebrai.[16] In 1113 he apparently received the forfeited lands of another of Duke Robert's supporters; this time the honour of Eye in Suffolk, which had previously belonged to Robert Malet.[17] Five years later he received important lands on the southern frontier of Normandy which had been forfeited from William Talvas the son of Robert of Belesme;[18] they included the towns of Séez and Alençon, which were naturally hostile to the Normans, and Stephen, still only a youth, promptly lost them to their former owner who had allied with the count of Anjou.[19] Another rich fief which he received from the king was the Honour of Lancaster, or forfeited lands of Roger of Poitou; Stephen's tenure of it was marked by the foundation of Furness Abbey (1126) with monks from the Abbey of Savigny in his Norman county of Mortain.[20] Finally, in 1125, Henry I gave him the hand of Matilda, the only daughter and heiress of Eustace III Count of Boulogne, who, quite apart from his continental possessions, was one of the richest landowners in England.[21]

Some idea of the final extent of Stephen's land can be got from the Pipe Roll of 1130 which records the exemptions from danegeld allowed to tenants-in-chief.[22] Stephen's are set out in the table printed overleaf.

As the danegeld was levied at the rate of two shillings a hide in 1130, and as the exemptions were only for the *demesne* lands of

15 *OV* vi. 42: 'Porro Stephanus, Stephani Blesensis tertia proles, ab avunculo rege arma militiae accepit, et, capto apud Tenerchebraicum Guillelmo comite Moritolii, comitatum ejus dono regis obtinuit.' The implication that Stephen fought at the battle and captured the count himself is probably accidental, for in his account of the battle *OV* says it was the Bretons who captured him: 'Britones autem Guillelmum comitem ceperunt, quibus rex et amici ejux vix abstulerant' (vi. 90). In 1118 Orderic describes Stephen as a young man (*juvenis*) and adolescent (*adolescens*) (*OV* vi. 196, and 204–6) which could hardly have been possible if Stephen had been knighted by 1106.

16 *OV* vi. 174.

17 *Reg.* ii. 932 n.

18 These lands were given in the first place to Stephen's elder brother, Theobald, but Henry allowed him to give them to Stephen, in exchange for his portion of his father's inheritance *OV* vi. 196.

19 *OV* vi. 202–6.

20 *Book of Seals*, no. 423.

21 The English Honour of Boulogne was centred on Colchester and London.

22 *The Pipe Roll of 31 Henry I*, ed. Joseph Hunter (London, 1833, reprinted 1921).

7

Page	County	£	s.	d.	Remarks
4, 6	Oxon			6	
9	Notts and Derby	5	2	8	
11, 16	Dorset	1	3		
41	Hants	2	11	8	*auxilium* civitatis (Winchester)
46	Cambs	5	3	9	
46	Hunts	1	12	6	
50, 51	Surrey	7	17		
52	Southwark		11		
57	Essex	22	16	4	
62	Herts	7	15	1	
66	Kent	1	11		
84	Northants		13	6	
87	Leics	3	10		
95	Norfolk	9	10	3	but £9 18s. 10d. last year (p. 93)
99	Suffolk	45	19	9	but £48 4s. 6d. last year (p. 98)
101	Bucks	2	2	7	
103	Beds	3	18	6	
104	Bedford town		1		
114	Lincs	9	7	9	
135	Rutland		10		
138	Colchester		16	6	but £1 2s. 6d. last year
150	London		5		
151, 152	Middlesex		13	4	
	Total	£133	18	2	

Table 1. Stephen's Danegeld Exemptions in 1130

tenants–in–chief, it follows that Stephen must have had 1,339 hides in demesne. A hide was more like a rateable value than a fixed area, but if we attribute to it the conventional figure of 120 acres, we would have an approximate figure of 160,680 acres for Stephen's demesne land. If we were to add in the land which he had sub–infeudated to his men, we could probably treble the figure, getting a round number of about half a million acres in England. In addition to this there were his lands in Normandy and the County of Boulogne. It is impossible to give a comparable figure for these, but it is known that the County of Mortain was subsequently reckoned at 29½ knights' fees and that Henry II put its value at £1000 a year.[23]

23 T. Stapleton, *Magni Rotuli Scaccarii Normanniae* (2 vols, London, 1840–4, i. p. lxiii; R. W. Eyton, *Itinerary of King Henry II* (London, 1878), 102).

It may be thought surprising that Henry I should have bestowed such enormous lands on any of his nobles, for he was renowned for the way in which he raised 'new' men from the dust, surrounding them with wealth and exalting them above distinguished lords of castles. But the point about Henry's 'new' men was not that they should necessarily be low-born (which he probably found unpleasant), but that their fortune should depend entirely on him. The 'new' men were created in order to resist the disinherited supporters of Duke Robert and the Clito, and Henry ensured that they had no option in the matter by giving them the very lands which the disinherited were so anxious to recover. Stephen received, as we have already seen, the forfeited fiefs of William Count of Mortain, Robert Malet and Roger of Poitou, and it was therefore impossible for him to make peace with them or their heirs without divesting himself of his honours. That was why it was safe for Henry to exalt him still further by putting him forward for the hand of Matilda of Boulogne (1125). She had to be found a husband because her father wanted to retire to a Cluniac monastery; but any husband proposed had to be of very noble birth, because the lady was descended from Charlemagne, and her uncles, Godfrey and Baldwin, were the first crusader kings of Jerusalem. That was why Henry chose Stephen. His birth was unexceptionable, and yet he was bound to Henry's interests as closely as if he had been his creature.

Boulogne, quite apart from the English lands of its count, was a county of great strategic and economic importance. In the twelfth century it was relatively more important than it is now, because the rival ports of Calais, Dunkirk and Ostend had not yet come into existence, being little more than sandbanks in the great Gulf of Itius which stretched northwards from Cap Gris-Nez and extended inland almost as far as Saint-Omer.[24] Consequently it was the ships of Boulogne which tended to dominate the channel, and the count's port of Wissant seems to have handled most of the cross-channel traffic.[25] This put him in a very advantageous position, for it meant that a large part of the English wool trade passed through his county on its way to the cloth towns of Flanders. There an unwise or unfriendly count could have levied exorbitant tolls, while a prudent and sympathetic count would act as an honest middleman, promoting the interests of both the

24 See, for example, the map in F. L. Ganshof, *La Belgique Carolingienne* (Bruxelles, 1958).

25 For the fleet of Boulogne, see *OV* ii. 204–6 and vi. 520, where he describes its attacks on Dover in 1067 and 1138; cf. P. Héliot, *Histoire de Boulogne et du Boulonnais* (Lille, 1937), 73: For Wissant, see Héliot, *op. cit.* 94 and clause 17 in William Clito's charter to Saint-Omer in 1127 (A. Giry, *Histoire de Saint-Omer* (Paris, 1877) 373).

English in Flanders and the Flemings in England. This was the part for which Henry I intended Stephen, as subsequent events were to show.

On 2 March 1127 Charles the Good, Count of Flanders, was murdered in the church of St Donatian at Bruges. As he had no children or designated heir, there was a disputed succession and the county was in an uproar. Eventually King Louis VI of France appeared with an army and exercised his feudal right of naming a successor. As we have already seen, he chose William Clito, and Henry I of England found it a matter of life and death to thwart him. He mobilized Stephen, and Stephen dutifully made war on the Clito, but he seems to have had the worst of it, for the Clito (whose military strength was truly formidable) devastated his territory and forced him to make a three-years' truce.[26] In the event, however, this reverse was not disastrous to Henry, for his strongest card was in the Flemish towns which, since they were dependent on English wool for their livelihood, could be threatened or bribed into rebellion against the Clito. The towns soon proved that they were the key to the whole country, since it was only their wealth that made Flanders worth anyone's having. In the end it was they who decided that their count should be neither the Clito who was unacceptable to the English, nor Henry I who was unacceptable to the French, but Thierry of Alsace who, having kept clear of the feudal quarrels of France and Normandy, was more or less acceptable to all.

The point is of some importance because it seems to have provided Stephen with a useful lesson in the realities of economic power. As an aristocrat, wealthy landowner and courtier he might easily, in any other place than Boulogne, have spent his life in ignorance of the social and economic revolution which had been effected in the towns of Flanders. They formed a society which was based, not on nobility of birth and land, but on industry, commerce and money. They had established a new economy based on the wool and cloth trades, which extended from England to Italy and from Spain to Scandinavia. They were conscious of their power, and after the murder of Count Charles the Good they had shut their gates, and refused to open them for any claimant count except on their own terms. The burghers of Bruges, for example, admitted the Clito only on condition that he gave them a formal charter exempting them from toll and land-tax.[27] When he broke the terms of the charter, they revolted and elected Thierry as

---

26 *OV* vi. 370–2.
27 *The Murder of Charles the Good by Galbert of Bruges*, trans. J. B. Ross ('Records of Civilization' series, Columbia, 1960), 203; cf. Giry, *op. cit.* 47–9.

Count; and though worsted in battle they emerged victorious, because the Clito was killed as if by the judgment of God. The fact seems to have impressed Stephen deeply, for when, seven years later, he won the English throne, he allowed the Londoners to claim that they had 'elected' him, just as the burghers of Ghent, Bruges, Lille or Saint-Omer had 'elected' their count. We do not know what privileges he gave them in return, but they were probably considerable, because the Londoners supported him through thick and thin, and rescued him from disaster when his cause seemed lost. It can hardly have been a coincidence that the man who won such ardent support from the traders of London was also the man who controlled the shortest route to the cloth towns of Flanders. When the burghers of Saint-Omer had admitted the Clito in 1127 they had made him promise that if ever he made peace with Stephen Count of Boulogne he would see that they were exempt from toll and *sewerp* at Wissant.[28] A similar privilege would presumably have been acceptable to the Londoners, and might well have been sufficient to make them his most devoted subjects. But whatever it was he gave them, he had learnt from living in Flanders that townsmen were not to be despised. Whatever else they lacked, they had money in abundance; and money gave them the power even to be kingmakers.

28 Giry, *op. cit.* 373, para. 17.

CHAPTER TWO

The Succession, 1135–1136

Waiting for the death of Henry I must have been like waiting for the Bomb. When he died (1 December 1135) there was a sort of hushed suspense while people listened for the explosion. The feeling is vividly conveyed in the letter which Peter the Venerable, abbot of Cluny, wrote to Stephen's mother, who of course was also Henry's sister, announcing the news of his death. Adela was then a Cluniac nun, and the letter makes it clear that Peter's information came from one of his Cluniac monks, Hugh Archbishop of Rouen, and that he had written for further news both to him and to Adela's youngest son Henry, also a Cluniac monk, who was bishop of Winchester.

> *To our venerable and dearest sister the lady Adela, Brother Peter, humble abbot of Cluny, sends greeting and every blessing from God.* If we have not sent news till now to Your Charity about the death of our ever-beloved lord the King of England, the reason is that great grief, which we still cannot banish, has prevented it; and we shrank, not without cause, of being the first to bear tidings of so great a calamity. But as you have asked to know all that we know, know that as yet we having been informed of nothing, except that he was confined to bed for eight days in a town near Rouen, that the lord archbishop of Rouen remained assiduously at his side, and that fortified by the sacraments of the church, in deep penitence and confession of the faith, he passed away from this life on December 2 [sic]. His body, as he had commanded, was brought to Rouen, and from there was taken to England by his son Earl Robert,[1] to be buried at Reading. All Normandy is shaken with internal and external war. Of the state of the kingdom across the sea we have heard nothing certain, for those who brought us the news had fled in all haste from Normandy. But we have already sent two runners, one to my lord of Rouen and the other to my lord of Winchester, and they will immediately inform us of anything they hear about them or from them. For the eternal salvation of the dead

1 Natural son of Henry I, see p. 13.

King we have arranged services as great as have ever been arranged for anyone at Cluny. I think it is unnecessary for me to tell you what you should be doing for him.[2]

The unwritten words almost shout from the page. 'I know why you are anxious,' the abbot is saying, 'but I do not know who has become king in your brother's place. It may be your son; it may be someone else.'

There were three principal contenders for the succession, and one 'fancied outsider'. The least popular was the official candidate whom Henry had designated and to whom the English barons had sworn allegiance (December 1126), his daughter the Empress Matilda. She was unpopular because she was a woman, and because her husband, Geoffrey Count of Anjou, was the hereditary enemy of the Normans, and actually at war with Henry at the time of his death. But more important still was the fact that in the course of hostilities, both past and present, Geoffrey had naturally made friends and allies of those Normans whom Henry I had exiled and disinherited, those most in evidence in 1135 being William Talvas the son of Robert de Belesme and Amauri Count of Evreux. This made it inevitable that there would be opposition from Henry I's 'new men' for they had been consistently rewarded, as we have already seen, with the estates of the disinherited. Their self-interest was bound to make them prefer a successor who was already committed to the new order, and they therefore focused their attention on the two men who were both of royal birth and 'new', Robert Earl of Gloucester, the illegitimate son of the king, and Stephen.

In wealth and influence these two were very equal. Their English demesne lands were comparable in extent—Robert's has been calculated as 1564½ hides in demesne as opposed to Stephen's 1339[3]—both were reputedly good knights, and though Stephen was only the nephew of the king, Robert was illegitimate. Either could have been considered worthy , but they were so jealous of each other that it was a foregone conclusion that neither would concede the slightest superiority to the other. Even when it came to taking the oath to the

2 Peter the Venerable, *Letters*, Bk i, no. 15, printed in M. Marrier and A. Duchesne, *Bibliotheca Cluniacensis* (Paris, 1614), cols. 635–6; cf. M. A. E. Green, *Princesses of England*, 68.

3 For Robert's lands, see Robert B. Patterson in the *American Hist. Rev.*, lxx (1965), 994. While Stephen's main demesne holdings were denoted by danegeld exemptions in Suffolk (£45 19s 9d.), Essex (£22 16s. 4d.), Norfolk (£9 10s. 3d.) and Lincolnshire (£9 7s. 9d.), Earl Robert's were in Gloucestershire (£32 16s. 4d.), Dorset (£22 10s.), Wiltshire (£12 7s. 6d.), and Devon (£10 5s.). Though Robert had more land than Stephen in England, it is probable that in all Stephen had more than him because of the County of Mortain. The continental lands of the County of Boulogne would have been a bonus for Stephen.

empress as Henry's heir (1126), they had quarrelled over which should have the honour of taking it first.[4] Consequently there were many Normans who, though unwilling to accept Matilda, thought it dangerous to elevate either Robert or Stephen, and inclined towards an 'outsider' or compromise candidate in the person of Stephen's elder brother Theobald, who was already Count of Blois, Chartres and Champagne. His hereditary claim was of course excellent, and as an ally of Henry I he was connected with the 'new men' rather than the disinherited, so he might have done very well. Unfortunately he did not want the kingdom, at any rate not badly enough to make a fight of it.

In such a situation it was virtually inevitable that the death of Henry I would be the signal for civil war. The only possible hope, and it was a desperate one, was that Henry might be persuaded to change his mind, disinherit the empress, and throw all the weight of his authority into the designation of either Stephen or Robert. The agony must have been intense when he lay dying at his hunting lodge of Lyon-la-Forêt. With him were the archbishop of Rouen and the bishop of Evreux who were both to support Stephen, and five earls—four of them supporters of Stephen, and the fifth Robert of Gloucester himself—but it is clear that Henry remained unmovable.[5] Quite apart from Peter the Venerable's letter already quoted, we have the text of the letter which the archbishop of Rouen wrote to the pope announcing the news of Henry's death, and though he was a supporter of Stephen's he does not say a word about the king's wishes for the succession. When Stephen subsequently claimed that Henry had in fact changed his mind and designated him, his witness was not the archbishop or bishop or any of the four friendly earls who were there, but Hugh Bigod whose testimony cannot but be suspected. As the bishop of Angers later put it to Stephen's advocate: 'As for your statement that the king changed his mind, it is proved false by those who were present at the king's death. Neither you nor Hugh could possibly know his last request, because neither of you was there.'[6]

---

4 William of Malmesbury, *Hist. Nov.* para. 452. John of Worcester (ed. Weaver, 27) inverts the situation and makes Robert insist that Stephen, being older, should take the oath before him.

5 For the list of those present, see *OV* vi. 448.

6 *Historia Pontificalis of John of Salisbury*, ed. and trans. M. Chibnall (London, 1956), 85. I might add that, having myself seen Muslim soldiers 'converted' and baptized in their last moments by a well-intentioned priest, I have no difficulty in appreciating that anyone who intended to see a sign of assent from the dying king could have done so. I would also guess that Hugh Bigod was present when the king fell ill but left before his actual death so as to prepare Stephen and his associates for the news.

When one thinks about it, one realizes that if Henry had changed his mind, he would have only made a bad situation worse. When he had given his daughter in marriage to Geoffrey of Anjou, he had promised that unless he had another child by his lawful wife the inheritance would be his.[7] If he now went back on his word, Geoffrey would be bound to fight; indeed the very reason for the present hostilities was that Henry, refusing to share his power with anyone, had refused him the Norman castles which he had promised to hand over as security for the inheritance.[8] A peaceful succession could not be secured; the various contenders would fight in any case, and all that Henry could usefully do was to show where his affection lay, by leaving Earl Robert '60,000 pounds' from his treasury at Falaise as a donative for his servants and mercenaries.[9] If with the 5,000 pounds which the Conqueror had left him, Henry had been able to win both England and Normandy, what might not Robert do with 60,000?

Henry died on 1 December 1135, and immediately Normandy was in an uproar. At first there was no clear alignment of parties, but every man was for himself. As Orderic put it:

> Already everyone covets the pillage of his neighbour's property, and abandons himself to unbridled injustice . . . .The Normans abandon themselves to robbery and pillage; they butcher one another, make prisoners and bind them in fetters, burn houses and all that is in them, not even sparing monks or respecting women.[10]

Amid this turmoil, the earls who had been at Henry's deathbed bore his body to Rouen (2 December) where it was embalmed, the bowels being buried in the church of St Mary du Pré. The body was then taken overland to Caen where it rested almost four weeks in St Stephen's Church (the 'Abbaye aux Hommes') awaiting a favourable wind for the passage to England. It was buried at Reading on 4 January 1136, thirty-three days after the death of the king. Meanwhile the Norman barons, attempting to settle the succession, had sent for Theobald Count of Blois. On 20 December they had almost decided to elect him, when a messenger arrived from England to say that Theobald's

---

7 *Symeon of Durham, Hist. Reg.* (R.S.) ii. 282.

8 *OV* vi. 444 'Gener enim ejus Josfredus Andegavensis magnas potentis soceri gazas affectabat, castella Normanniae poscebat, asserens quod sibi sic ab eodem rege pactum fuerat, quando filiam ejus in conjugem acceperat. Animosus autem sceptriger neminem sibi, dum vitales carperet auras, voluit praeficere, vel etiam in domo sua seu regno sibi coaequare, diligenter revolvens divinae dictum sophiae, quod nemo potest duobus dominis servire.' Cf. Robert de Torigni, in *Chronicles* iv. 128.

9 *OV* vi. 448. Orderic's figure of 60,000 should probably not be taken too literally.

10 *OV* vi. 452.

brother Stephen had already been accepted as king.[11] While they had been thinking, Stephen had acted.

The speed of Stephen's action has not ceased to provoke amazement and admiration. He was at Boulogne when he heard the news of Henry's death.[12] He set sail for England at once—the winds did not present much difficulty for the short crossing from Wissant—and made straight for London, which received him as king. The *Gesta Stephani* describes the Londoners' action as a formal election, which from their own point of view it probably was, but it would be a mistake to understand it as anything which had legal binding on the kingdom as a whole. It should rather be viewed as a declaration to receive Stephen and to fight for him as king; and as such it would have been strictly parallel to the declarations made by the Flemish towns in 1127, and for which they were rewarded, as we have already seen, with handsome charters of liberties.[13] Moving on, Stephen seems to have met a little opposition in the country near London,[14] but overcoming it quickly, made a dash for Winchester where he was welcomed by his brother Henry who was the bishop, and accepted by the citizens. There also, thanks to the assistance of his brother, he was recognized as king by Roger Bishop of Salisbury who, as justiciar, controlled the government of England, and by William Pont de l'Arche who kept the royal treasury. Then, having already secured the vital organs of the kingdom, he asked the archbishop of Canterbury, William de Corbeil, to anoint him king. William showed some scruple about the oath which he, Stephen, and all the other notables had taken to the empress in 1126. But Stephen's supporters claimed that the oath was null and void because it had been exacted from them by force. They also produced the story—the first we hear of it—about Henry's deathbed change of mind, and Hugh Bigod took an oath to vouch for its truth. Consequently the archbishop anointed Stephen king on 22 December 1135. It was not just a ceremony; it was an action which was thought to have *made* Stephen king. Henceforward even his enemies could not deny that he was king, even if they thought he was the wrongful king; and conversely they could not, and did not style the empress queen, for though the kingdom might be hers by right, she had not been anointed. The only possibility

11 Robert de Torigni in *Chronicles* iv. 128–9; cf. *OV* vi. 454. Orderic says that the meeting of the Norman barons was at Neufbourg, Robert de Torigni that they heard the news at Lisieux.

12 Robert de Torigni in William of Jumièges, ed. Marx, 329; cf Wm. Malmesb, *Hist. Nov.* para. 460.

13 *Supra*, p. 11.

14 G.S. 6–8.

left open to her was to appeal Stephen before the pope of having defrauded her of her right and of having broken his oath. This she did but the pope, though he considered the matter (with the help of Peter the Venerable) at the Lateran Council of 1139, in effect declared the accusations not proven, and recognized Stephen as king.[15]

There can be little doubt that the man who was really responsible for Stephen's success was his brother, Henry of Blois, bishop of Winchester. It was he who secured the government machine and treasury by winning over Roger of Salisbury and William Pont de l'Arche, and it was he who gave the archbishop the biggest inducement to anoint Stephen, by going surety for the solemn oath which Stephen took to restore and maintain the freedom of the Church. It was he also who had the ecclesiastical position and Cluniac connections to secure the ear of the papacy. But he was absolutely sincere in his desire to secure the liberty of the Church; he made Stephen promise it, not as a bribe which might be forgotten, but as the price which any king ought to pay for the friendly cooperation of the Church, and he saw to it that the general promise was made specific. As soon as Stephen had been recognized by the pope he issued a charter which, though sometimes called 'the second'[16] or (from its place of issue) 'the Oxford' charter of liberties, was really a charter of liberties for the Church. In its general form it is not unlike the charters which the towns of Flanders had demanded in 1127 for the recognition of their new count. It suggests a contract or treaty rather than a grant made as a matter of course, and instead of starting with the normal 'Stephen King of the English', it opens with an enumeration of the benefits which Stephen had received from the Church, in order to explain his present concessions:

I, Stephen, by the grace of God elected King of England by the assent of clergy and people, and consecrated by the lord William archbishop of Canterbury and legate of the Holy Roman Church, and afterwards confirmed by Innocent bishop of the Holy Roman See, out of respect and honour of God, concede that the Church shall be free and confirm to it the reverence which I owe.[17]

15 John of Salisbury, *Historia Pontificalis* ed. Chibnall, 83 ff. Cf. Adrian Morey and C. N. L. Brooke, *Gilbert Foliot and his letters* (Cambridge, 1965), 105 n.

16 The 'first' charter, given at London and witnessed only by William Martel simply confirmed 'the good laws' of Henry I (*Reg.* iii. 270).

17 *Reg.* iii. 271; cf. the charter of William Clito for Saint-Omer (1127), in Giry, *op. cit.* 371. 'Ego Guillelmus dei gratia Flandrensium comes, petitioni burgensium Sancti Audomari contraire nolens, pro eo maxime quia meam de consulatu Flandriae petitionem libenti animo receperunt, et quia honestius et fidelius coeteris Flandrensibus erga me semper se habuerunt, lagas seu consuetudines subscriptas perpetuo eis jure concedo et ratas permanere praecipio.'

In the detailed clauses which followed, he promised not to commit simony (i.e. accept gifts for the preferment of clerics); recognized that the clergy were subject to canon law and under the jurisdiction of their bishops; confirmed all privileges, customs and lands which the Church held at the death of the Conqueror; promised to investigate cases of church lands lost before that date, and to confirm all lands given since; promised peace, justice and the return to churches or the kingdom of all lands afforested by Henry I; confirmed that bishops or abbots might distribute their property reasonably before their death; put strict limits on the rights the king could enjoy in vacant sees; and generally promised to correct the unjust practices or exactions of his officials.

It was everything that the Church could possibly have desired, and a master-stroke of Cluniac policy. Cluniacs had always believed that the most effective way for the Church to gain its liberty was not by fighting the secular power, but by co-operating with it and converting it. They specialized in important people; Stephen's uncle, King Henry I, had founded a Cluniac abbey, his mother and father-in-law had both become Cluniacs in old age, and his brother the bishop of Winchester was a very important Cluniac monk. Now that Stephen had secured the throne, it might be hoped that there would be a glorious *condominium* in England with two brothers, bishop and king, wielding the spiritual and secular swords in loving harmony. Henry the bishop had secured Stephen the kingdom of the English, and Stephen in return would advance the kingdom of God.

Having been accepted by the Londoners, having secured the central administration, and having been anointed by the Church, Stephen was able to face the problem of the nobles. Somehow or other they had to be persuaded to recognize him. Some barons presented little difficulty; they were the men who, in the spirit of gamblers, rallied to Stephen with the utmost speed, in the expectation that those who took the risk of recognizing him first were likely to receive the greatest rewards. One of them, Hugh Bigod, whose oath about Henry's deathbed wishes had proved so timely, seems to have been disappointed—we know that though he was given custody of Norwich castle he aspired to make it his own[18]—but in general Stephen seems to have fulfilled the expectations which had been raised. We know, for example, the terms which he made with Miles of Gloucester, who had evidently rallied to him by the time of Henry's funeral (4 January), and

---

18 His first revolt is said to have been at the end of April 1136 (H. Hunt, 259), but the chronology of his revolts is difficult. He was a frequent witness of Stephen's charters down till 1139, but after that seems to have been mainly, if not wholly, in revolt.

was a valuable supporter both for his own sake and also for the proximity of his estates to those of Robert Earl of Gloucester. Miles was one of Henry's 'new men' and an important official, the local counterpart of Bishop Roger of Salisbury. Like his father and grandfather he was sheriff of Gloucestershire (hence his name), but by the end of Henry's reign he was also sheriff of Staffordshire, a justice itinerant, justice of the forest and constable of the king. Naturally he wanted Stephen to continue him in these offices as well as to confirm his lands, and Stephen did so. But he also asked for, and got, an undertaking from the king that he would not permit him to be impleaded in his court concerning the lands he held on the day when King Henry was alive and dead. The point was that, being a favourite of Henry I and all-powerful in the counties which he administered, he had had every opportunity to enrich himself with other people's lands, and was anxious that his own title to them should not be questioned. Stephen's charters confirmed everything that he possessed, no matter how it had been acquired, but it also granted him one thing more. Under Henry I Miles had held Gloucester Castle from Robert Earl of Gloucester; now he was to hold it from the king direct as his 'patrimony' Stephen had no objection to embroiling him with Earl Robert. It might even help him to be loyal.[19]

A larger problem was posed by those nobles who were openly hostile. The first to declare himself was King David of the Scots, who ranked as an English earl in respect of his honour of Huntingdon and who as the maternal uncle of the empress was naturally one of her supporters. As soon as he heard the news of Stephen's accession, he crossed the border and captured Carlisle, Wark, Alnwick, Norham and Newcastle upon Tyne. Clearly he did not think that Stephen would be able to muster an army against him, since few of the greater nobles had yet submitted. But Stephen, having both the royal treasury at his disposal and also contacts with Flanders, the inexhaustible source of mercenary soldiers, raised a force 'as big as any that could be remembered in England', and reached Durham by 5 February.[20] That persuaded David to parley, and Stephen proceeded to purchase his support. He could not induce David to do him homage personally, but the two kings agreed that the earldom of Huntingdon should be held by David's son Henry, and that Henry should do homage to Stephen for it and attend Stephen's court, which put him temporarily in the

19 *Reg.* iii. 386–7; cf. *G. de M.* 11–14, and Davis in *Stenton Miscellany*, 142–4.
20 The phrase about the size of the army is from H. Hunt, 258–9; the evidence for it being composed of mercenaries is in Ric. Hexham (*Chronicles* iii. 145).

position of a hostage. It was alleged that Stephen promised not to revive the earldom of Northumbria for anyone without first giving judgment on Henry's claim to it in his court, but certainly King David, though he restored Wark, Alnwick, Norham and Newcastle, was granted Doncaster and Carlisle, with which went much of Cumberland and Westmorland. The price may not have seemed very large, but the difficulty was that such grants could only be made at the expense of other people. In surrendering Carlisle and reserving some right in the old earldom of Northumbria, which included Lancashire north of the Ribble, Stephen had given or half-promised lands which were claimed or coveted by the Earl of Chester. As a result, when Stephen brought the Scottish prince to court and treated him with honour, the Earl of Chester went away in a rage, and when Stephen seated him at his right hand, the Archbishop of Canterbury left because that place should have been his.[21] King David was able to make these incidents the pretext for not letting his son attend Stephen's court again, and in the long run no one was satisfied.

In the short run, however, the Scottish treaty was a triumph. The speed with which Stephen had acted impressed his enemies and induced them to recognize him as king by attending Stephen's Easter Court (22 March). While at his coronation there had been only three bishops (Canterbury, Winchester and Salisbury) and only a handful of nobles, Stephen's activity during the first three months of his reign had now ensured him the attendance or service of almost all the bishops of England and Normandy and almost all the nobles.[22] If it was the anointing that had made him king, it was the Easter Court which showed that he *was* king, and accepted by his kingdom. Stephen therefore prolonged his Easter Court, eventually moving it to Oxford, so as to impress the hesitant with his magnificence and give them every opportunity to come and do him homage. The result was spectacular, for before the end of April even Robert Earl of Gloucester appeared. William of Malmesbury, who had every reason to know, is at pains to

21 John of Hexham in *Symeon of Durham* ii. 287, and Ric. Hexham in *Chronicles* iii. 146; cf. Davis in *E.H.R.* lxxv (1960), 658–9.

22 The names of those present were recorded, as Round pointed out (*G. de M.* 19) in some very long witness-lists for charters, one charter having as many as fifty-five witnesses, the point being to record not only their witness to the grant but also their attendance at Stephen's court. There were twelve English bishops present, two more (Coventry and Durham) arrived shortly afterwards, one (Exeter) was apparently ill, and one (London) was vacant. Five out of the seven Norman bishops attended, the absentees being John of Lisieux, who as head of the Norman Exchequer seems to have been required in Normandy, and Richard of Bayeux who was the natural son of Robert Earl of Gloucester.

explain that his arrival did not imply any real change of heart on the earl's part, but was due to the realization that, having been outmanœuvred by Stephen's speed, he would only succeed in isolating himself if he now remained sulking in Normandy. If he wanted to build up a party of supporters now, he would have to go to Stephen's court to find them, because that was where all the nobles were. He therefore disguised his real intention, and did homage to Stephen in a very conditional form, after he had made agreements with him about his lands and possessions.

> And so he did homage to the king conditionally, that is to say for as long as the king kept the agreements and kept him in his dignity entire; for he already long observed the King's disposition, and foresaw that his promises would be worthless (*instabilitatem fidei ejus previdebat*).[23]

Stephen's triumph must have seemed complete, and we may well imagine him with thoughts as optimistic as his father's had been at Constantinople or Nicaea. But there were difficulties in the situation which he would soon have to face, and the real testing time was still to come. It was easy to win friends when one had only to make promises, more difficult to keep them when the promises had to be fulfilled.

23 William of Malmesbury, *Hist. Nov.* para. 463

CHAPTER THREE
Mistakes,
1136–1139

The first mistake which Stephen made concerned a baron called
Baldwin de Redvers. He was bound by close ties to Henry and his
family, since his father had been one of the barons of the Cotentin who
had supported him as early as 1090 against both his brothers. He was
therefore likely to support Henry I's daughter and few can have been
surprised when he did not attend Stephen's Easter Court. After the
submission of Robert of Gloucester, however, it would seem that he
changed his mind and offered the king homage provided that he was
confirmed in his lands.[1] Stephen refused. We may suppose that
Baldwin's offer was altogether too late, that he had been contumacious
in not attending the Easter Court, and that it would in any case have
been impolitic to reward conspicuous late-comers in the same way as
those who had rallied promptly. In itself this decision was not a
mistake. The right to confirm a baron's lands clearly implied the right
not to confirm them, and forfeitures were common under the first three
Norman kings—in one part of the country only half the barons who died
between 1086 and 1118 had been succeeded by their legitimate heirs.[2]
The Redvers, though noble, were 'new men' in England, having

1 The reasons for Baldwin de Redvers's rebellion are here reconstructed from (*a*)
the direct statement of Ric. Hexham (*Chronicles* iii. 146): 'Eodem quoque anno
Baldewinus de Redwers, quia non potuit quendam honorem habere, quem a rege
postulaverat, Execestram oppidum suum contra illum firmavit'; (*b*) the fact that he does
not attest Stephen's 'Easter court' charters, or indeed any other charter of King Stephen
until the Treaty of Westminster (1153); (*c*) the *Gesta Stephani.*

2 The district was Lindsey where a survey now dated *c.* 1115–18 gives the relevant
facts. R. E. C. Waters, *Survey of Lindsey 1114–16* (Lincoln, 1882), 19: 'It appears from the
Roll that out of thirty-eight barons, who had died since *Domesday*, only nineteen were
succeeded by their legitimate heirs.' On the question of hereditary tenure in England
at this date, see R. H. C. Davis, 'What happened in Stephen's reign, 1135–54', *History* xlix
(1964), 1–12, and Appendix IV 'Politics and Property', pp. 150–3 below.

received nearly all their estates, which were mainly in the Isle of Wight and Devon, from Henry I, and there was nothing outrageous in the idea of declaring them forfeit because of Baldwin's contumacy. The only difficulty was in the execution of the sentence, for Baldwin was certain to resist and might find allies.

Baldwin was castellan of the royal castle of Exeter, and his plan was to capture the city and the surrounding district as well. Stephen was warned by the citizens, however, and made a dash for the city, arriving just in time to secure it and besiege Baldwin's men in the castle. He set about the siege with commendable vigour, and in addition to his mercenaries brought up a large baronial army in order to display that the splendour of his Easter Court was not mere show, and that the barons who had attended it would also fight for him. In this respect the prize exhibit of the army was Robert Earl of Gloucester.[3] His presence was a great acquisition as it enabled Stephen not only to show him off, but also to keep an eye on him. But there was a corresponding disadvantage in the presence of Earl Robert and other dubious supporters, as was amply demonstrated when the besieged garrison received reinforcement under the very noses of the king's army. One of Baldwin's men, Judhael of Totnes, succeeded in bringing a force into the city as if it were part of the royal army, mingled freely with the king's troops, got a message to the besieged, and having taken up a position by one of the gates, got himself whisked into the castle by a sudden sortie of the garrison. The king's forces said that they had been unable to recognize him or his men because they were wearing armour like everyone else, and claimed that they had all been taken by surprise; but it is doubtful if anyone can have seriously believed that none of them had connived at the plot.[4]

Stephen put a good face on the matter, cheerfully saying that the more of his enemies were shut up inside, the better it would be for him. He pressed the siege, and when the besieged ran out of water, he had them at his mercy. The *Gesta Stephani* describes how they tried to negotiate for terms, and how Henry Bishop of Winchester,

> observing their sagging and wasted skin, the look of torpor on their faces, drained of the normal supply of blood, and their lips drawn back from gaping mouths, perceived that they were suffering from agonies of thirst, and that therefore it was anything but wise to give them permission to

3 *Reg.* iii. 952; cf. iii. 284; cf. *G.S.* 40 which refers to those 'qui tunc cum rege dolose militabant'.

4 *G.S.* 38. The story shows that the knights cannot have been wearing armorial bearings.

leave the castle, it being certain that they would very soon surrender on whatever terms the besiegers desired.[5]

He persuaded Stephen to reject the deputation, and even to be unmoved by the pleas of Baldwin's wife who came 'barefooted, with her hair loose on her shoulders, shedding floods of tears'. In his view it was essential to punish the besieged as rebels—which meant death or mutilation—in order to demonstrate that there was no longer any question who was king. Earl Robert and his supporters were equally determined, and for the same reason, that the besieged should not be so punished. On the contrary, they were determined to demonstrate that though they might be in the king's camp, their sympathy lay with the besieged. They approached the king in a body, plied him with specious arguments and flattery, and (as the *Gesta* puts it) 'suddenly changed him into another man'. He allowed the besieged not only to go free, but also to take their possessions with them and to adhere to any lord they wished, which suggested that they had been fighting a just and honourable war instead of a rebellion. It availed Stephen little that he subsequently captured Baldwin's castle at Carisbrooke in the Isle of Wight, and forced him to take refuge with the Count of Anjou, for the mistake which he had made at Exeter could not be redeemed. He had shown everyone that though his army might be large, part of it was half-hearted; and that his own determination could be shaken.

The second mistake which Stephen made was in Normandy. The duchy had been in a state of uproar since the death of Henry I. In addition to the general disorder which we have already described (p. 15), the southern frontier of the duchy had been greatly weakened by the loss of Séez to William Talvas and Theobald of Blois,[6] and of Argentan, Exmes and Domfront to Geoffrey of Anjou. Roger de Toeni was in revolt in the south-east, Rabel de Tancarville in the centre, and everywhere there was incipient war. No one expected things to improve until the new king came to put them right in person, and yet it was fifteen months before he arrived.

He landed at La Hougue near Cherbourg in the third week of March 1137, proceeded at once through Bayeux to Evreux which he reached before 25 March,[7] and made peace with his brother Theobald, soothing

<hr />

5 *G.S.* 40.

6 Séez had been part of the honour of William Talvas before Henry I had disinherited him, but Theobald was also interested in it, since Henry had subsequently given it to him. He in turn had given it to Stephen in exchange for other lands (p. 7, n. 18), but now that he was jealous of Stephen as King, he seems to have revived his claim. The territory was in any case on the borders of his county.

7 *OV* vi. 480 and *Reg.* iii. 594, 69, 843.

his wounded vanity with a pension of 2000 marks a year. The order in which he made his next movements is not clear,[8] but in May he met King Louis VI of France, was invested with the duchy of Normandy to be held as a fief of the French crown, and made an alliance with him in order to secure his eastern frontier while he turned his attention to Geoffrey of Anjou in the south. Geoffrey, rather tactlessly keeping the real heiress, his wife, in the background, had invaded Normandy at the beginning of May. Starting from Exmes, he had advanced north-westwards to Argences, thus joining forces with the rebellious Rabel de Tancarville at Mézidon, and putting himself within ten miles of Caen which was in the custody of Earl Robert of Gloucester. Obviously he was hoping that the earl would seize the opportunity to throw off his allegiance to Stephen, but he was disappointed. The earl remained loyal, and Stephen, having captured Mézidon, collected a large army at Lisieux in June for a counter-offensive.

The plan was to march on Argentan, which had been held by the Angevins since December 1135, besiege it, and try to force Geoffrey to give battle in its defence. But Stephen had got no further than Livarot when his army was convulsed by internal feuds, and suddenly disintegrated. All our sources agree that the Norman barons were jealous and distrustful of Stephen's Flemish mercenaries commanded by William of Ypres, and that somehow or other a battle broke out between them. Stephen's supporters said that the trouble started when a Fleming seized a pipe of wine from a Norman knight, but Earl Robert of Gloucester declared that he had discovered an ambush which had been laid for him by Stephen at the instigation of William of Ypres, and claimed that Stephen eventually admitted as much.[9] Whatever the cause of the trouble, there was considerable slaughter, and most of the barons collected their vassals and left the royal camp without taking leave of the king, which in normal circumstances would have been considered an act of rebellion. Stephen apparently pursued them as far as Pontaudemer, thirty miles away, and succeeded in detaining one or two of them, but he did not dare to summon the Norman army again. Earl Robert of Gloucester had by the most incredible luck (or was it design?) evaded having to fight against the Angevins, and Stephen had to spend the rest of his stay in Normandy trying to patch up relations with the earl and other barons as best he could. In this he was greatly

8 Orderic and Robert of Torigni give different itineraries which cannot be reconciled in detail.

9 There can be little doubt that the stories in *OV* vi. 484–6, Robert de Torigni (*Chronicles* iv. 132) and William of Malmesbury (*Hist. Nov.*, para. 466) all refer to the same event.

helped by the archbishop of Rouen, but he must have realized that the reconciliation effected was only nominal. He was probably relieved to find an excuse for returning to England at the end of November. According to Orderic,

> He appointed William de Roumare and Roger the vicomte with others as justiciars of Normandy, commanding them to accomplish what he himself had been unable to effect in person, namely to do justice to the inhabitants and procure peace for the defenceless people.[10]

It was a mistake for Stephen to abandon the struggle so easily, for Normandy was more important than he realized. It lacked the administrative system of England, had a long tradition of rebellion and unrest, and in a strictly financial sense was probably more trouble than it was worth; but it was the key to security in England. That was why Henry I had found it necessary to conquer it from his brother, and why, when he had conquered it, he spent more than half his time there. England could look after itself with a man like Roger of Salisbury at the helm, but Normandy needed the presence of the king and his army in order to keep the peace. For Stephen there was an even greater reason for keeping Normandy secure. His great rival, King Henry's daughter, was married to Geoffrey of Anjou, and Geoffrey had made it very clear that he intended not only to invade Normandy but also to conquer it. If he succeeded, the matter would not rest there. The Norman barons, having fiefs on both sides of the channel, would never willingly contemplate a renewal of the situation as it had been under Duke Robert, when England and Normandy were at war, and every baron forfeited his lands in one country or the other. That was why they had abandoned Theobald as soon as they learnt that Stephen had been accepted in England.[11] But then they had thought that with their help Stephen would be able to establish himself in Normandy. If he did not try, it would be necessary to consider the alternative of the Angevins for both countries.

The third mistake concerned Stephen's brother, Henry of Blois the bishop of Winchester. We have already seen how it was largely due to him that Stephen had secured the throne, and how he was ambitious for a free and friendly partnership between Church and king (pp. 17–18), and it would have been only natural for him to expect that when the archbishop of Canterbury died, as he soon did (21 November 1136), he would himself be appointed in his place. The archbishop was not only the effectual head of the English Church—whatever York might

10 *OV* vi. 494.
11 *OV* vi. 454.

say—but also by tradition the first adviser of the king. Henry was virtually both these things already—Orderic thought he had actually been elected—and all he needed was the formal position. But Canterbury was kept vacant for more than two years, and when it was filled, the election (though canonical) was obviously engineered so as to exclude him. It was made at Westminister on 24 December 1138 in the presence of the king, the papal legate (Alberic of Ostia) and several nobles and bishops, at a moment when Bishop Henry had gone from Westminster to St Paul's for an ordination of deacons, and the person elected was Theobald Abbot of Bec. When he was told what had happened, Henry was furious and abandoned the ordinations unfinished, obviously believing that he had been got out of the way on purpose. He could not dispute the election because it was canonical, and he was doubtless told that there were difficulties about the translation of a bishop from one see to another, but he obviously thought that the whole business was a dirty trick, and that the person responsible was Stephen.[12]

What must have galled Henry particularly was that the man who had been chosen instead of him was almost unknown, his main qualification apparently being that he was 'not Henry'. It could be argued that as abbot of Bec, like Lanfranc and Anselm before him he was an obvious candidate for Canterbury, but Theobald had only been abbot for two years. Who would have known about him? That was probably what Henry of Blois minded most, for the obvious person was Waleran Count of Meulan, lay patron (or *advocatus*) of Bec.[13] He and his twin brother, Robert Earl of Leicester, were favourites with Stephen but hated by Bishop Henry.[14] If the Canterbury election had been made at their instigation, it meant that Bishop Henry had not only lost his position as first adviser to the king, but lost it to men whose policy was repugnant to him.

Since Waleran, the elder and more vigorous of the twins, was largely responsible for Stephen's fourth and most spectacular mistake, it is not irrelevant to take a look at him.[15] In many ways he was just the sort of friend one would have expected Stephen to make, having interests in France as well as Normandy (for Meulan was in the Vexin),

12 *OV* vi. 478; Gervase of Canterbury (R.S.) i. 109; Ralph Diceto (R. S.) i. 252. The evidence is reviewed in detail in Saltman, *Theobald* 7–13.
13 *C.D.F.* 373.
14 The *Gesta Stephani* which generally reflects Henry's views is full of 'digs' about Waleran and his family. See *E.H.R.* lxxvii (1962), 22 n.
15 Most of the following paragraph is derived from G. H. White, 'The career of Waleran Count of Meulan and Earl of Worcester', *T.R.H.S.*, 4th series, xvii (1934), 19–48, but see also Appendix II below.

and being not only head of the great Norman family of Beaumont but also descended (through his grandmother) from the French royal family. His father, a close adviser of Henry I and noted for the diplomatic skill and ingenuity with which he had opposed St Anselm in the investitures contest, had died in 1118 when Waleran and his brother were only fourteen. Thenceforth the twins had been educated at the king's court and were considered infant prodigies. When the pope visited Normandy, and they were boys of fifteen, they had distinguished themselves in a disputation arranged for them with the cardinals, their ingenious sophistry (*tortilibus sophismatibus*) carrying all before it.[16] In Waleran's case his cleverness did not prevent his revolting against his patron the king (1123–4), but it did enable him to regain favour completely when he had been defeated.

It also enabled him to cultivate Stephen's friendship while Henry I was still alive, and when Stephen became king his rise was meteoric. By Easter 1136, Stephen had given him all the castles in the valley of the Risle, had put him and his twin brother in charge of Normandy, and had betrothed him to his own daughter although she was only a child of two. Waleran, who was a skillful soldier, succeeded in repelling Angevin invasions of Normandy in 1136 and 1138, and on a brief visit to England in the winter of 1137–8 also drove a Scottish army from Wark. He was a very useful man, and no doubt deserved his reward, but as his own power rose, so did that of his family. Even at the beginning of the reign his twin brother Robert was Earl of Leicester, his half-brother William de Warenne was Earl of Surrey, and his first cousin Roger de Beaumont (whose wife was Waleran's half-sister) was Earl of Warwick. In 1138 Waleran himself was created Earl of Worcester, his young brother Hugh Pauper was created Earl of Bedford, and his brother-in-law, Gilbert de Clare, was created Earl of Pembroke. When the monks of St Evroult elected a new abbot in 1137 they chose one of their number who had been the confessor and administrative adviser of Waleran's father,[17] and when a new bishop was needed for Evreux (1139) the man chosen was Waleran's first cousin Rotrou. Instead of being governed by Henry I's 'new men', it looked as if England and Normandy would soon be ruled by the Beaumonts.

One of the biggest obstacles in their way was that the central goverment in England was still managed by Henry I's justiciar, Roger Bishop of Salisbury, with the assistance of his nephews, Alexander Bishop of Lincoln, Nigel Bishop of Ely the king's treasurer, and Roger le

16 William of Malmesbury, *Gesta Regum* (R.S.) ii. 482.
17 *OV* vi. 488.

Poer—so-called because he was the only one without a bishopric—the king's chancellor. Between them they controlled the entire central administration, both chancery and exchequer. Under Henry I Bishop Roger had acted as regent whenever the king was in Normandy with the result that he could, and did, issue writs in the king's name; and through the exchequer he had a hold on all the sheriffs, who represented royal power in the countries. To Henry I such concentration of power in the hands of one clerical family had not seemed dangerous, because he himself understood the workings of the bureaucracy and consequently knew what was going on. But Stephen probably found the intricacies of chancery and exchequer so much double-Dutch, and it would have been easy to persuade him that Roger of Salisbury's power was a menace to his own, especially as the bishop and his nephews had large forces of knights, and stone castles at Sherborne, Devizes, Malmesbury and Newark. What was to stop them sending orders to the sheriffs which would assist a landing of the empress?

We will never know whether the suspicions harboured against the bishops were justified or not, but it is clear that no one had any firm evidence against them.[18] The problem of arresting them was therefore very difficult, for no king could survive if he arrested prominent subjects for no stated reason. Yet how could evidence be discovered without putting the bishops on their guard and thus encouraging them to revolt while they were yet free? It was the ingenious mind of Waleran which produced an answer. All that was necessary was to stage an 'incident' at court which would result in the bishops breaking the king's peace by becoming involved in a mêlée in his presence; for after the affair at Livarot, it would be appreciated that armed combat amongst the king's supporters had to be dealt with severely. Accordingly in June 1139, when the court came to Oxford, Count Alan of Brittany was put up to start a quarrel with Bishop Roger's men over their quarters. He did so, at dinner-time, with such good effect that at least one man was killed and many wounded. Stephen summoned the bishops to satisfy his court for the disturbance of its peace, 'the means of satisfaction to be surrender of the keys of their castles as pledges of their faith'.[19] The Bishop of Ely fled to Devizes Castle and prepared it for a siege, but the other members of the family were held by the king. When Stephen marched against Devizes and threatened to hang the

18 *Hist Nov*. para 468, 'pro sola suspicione' chimes in well with *G.S.* 74 which also harps on 'suspicion'.
19 *Hist. Nov*. para. 469.

ex-chancellor in front of its walls, the castle quickly surrendered, and all three bishops submitted to the king on the terms required, that is to say they surrendered their offices and their castles but were free to return to their sees.

The incident proved itself to be one of the turning points of Stephen's reign, so it is necessary to be quite clear about what was intended as well as about what happened. The idea—surely worthy of Waleran of Meulan's ingenious father— was to draw a very strict line between the functions of the three bishops as bishops and ministers of the crown. As bishops they were to be left unmolested in control of their sees, and as ministers of the crown they were to be broken. A new chancellor was appointed, Philip d'Harcourt who was a protégé of Waleran's and dean of 'his' college of Beaumont-le-Roger. So far as can be seen, he had had no previous experience of the chancery in England; but this lack may have been thought desirable because a 'new deal' was clearly intended. The royal seal was changed so that it would be easy to tell at a glance if any particular grant had been made under the old dispensation or the new, and it is likely that widespread changes were expected in local government, so as to get rid of any of Roger of Salisbury's associates who were sheriffs.

This latter development has received less attention from historians than it deserves. It is well known that most of Henry I's sheriffs were lesser barons who had risen to power, not through any influence in the counties, but through hard work in the central administration.[20] Many of them must have had their careers made for them by Roger of Salisbury, and could be expected to be in a dangerous state of mind if he was dismissed. It would therefore be necessary to watch over their activities and, if necessary, replace them. This meant that Stephen would have to find a new set of local governors who could oversee the work of the sheriffs and suppress incipient rebellion. Both inclination and policy would probably lead him to pick his men from the upper nobility, and particularly from Waleran's friends. Notions of honour and dignity would then urge that their office be styled that of earl (*comes*), while a sheriff (*vicecomes*) was retained as their subordinate to manage the more tedious routines of government.

20 Judith A. Green, *The Government of England under Henry I* (Cambridge, 1986), 285–6 shows that of the 20 sheriffs in office in 1129–30, three (or possibly four) came from the greater and five from the lesser landholding families, while twelve were 'of unknown social origin'. She reckons (pp. 207–8) that 'over the reign as a whole, the number of counties in the hands of *curiales* was small, probably only three or four at any one time with the exception of 1130', but in that exceptional year the number of counties in the hands of *curiales* (thanks to Richard Basset and Aubrey de Vere) was fifteen—exactly half of the total.

This would seem to have been the real reason for Stephen's prolific creation of earldoms. He was not bestowing empty honours, but trying to ensure that local government was controlled by his friends rather than by the bureaucrats whom Henry I and Roger of Salisbury had installed. The reasons for thinking this are set out in detail in Appendix I, together with a full list of the earls, but for our present purpose the most significant facts are perhaps the dates of the new earldoms, for they were nearly all created in the years 1138–40, immediately before or after the arrest of the bishops. By the end of 1138 ten or eleven counties would have been under the control of earls committed to Stephen's cause, and by the end of 1140 another eight or nine. The only one of the new earls to have had administrative experience was Geoffrey de Mandeville, who had been sheriff of Essex before he was made earl.[21] The others were primarily military men and designedly so, for quite apart from the potential danger of Bishop Roger's men, there was a whole crop of local rebellions by men who were disappointed in the grants they had received from the king. In 1138, for example, Miles de Beauchamp revolted at Bedford, Geoffrey Talbot at Hereford, William fitz Alan at Shrewsbury, Ralph Lovel and William de Mohun in Somerset, and Walchelin Maminot at Dover (though he was easily defeated by the queen's navy from Boulogne). The responsibility of the new earls was to protect their earldoms. York defended England from the Scots, Pembroke kept the southern Welsh in check, Cornwall was in opposition to Baldwin de Redvers in Devon, and Worcester, Hereford and Wiltshire almost encircled the earl of Gloucester.

It may be that such military and aristocratic government was necessary at this juncture of the reign. It may be that Roger of Salisbury and his nephews were plotting against the king and would have been able to carry some of 'their' sheriffs with them, but even if both suppositions were correct, the arrest of the bishops, at any rate in the way in which it was carried out, was a disastrous mistake. The disturbance at court was universally recognized as a contrivance, and since it was clear that though Stephen suspected the bishops he had no evidence against them, the whole affair was seen as a clever but dishonest trick. Henry I, when a baron had defied him to his face, had still refused to arrest him at court, because he was in the king's peace and therefore under safe conduct. 'As you have come to court,' he said, 'I will not arrest you; but you will repent of your evil designs against me.'[22] He had been able to take this firm and kingly line because he was confident that he would be

21 *Reg*. iii. 40, 543.
22 *OV* vi. 214.

able to deal with the man in due course. Stephen had no such confidence. He dared not warn the bishops of his intention or give them time to raise an army, but thought that the only way in which he could possibly catch them was by a trick, when they were disarmed and 'in his peace'. Apparently he did not realize that in so doing he was proclaiming both his own weakness and his perfidy.

The perfidy was doubly apparent because by condemning the bishops in his own court he had broken his promise to the Church. In the charter of liberties which he had granted in 1136 (p. 17), he had specifically stated that 'justice over ecclesiastical persons and all clerics and their belongings . . . should be in the hands of bishops'. Had he forgotten that this charter was the price which he had paid the Church for making him king? Did he think that his brother Henry would acquiesce in such a breach of faith, or imagine that by keeping him out of Canterbury he had rendered him powerless? If so, he was very badly mistaken. Henry had not let matters rest after his defeat in the Canterbury election. Within three months he had secured from the pope a legatine commission, though he apparently agreed not to produce it unless his suspicions of Stephen's intentions were proved correct. He now produced it, and as papal legate (and thus superior to the archbishop of Canterbury) summoned the king to appear before a council of the Church to be held at Winchester on 29 August 1139.

William of Malmesbury was present at the council and has left us a vivid account of the proceedings. He tells us how the king sent earls to the council to enquire why he had been summoned:

> The legate [Henry] answered in brief that one who remembered he owed obedience to the faith of Christ should not complain if he had been summoned by Christ's ministers to give satisfaction when he knew himself guilty of an offence such as our times had nowhere seen; for it belonged to pagan times to imprison bishops and deprive them of their property.[23]

After some consultation, the earls decided that the charge should be answered, and thus recognized the competence of the court, which was in itself a victory for the Church. Stephen's case, presented by his chamberlain Aubrey de Vere, was in substance that the bishops had been arrested not as bishops but as servants of the king, since they 'managed his affairs and received his pay', and this reply was eventually upheld, to the evident chagrin of Bishop Henry, by the archbishop of Rouen. He gave it as his opinion that the root of the matter, and the actual cause of the bishops' arrest, was the castles which they had

23 *Hist. Nov.* para. 472.

refused to surrender to the king. If they wished to claim that these castles were church property and sacrosanct, they would first have to 'prove by canon law that they were entitled to have them'.[24]

This judgment, besides upholding the conduct of the king, implied disapproval of Bishop Henry's behaviour, for he had built more castles than any other bishop, at Winchester, Merdon, Farnham and Bishop's Waltham (Hants), Downton (Wilts) and Taunton (Som).[25] It was not surprising that the council broke up in confusion, with both sides threatening to appeal to Rome, and the king's men forbidding the bishops to do so. Stephen may well have thought he had carried the day, but he had allowed the Church to sit in judgment on him, and had forced his brother, now papal legate, into open opposition.[26] It was not an enviable position to find himself in, twenty-nine days before his rival, the empress, was to land in England.

24 *Ibid.* para. 475.
25 Winchester Annals, in *Annales Monastici* (R.S.) ii. 61.
26 Since the council broke up without condemning Stephen, there was no question of anyone having to shun him, let alone to renounce their allegiance. But relations between King and Church did cool; the number of bishops at court at any one time in 1140 was never great, and Henry Bishop of Winchester, finding his personal influence reduced, spent much of his time on fruitless peace negotiations (p. 43 below). Full details of ecclesiastics at court in 1140 are given by Kenji Yeshitake 'The arrest of the bishops in 1139 and its consequences' in *Journ. Med. Hist.* 14 (1988), 97–114.

CHAPTER FOUR

The Empress and her Party, 1136–1140

So far we have been considering the successes and failures of King Stephen. It is now time to look at events from the viewpoint of the empress, for just as two rivals can both have their victories, so they can both have difficulties and both make mistakes. The first difficulty that Matilda had to face was that she was a woman; the second was her husband. The trouble with him was not simply that he was only a count whereas her first husband had been an emperor; nor simply that she was eleven years older than he; nor even that their personalities were incompatible. The real trouble was that Geoffrey was an Angevin and proud of it, making no attempt to disguise the fact that it was his typically Angevin ambition to conquer Normandy. When he invaded Normandy after Henry I's death (as also before), he made no pretence of acting merely on his wife's behalf. He claimed the duchy for himself, invaded it at the head of his Angevin army, and kept his wife firmly in the background. The Normans called his soldiers 'Guiribecs' and claimed that they burnt villages, desecrated churches, slew priests, pillaged indiscriminately, and slaughtered all the flocks and herds they came across, eating the flesh 'raw or half-cooked without any salt or bread', and sending the hides back to their own country in carts.[1] It would not be easy to persuade the Normans that the leader of such an army was their rightful duke; and if he was to succeed at all, the first essential was to win the support of a noble who was essentially Norman and whom other Normans would respect.

The man ideally qualified for this role was Robert Earl of Gloucester. As King Henry's son and one of the greatest nobles of his court, he was irreproachably Norman; he was widely respected as a man

1 *OV* vi. 468, 472.

of honour; and having himself negotiated Matilda's marriage on his father's behalf, he could not complain of her Angevin husband. In his conduct after his father's death, however, Earl Robert disappointed Matilda greatly. After three months' hesitation he recognized Stephen as king, and though he subsequently claimed to have done so only as a temporary expedient in order to make contact with the nobles in England, his presence in Stephen's army at Exeter was undoubtedly a severe blow to his sister's cause. In Normandy he held Caen and Bayeux and kept everyone in suspense as to what he intended to do next. For fear of antagonizing him Stephen did not dare remove him, nor Geoffrey attack him, and perhaps Robert had hopes of establishing a neutral position for himself there. It is more probable however that he was simply finding it difficult to make up his mind. After the affair of Livarot, when he claimed that Stephen had tried to ambush him, it was still a year before he decided to support his sister and submit Caen and Bayeux to Angevin rule (June 1138), and even then the formal niceties of feudal law took precedence over decisive action. He sent envoys to Stephen to announce his 'defiance', and himself remained immovable in Normandy.

'Defiance' or *diffidatio* was a formal renunciation of fealty. It released Earl Robert from the homage he had done Stephen, and meant that in future he owed him no service or loyalty. It also released Stephen from every obligation to Earl Robert, and gave him the opportunity, which he took, of declaring his lands forfeit. Robert should therefore have been ready to cross over to England at once in order to help his vassals to defend his (and their) lands, but he was too slow. One of his vassals, Walchelin Maminot, who was in charge of Dover, revolted in order to secure him a port of entry, but before he had been able to make use of it, Stephen's queen, Matilda of Boulogne, blockaded the place by land and sea— her ships from Boulogne were invaluable—and forced it to submit to her.[2] As a result Robert remained in Normandy, and wasted sixteen months while his English vassals were left to fend for themselves. This meant that Stephen was able to seize their lands and castles piecemeal without any fear of coordinated resistance. All that the depressed vassals could do was to retreat to the earl's castle at Bristol and prepare for a desperate defence.[3]

Stephen immediately summoned a vast army and marched on Bristol. There were no great difficulties in his way, because he had a

2 *OV* vi. 520.
3 William of Malmesbury (*Hist. Nov.* para. 467) says that only Bristol remained to the earl but was probably exaggerating.

garrison at Bath which had resisted the attacks of the earl's men, and the sheriff of Gloucestershire, Miles of Gloucester, was still loyal. But, as had been said of Stephen's father, 'there's no use making a good beginning unless you go through to the end', and when the army reached Bristol, those who secretly sympathized with the earl managed to weaken Stephen's resolution. The *Gesta Stephani*, whose author may well have been present, describes how some of the king's advisers recommended a full-scale siege, and urged that the river should be blocked with 'a huge mass of rocks, beams and turves at the point where the approach to the town narrowed', so as to prevent the passage of boats and flood the city.

> But others, and especially those who only pretended to serve the king but really favoured the earl, confuted the sound and acceptable advice of these men, and urged that it would be a waste of time and a profitless labour to try to block up the unfathomable sea with masses of timber and stone, since it was very clear that anything rolled in would either sink and be swallowed up from the mere depth of the water, or else would be entirely washed away and brought to nothing by strong flooding tides.[4]

They persuaded Stephen that it would be better to turn his attention to other places where quick victories could be won with little effort, and consequently he led his army away from Bristol in order to capture Castle Cary from Ralph Lovel, and Harptree from William fitz John. If he had succeeded in taking Bristol, these other castles would probably have fallen in any case, but Stephen was apparently pleased with his victories, since he had demonstrated that Earl Robert could not, or would not, leave Normandy in order to defend his English vassals.

Because of his delay in crossing over to England, Earl Robert had also lost the opportunity of co-ordinating his activities with those of King David of Scotland, who had invaded Northumbria earlier in the year. King David was Matilda's uncle and suffered from exactly the same disadvantage as her husband, in that most people thought he wanted to invade the kingdom anyway, and that his niece's cause was merely a good excuse. When, at the end of July 1138, he crossed the Tees and entered Yorkshire with an army which included a large number of 'Pictish' troops from Galloway, it was regarded almost as a barbarian invasion. Though Stephen was busy with rebels in the South, Archbishop Thurstan assembled the barons of Yorkshire and persuaded them to fight. He ordered all men to defend the Church of Christ against the barbarians, and instructed all priests to lead their parishioners with crosses, banners and saints' relics to the

---

4 G.S. 66. This presumably refers to the Avon gorge.

meeting-place of the magnates. There he had a standard made as the emblem of resistance. It consisted of a ship's mast mounted on a carriage, adorned with the banners of St Peter of York, St John of Beverley, and St Wilfred of Ripon, and surmounted by a silver pyx containing the Body of Christ. Round this standard the army assembled and drew up for battle in a plain near Northallerton on 22 August 1138. The Scottish attack was led by the 'Picts' from Galloway, who had demanded the position of honour as of native right, claiming that lacking armour though they were, they would be invulnerable to troops in armour. They soon discovered their mistake. They could make no headway against the English knights who had dismounted and taken up positions in the front rank, in order to protect the archers whose arrows 'buzzed like bees and flew like rain'. The slaughter was immense, and within two hours the Scots had been routed.

The Battle of the Standard was a severe blow for the empress. Her uncle had not only been defeated, but had also succeeded in uniting the barons of Yorkshire against him and identifying her cause with a horde of barbarian Picts. When taken in conjunction with the fact that Earl Robert had lost nearly all his lands in southern England, it made 1138 a year of disasters for her. If she was to retrieve them, she would have to cross to England herself in order to rally fresh support, but the difficulty was to see how she could get there, because all the south-coast ports were now under Stephen's control and a voyage round Land's End to Bristol was too hazardous to be attempted. In August 1139 she sent Baldwin de Redvers from Normandy to capture Wareham, but after a temporary success he was forced to withdraw to Corfe Castle.[5] It looked as if, lacking a port to land at, the empress would be forced to spend yet another winter in Normandy.

Then her luck turned. She received from William d'Aubigny *pincerna*, now married to King Henry I's widow, Queen Adeliza, an invitation to land at Arundel.[6] She accepted it, and on 30 September 1139 arrived there with Robert Earl of Gloucester and a force of 140 knights. As soon as they were admitted to the castle, Earl Robert committed his sister to Queen Adeliza's care and rode off with a dozen knights to rally support at Wallingford and Bristol. He apparently thought that the English barons would rise as one man and that an immediate advance on London would be possible. He must have been encouraged by the speed with which Brien fitz Count the lord of Wallingford joined him, but he was both shaken and surprised when he

5 G.S. 84.
6 Robert de Torigny, in *Chronicles* iv. 137.

learnt that Stephen had marched on Arundel and so terrified Queen Adeliza that she had surrendered the empress to him. He eventually learnt that Queen Adeliza's submission had not been unconditional and that she had received an undertaking from Stephen that he would give the empress a safe-conduct to Bristol, but to judge from William of Malmesbury's account, Earl Robert was as angry at the way in which things had turned out as were most of Stephen's supporters.[7] They were as indignant that Matilda had been allowed to leave Arundel, as Earl Robert was that she had not been allowed to stay.

The man who persuaded Stephen to give the empress free passsage to Bristol was his brother, Henry of Blois, Bishop of Winchester, and it has sometimes been thought that he gave it treacherously in order to gain his revenge for Stephen's treatment of both the Church and himself.[7a] It is more likely however that the advice was not dishonest but mistaken. The mistake, a very easy one to make so soon after the arrest of the bishops, would have been the assumption that a really large number of nobles would rise to the support of the empress as soon as they heard that she had landed and was in danger. In this case a lengthy siege of Arundel whose castle, built by Robert de Bellême, was one of the strongest in the land, would have been extremely dangerous. But by granting the empress free passage to Bristol, Stephen ensured that if armies of rebels were to march across England to the empress's support, they would be marching away from London and the English Channel, and not towards them. None the less, most people thought that the empress had had a lucky escape in being allowed to leave Arundel, and would have expected the number of her adherents to be relatively small. It could hardly have been expected that many barons would risk forfeiting their lands and their lives simply out of loyalty to the empress, for nearly all of them had already forsworn her once by recognizing Stephen as king. With a few gallant exceptions, the men who could be counted on were those who already had a grievance against Stephen, and who had nothing to lose by revolt because they were 'disinherited'.[8]

7 *Hist. Nov.* paras. 478, 506; cf. John of Worcester, 55, who gives the excuse offered by Adeliza to the king. It is odd, but apparently true, that she and her husband remained loyal to Stephen for the rest of their lives; cf. Gervase of Canterbury (R.S.) i. 110.

7a One fact which may suggest that he had formed some connection with the empress is that he was selected as one of the two people to escort her to Bristol, the other being Waleran of Meulan (*Hist. Nov.* ch. 478). In order to avoid the risk of treachery it would have been normal for Stephen to nominate one of the escorts and the empress the other. Since it is hard to believe that Waleran of Meulan was not Stephen's nominee, it would seem that Bishop Henry was the empress's.

8 Cf. *Hist. Nov.* para. 488: 'quorum erat maior exheredatorum numerus'.

The 'disinherited' were those who had not received from Stephen the lands which their fathers had held before them, or which they themselves had held under Henry I. A few of them, like Baldwin de Redvers (p. 22) had been disinherited deliberately for their failure to recognize Stephen as king, but most of them were men whose inheritances were disputed by others. An extreme example was Robert of Bampton who lost Uffculme at the beginning of Stephen's reign, because Glastonbury Abbey was able to establish the rights it had had before the Norman Conquest.[9] Most of the 'disinherited' had shorter histories than this, and many of them had only lost their lands under Henry I, some of them by forfeiture for rebellion, others through the legal chicaneries of his justices. Two of the more prominent 'disinherited', for example, were Geoffrey Talbot and Gilbert de Lacy, who thought they had been cheated of their share of the Lacy inheritance by Miles of Gloucester in Henry I's reign.[10] Another, and fairly typical, case was William Peverel of Dover who had a claim through the wife of his uncle Hamo (whose heir he was) to the barony of Gerard de Tornai; Henry I claimed that the barony had escheated to the crown before Hamo's marriage took place, but Hamo claimed that his wife was still legal heir, and so did his nephew.[11] In many such disputes it was almost impossible to give a confident judgment, and when the lands had already been redistributed among other families, it was not possible to please everyone, or to be fair to all. There were too many claimants for too few baronies, and do what one might there would always be some men complaining that they had been disinherited. They formed a ready-made opposition to any king, and flocked to the support of the empress.[12]

It was impossible to form an effective party from the 'disinherited' alone, since the very fact that they were disinherited made their support less effective than that of men who were in possession of lands and castles. If the empress was to be a serious claimant to the throne, she would have to demonstrate that she had territory under her control, if only for her own security; hence the importance of the only three great landed lords who rose to her support at once, Robert Earl of Gloucester, Brien fitz Count and Miles of Gloucester. Brien, the illegitimate son of Count Alan 'Fergan' of Brittany, was lord of the castle and honour of

9 H. P. R. Finberg, 'Uffculme', in *Lucerna* (London, 1964), 204–21.
10 R. H. C. Davis in *Stenton Miscellany*, 140. Cf. W. E. Wightman, *The Lacy Family in England and Normandy, 1066–1194* (Oxford, 1966), 175 ff.
11 R. W. Eyton, *Shropshire* ii. 106.
12 R. H. C. Davis, 'What happened in Stephen's reign', *History* xlix (1964), 1–12. Appendix IV, below pp. 150–3.

Wallingford in Berkshire. He had been brought up at Henry I's court, almost as a foster-son of the king, and he undoubtedly felt a deep obligation to Henry's daughter. Though he had recognized Stephen as king and attended his court on at least three occasions,[13] he rose in revolt the moment that he heard of Matilda's landing and remained her most unselfish and chivalrous supporter. As a leader and as a general, however, he was not nearly so significant as Miles of Gloucester.

Miles, as we have already seen (p. 19), was one of Henry I's 'new men' or 'professional' barons whose services had been purchased by Stephen and who, as sheriff of Gloucestershire, constable of Gloucester castle, and a royal justice as well, was the local counterpart of Bishop Roger of Salisbury, the great justiciar. Indeed it may well have been the fact of Roger's arrest which finally decided him to revolt against Stephen, for though he was devoted to the empress, his local interests clashed with those of Earl Robert.[14] He did homage to the empress soon after she had arrived at Bristol, admitted her to Gloucester, and then proceeded to demonstrate that he was the one man amongst her supporters who could see the military situation with a professional eye, and take quick and decisive action.

The empress's position at Bristol was none too secure. Stephen had sent her there from Arundel with the expressed intention of isolating her, and now he was acting with vigour and speed. He marched from Arundel to Wallingford, where he constructed siege works. Then, leaving a task force to beleaguer the castle, he proceeded with the main body of his army against Bristol. On the way he secured a small castle at South Cerney near Cirencester and the important castle of Malmesbury, and he had just begun the siege of Trowbridge, which was held by Miles of Gloucester's son-in-law, Humphrey de Bohun, when he heard news of disaster in his rear. Miles of Gloucester had marched right across his flank, relieved Wallingford and routed the besiegers. If Stephen did not return rapidly from the west, he might even be in a position to advance on London. Stephen therefore abandoned the siege of Trowbridge and returned to London himself. Miles, for his part, returned to the west, and intent on diverting Stephen from any further assault on Wallingford, sacked Worcester (7 November). The manœuvre had the desired effect. Stephen marched on Worcester, arriving there on 30 November with Waleran of Meulan, whom he had recently made earl of the county. He had a big army, but Miles had no intention of

13 He witnessed for Stephen at Westminster and Oxford in 1136, and at Hereford in 1138 (*Reg.* iii. 271, 944, 383, 385).
14 R. H. C. Davis in *Stenton Miscellany*, 142–4.

meeting it. He had retreated in good time, avoiding any further action until the king moved away. This happened quite soon, for after capturing the castle at Sudeley, Stephen heard news of the death of Bishop Roger of Salisbury (11 December 1139) and rushed to Salisbury to secure the see. From there he was called to suppress other revolts, at Ely and in Cornwall, and while he was thus engaged, Miles of Gloucester recovered his castle of South Cerney and, having failed to recover Sudeley, joined Geoffrey Talbot in a successful siege of Hereford. By his astute generalship Miles had not only saved Wallingford but also secured the whole northern flank of the empress's position. He had also, as befitted a professional soldier, laid the foundations of a principality for himself in Herefordshire, for in addition to the city of Hereford which, owing to Geoffrey Talbot's death soon after the siege,[15] he was able to make his own, he was shortly to receive the castle and honour of Abergavenny from Brien fitz Count, as a reward for his services to Wallingford.[16]

Few of the empress's supporters had such spectacular success as Miles of Gloucester, but the tactics he had demonstrated were soon copied by others. When it was realized that Stephen's army, though infinitely superior to anything which the rebels could muster, could not be everywhere at once, potential supporters who had failed to make a move in October, began to rebel against the king. In January Nigel Bishop of Ely fortified the Isle of Ely, but he made the mistake of staying there long enough to be besieged, and eventually had to flee to Gloucester. In February William the son of Richard fitz Turold rebelled in Cornwall, marrying his daughter to Reginald fitz Roy who, as his name implies, was one of Henry I's illegitimate sons and an ardent supporter of the empress.[17] Stephen marched against him, installed Alan of Britanny as earl of Cornwall, and on his return through Devon did his utmost to force the earl of Gloucester to give battle. The earl retreated to Bristol, for he knew his forces were still too small to defeat the king, and that the best that could be done was to wear the king out with repeated marches and counter-marches.

The difficulty about such tactics was that though they weakened the king, they did little to strengthen the empress; and that if repeated

15 Geoffrey Talbot was killed in a skirmish at Bath on 20 August 1140. As the continuator of Florence of Worcester (ed. Thorpe, ii. 127) says, he was neither wholly for the earl of Gloucester nor wholly for the king. His main aim would have been to recover his share of the Lacy inheritance from Miles of Gloucester, and therefore he supported the side opposed to Miles. When Miles changed sides in October 1139, Geoffrey must have been disconcerted.

16 *Reg.* iii. 394.

17 *G.S.* 100–4.

indefinitely they would lead to a state of anarchy. This danger became particularly noticeable in March and April with regard to the activities of Robert fitz Hubert, a Flemish mercenary in the earl of Gloucester's pay.[18] On 26 March 1140 he captured Devizes by a surprise attack at night; and having captured it, he decided not to hand it over to his master but to keep it for himself. According to William of Malmesbury it was his ambition to acquire the whole district between London and Winchester,[19] but his most immediate aim was to gain possession of the castle at Marlborough. This was held by John fitz Gilbert, a baron whom most people considered to be a supporter of the empress, but whom some still thought a supporter of the king.[20] He outwitted fitz Hubert, and instead of being caught by him, captured him and handed him over (for the sum of 500 marks) to the earl of Gloucester. The earl took his prisoner to Devizes and (as Stephen had done with Roger le Poer) threatened to hang him if the garrison did not surrender. The garrison refused. Fitz Hubert was hanged; and the garrison continued to resist, until they somehow succeeded in negotiating a handsome sum of money for surrendering the castle not to the earl of Gloucester but to his adversary, Hervey Brito, the king's new earl of Wiltshire.

The confusion was such that it is impossible to establish the exact sequence of events during this year, let alone to disentangle the intentions and motives of the various nobles. The few facts which we know can be briefly stated. In the spring or early summer Stephen returned to Worcester and advanced from there on Miles of Gloucester; and Miles retreated to the safety of Gloucester, thus allowing the king to enter Tewkesbury and sack the palace of Miles's old rival, but present ally, Robert Earl of Gloucester.[21] In June Hugh Bigod revolted in East Anglia, but whether in the empress's interest or his own we do not know. Stephen captured Bungay Castle from him, made peace with him and left East Anglia, but apparently had to return there in August to go through the whole process again.[22]

In August the earl of Gloucester attempted, but failed, to take Bath. Early in September he and Ralph Paynel of Dudley raided Nottingham

18 It was from him that Stephen had recaptured Malmesbury in October 1139 (John of Worcester, 61).

19 *Hist. Nov.* para. 485.

20 In *Hist. Nov.* para. 485 and *G.S.*, 104–8, John fitz Gilbert is stated to have been a supporter of the empress. John of Worcester, 62–3, says he was *in regis fidelitate*, and alleges that when he handed fitz Hubert over to the earl of Gloucester, he himself urged the garrison of Devizes not to surrender, promising them that neither he nor the earl would harm their former leader.

21 John of Worcester, 60.

22 Annals of Waverley, in *Annales Monastici* (R.S.) ii. 228.

and sacked it; it was presumably intended as some sort of diversion, but why they chose Nottingham, and why they were aided by knights of the earl of Warwick is a complete mystery.[23]

In circumstances such as these one can but sympathize with the attempts of Henry Bishop of Winchester to negotiate a compromise peace between his brother and the empress. His motives in these negotiations have been doubted, because he might well have felt bitter about his brother's conduct towards both the Church and himself. But the evidence suggests that he was not attempting to avenge himself, but rather that he was genuinely concerned to mitigate the harshness of the civil war which his brother's folly had made inevitable. At the end of May (1140) he arranged a conference near Bath between Stephen's queen, Matilda of Boulogne, and the earl of Gloucester.[24] In September he crossed the channel to formulate new proposals, which obviously included Normandy since he enlisted the aid of the king of France and Count Theobald of Blois. In November he returned to England and put the proposals to both parties. The empress accepted them, but Stephen prevaricated, and so the war continued.

> Then at last (wrote William of Malmesbury) the legate [Henry] withdrew within himself, watching like the others to see how things would turn out. For what is the use of struggling against a racing stream? It is the extreme of folly, as someone says, to seek nothing but hatred by one's efforts.[25]

Time would show whether Stephen was right to reject all compromises in the hope of winning a decisive battle.

23 Continuation of Florence of Worcester, in *Florentii Wigornensis Chronicon*, ed. Thorpe, ii. 128. Ralph Paynel's instigation of the raid is presumably to be connected with the fact that after the battle of Lincoln the empress gave the custody of Nottingham to William Paynel of Drax, who was probably Ralph's first cousin (John of Hexham in *Symeon of Durham* (R.S.) ii. 309 and *E.Y.C.* vi. 48). *G.S.* 78 suggests that the Earl of Warwick did not join the empress till after the battle of Lincoln.

24. *Hist. Nov.* para. 486. It may well be true, as William of Malmesbury suggests (*Hist. Nov.* para. 502), that Henry had concluded an agreement with Robert Earl of Gloucester, limiting the number of knights with which he would serve the king to twenty. This would not have been an act of treachery, so much as an attempt to limit the scope of hostilities, exactly parallel to the well-known treaty between the earls of Chester and Leicester (1148–53), pp. 111–12.

25 *Hist. Nov.* para. 486.

CHAPTER FIVE
Disaster,
1140–1141

During 1140 Stephen's main adviser was Waleran of Meulan. Henry of Blois's influence continued to wane, and it is probable that Stephen and Waleran found that one of the main uses of his peace negotiations was that they kept him out of the way. In March, when it became necessary to nominate a new bishop of Salisbury, Henry, who as papal legate naturally expected to have a decisive say in the appointment, proposed Henry de Sully who was his and Stephen's nephew; but Stephen passed him over in favour of Waleran of Meulan's protégé, Philip d'Harcourt, whom he had already made his chancellor the previous summer. For Philip the promotion may well have suggested yet greater advancement, for when Roger of Salisbury had been raised from the chancellorship to the see of Salisbury, he had become the king's justiciar, in control of his whole administration. Henry of Blois could obviously not tolerate that; nor indeed could he turn a blind eye to simony or to the fact that the chapter of Salisbury had refused to accept Philip as bishop. He used his power as legate to oppose the nomination; and though Philip appealed to Rome he got nothing for his pains, though it subsequently emerged that in the course of a brief stay at Salisbury he had purloined a relic described as 'one arm covered with gold plate and adorned with precious stones'.[1]

One would have thought that by this time Stephen would have known that it was both useless and dangerous to try to thwart his brother in ecclesiastical affairs, but one of the qualities which he seems to have inherited from his father was his unwarranted and irrepressible

---

1 This was restored to Salisbury between 1147 and 1153, probably in 1148 at the Council of Reims. Bourrienne, *Antiquus Cartularius Ecclesiae Baiocensis*, i. 80–1, reading in the first line *T* (*heobaldo*) for *Thoma*.

optimism. He seems to have thought that because he could muster a larger army than the empress, everything was bound to turn out to his advantage. He did not realize that an army was useless unless it was in the right place at the right time, and that this could only be ensured if the king knew in advance where trouble was to be expected. One of the great qualities of Henry I, according to Orderic, had been that 'he penetrated everyone's secrets and clandestine operations, so that the people concerned were at a loss to understand how the king obtained his knowledge'.[2] Presumably he had used his sheriffs as a secret service, for in the small world of Norman England it would have been easy for them to know which barons were meeting which, and to guess the reason, since as the king's financial agents they would have had an accurate knowledge of everyone's grievances. By 1140, however, the king's intelligence service had clearly broken down, perhaps because Stephen had replaced too many sheriffs, perhaps because Waleran of Meulan and Philip d'Harcourt could not command their confidence as Roger of Salisbury had done. We can only say that during 1140 Stephen was always one move behind, instead of ahead of, the rebels, rushing from one end of the country to the other in an attempt to suppress each new revolt as it occurred. He tried to ease the situation for himself by appointing new earls to act as military commanders in specific counties—in this year he appointed Alan of Richmond to Cornwall, Hervey Brito to Wiltshire, Robert Earl of Leicester to Herefordshire, and Geoffrey de Mandeville to Essex—but military expedients were no substitute for administrative efficiency. They might succeed in suppressing rebellions, but they could not, and did not, prevent them happening.

One way in which an attempt might be made to bolster up Stephen's position was by means of foreign alliances. The person who seems to have been most keenly alive to this possibility was Stephen's queen, Matilda of Boulogne.[3] She had few illusions about the dangers of her husband's situation—as we have already seen (p. 43), she took part in Henry of Blois's negotiations with Robert Earl of Gloucester in May 1140—and was prepared to use her own connections to good advantage. In February 1140 she betrothed her eldest son Eustace to Constance, sister of King Louis VII of France, and thus formed an alliance which was both sensible and 'natural', since Louis was as anxious as anyone to prevent the Count of Anjou from becoming too powerful. The marriage was solemnized by the end of the year, when Eustace cannot

2 *OV* vi. 100.
3 There is a good life of her in Mary Ann Everett Green, *Lives of the Princesses of England* (London, 1849).

have been more than fourteen years old, but it came too late to be of any immediate use before the disaster of 1141.[4]

Another treaty which Stephen's queen helped to negotiate was the second treaty of Durham which had been concluded with the Scots on 9 April 1139, but of which the results only became apparent in 1140.[5] King David was the queen's uncle— it is a confusing fact that he was uncle to both Matilda the empress and Matilda the queen—and Stephen seems to have thought that this fortunate relationship could ensure a lasting peace, if it were coupled with a particularly large bribe. Thus in spite of the Battle of the Standard, the second Treaty of Durham was even more generous to the Scots than the previous treaty had been (pp. 19–20). King David's son, Henry, was given back all the lands which he had held before 1138 except for Newcastle and Bamborough, and for these he was to be compensated with two towns of equal value in the south. In addition he was given the earldom of Northumbria, which included the present counties of Northumberland, Durham, Cumberland, Westmorland and Lancashire north of the Ribble; and though Stephen stipulated that the laws established in them by Henry I should remain inviolate, he allowed the barons of Northumbria to do homage to the new earl for their lands, saving only the fealty which they had done to himself as king. In return for these substantial concessions King David and his son were required to give nothing except a promise of lifelong peace and good faith, with four hostages as pledges of their word.[6]

It was an unfortunate treaty, because it was not 'natural' in the way that the French alliance was. David's natural inclination was to invade England wherever he could, and if circumstances were sufficiently favourable no treaty would ever prevent him. It was pure waste of land and money to pay for promises to the contrary. There was far more to be said for rewarding David's enemies than for rewarding him, especially as the barons of Yorkshire had already demonstrated that nothing united them so well as a Scottish invasion. One magnate in particular would probably have served Stephen most faithfully if only he had been granted that part of Northumbria which he claimed as his own, and which had now been given to the Scots.

This man was Ranulf Earl of Chester, whose nickname was *aux Gernons* (moustaches). It was his grievance that Henry I had 'disinherited' his father, Ranulf *le meschin* (i.e. junior) in 1120 when, in

---

4 Continuation of *Florence of Worcester*, ed. Thorpe, ii. 125; *Henry of Huntingdon* (R.S. 265). The bride was in England by Feb. 1141. See p. 58.

5 John of Hexham, in *Symeon of Durham* (R.S.) ii. 300.

6 Richard of Hexham, in *Chronicles* iii. 178.

return for allowing him to inherit his uncle's earldom of Chester, he had forced him to surrender his lordship of Carlisle and Cumberland.[7] To him it was irrelevant that the earldom of Chester was far more valuable than Carlisle. It was a question of principle; Carlisle was his patrimony, and no king had any right to deprive him of it, except for treason. He lived for the day when he could recover it. If Stephen had granted it to him, he would have defended it and the whole Scottish frontier with his life. Now that Stephen had given it with the rest of Northumbria to the Scottish Prince Henry, he was prepared to revolt in order to win possession of what he considered to be his own.

It was in 1140 that he struck. In that year, according to John of Hexham, Prince Henry attended Stephen's court (presumably at Michaelmas), and it was Ranulf's plan to overwhelm him on his way back to Scotland. Stephen's queen got wind of Ranulf's intentions and, being a woman of honour, persuaded her husband to escort the prince back to his father's kingdom.[8] He did so, but by then the damage had been done so far as Ranulf was concerned. Either in preparation for the ambush, or else in an attempt to outface the royal escort, he had contrived to seize the King's castle at Lincoln. According to Orderic, the only writer to give any details, he and his half-brother, William de Roumare, sent their wives to visit the constable's wife in the castle. When they had been there some time, Earl Ranulf arrived also. Being dressed in his ordinary clothes and escorted by three knights, he had apparently come to fetch the ladies, but no sooner had he gained an entrance, than he and his knights seized every weapon they could find, ejected the royal garrison, and admitted the men of William de Roumare. They had become rebels against the King.[9]

At this point all the chronicle sources break down. John of Hexham mentions the obscure, but apparently important, fact that Earl Alan of Richmond captured the castle of *Galclint*, which may perhaps have been an old name for Belvoir;[10] and there is a gap in the *Gesta Stephani*,

---

7 R. H. C. Davis, 'King Stephen and the Earl of Chester revised', *E.H.R.* lxxv (1960), 659.

8 John of Hexham, in *Symeon of Durham* (R.S.) ii. 306.

9 Orderic, v. 125.

10 John of Hexham, in *Symeon of Durham* (R.S.) ii. 306. Arnold (*ibid.*) identifies the place as Gilling in Ryedale, near Helmsley, Yorks, but the context suggests both an important castle and Lincolnshire (cf. *ibid.* ii. 308). Cronne (*T.R.H.S.*, 4th series, xx (1937), 118) suggests Gaultney Wood in Rushton, near Kettering, Northants, but though this place was called Galklynt in the thirteenth century, it has no castle. Belvoir castle will fulfil all the conditions of John of Hexham's narrative, since it was (*a*) an important castle, (*b*) in Lincolnshire (then), (*c*) previously held by William d'Aubigny *Brito*, and (*d*) claimed by Ranulf Earl of Chester by the end of the reign. The name Belvoir is not in Domesday Book and is first found (as *Belveder*) in a charter of 1105 (*Reg.* ii. 689). It is not impossible

caused by the loss of two folios from the original manuscript. All we know is that the king eventually made some sort of pact with the two brothers and left Lincolnshire in peace, reaching London before Christmas.[11] We may imagine that his advisers had pointed out that though Ranulf had not yet sided with the empress,[12] a determined attack by the king would force him to do so, if only to get her assistance; that his quarrel with the Scottish prince was only natural and should on no account be confused with the totally different quarrel between king and empress; and that if ever the Scottish alliance should fail, his support would be invaluable. So Stephen swallowed his pride, made peace with the two brothers, and bestowed fresh honours on them, as had now become his custom.[13]

When he had got to London, however, the citizens of Lincoln secretly sent him a message complaining of the treatment they were receiving from the earl, and informing him that Earl Ranulf, his brother and both their wives were residing in the castle, completely off their guard. If the king came quickly he could easily surround the whole lot, and capture them before they had had a chance to seek aid from anywhere.[14] Stephen had just made peace with the brothers, but this was the sort of temptation he could not resist. It was clever; it required speed, which was his speciality; and it would recover Lincoln which was one of the most important towns of the realm.[15] He made a dash for it, arrived there before Twelfth Night (6 January 1141), and as expected found the place very scantily garrisoned. The citizens admitted him to the town, and he immediately set siege to the castle; but though he had been very quick, he had not been quick enough to prevent Earl Ranulf from escaping. The earl made for Cheshire in order to collect Welsh troops,

---

that an earlier name could have been used by a northern writer in 1141. Edmund King in 'The Parish of Warter and the Castle of Galchlin' (*Yorks. Arch. Journ.* 52 (1980), 49–58 (esp. 55–8)) offers *Galchlin* as an alternative reading of *Galclint* from a different MS. He also reviews the evidence for all the identifications suggested so far and adds a new one of his own, Gildersdale in the parish of Warter, but without reaching any firm conclusion.

11 *G.S.* 110; William of Malmesbury, *Hist. Nov.* para. 487; H. A. Cronne, 'Ranulf Gernons Earl of Chester, 1129–53', in *T.R.H.S.*, 4th series , xx (1937), 144–7.

12 *Hist. Nov.* para 487 is explicit that, so far from recognizing the empress, he had offended his father-in-law, the earl of Gloucester 'quia in neutro latere fidus videretur esse'; cf. *O.V.* vi. 540.

13 Perhaps it was on this occasion that he made William de Roumare Earl of Lincoln. See Appendix I.

14 *Hist. Nov.* para. 487; *G.S.* 110.

15 In 1204 Lincoln was the fourth sea-port of the realm; A. L. Poole, *From Domesday Book to Magna Carta, 1087–1216* (Oxford, 1951), 96.

appealed for assistance to his wife's father, Robert Earl of Gloucester, and promised fidelity to the empress.[16]

For the supporters of the empress this was the most wonderful stroke of good fortune. It presented them with an important new ally, and Earl Robert for once acted swiftly. He assembled an army and marched for Lincoln, joining forces on the way with the army which Ranulf had collected in Cheshire. It was not until they had almost arrived at the city that Stephen was aware of their coming. He held a council of war at which the older men advised him to entrust the city to a task force and himself withdraw so that he could return with a full-scale army levied from every part of England; but the younger men jeered and called their elders 'battle-shy boys'.[17] For Stephen, the situation must have been agonizingly similar to the one from which his father had run away at Antioch.[18] Knowing, as he must have done, that to refuse battle would mean being labelled as his father's son, instead of grandson of the Conqueror, it is not surprising that he disregarded the odds against him and decided to fight.[19]

The battle was fought on 2 February 1141, which was Sexagesima Sunday and the feast of the purification of the Virgin. It was the very day on which the earl of Gloucester's army arrived, and all contemporary accounts agree that it had just traversed a formidable obstacle. William of Malmesbury, who presumably had his story from the earl himself, says it was an unfordable river, that the earl swam across it, and (as a final touch of extravagance) that it was the raging Trent. The *Gesta Stephani* more soberly calls it a ford, and Henry of Huntingdon (who as a canon of Lincoln must have had local knowledge) describes it as 'an almost impassable swamp'. Probably it was the Foss Dyke, for there would have been swamps beside it if the Witham was in flood, and local tradition has it that the battle was fought on the level ground to the north of the city.[20]

The earl's army consisted of three principal divisions, his own, the earl of Chester's, and those disinherited by Stephen, who were granted the honour of striking the first blow, while on the flank was a mass of

---

16 See n. 12.

17 'Pueros imbelles', John of Hexham, in *Symeon of Durham* ii. 307; cf. Orderic, v. 126.

18 See p. 3, above. The parallel was exact, for the crusaders had captured the town of Antioch and were besieging the citadel when they were themselves surrounded by Karbōghā.

19 'Noluit gloriam suam fugae opprobrio deturpare', *G.S.* 112.

20 Sir James H. Ramsay, *The Foundations of England* (London, 1898), ii. 397–9, discusses the site of the battle and gives a map.

ill-organized Welsh.[21] Stephen's army included a number of great men, William of Ypres his mercenary captain, and earls Waleran of Meulan, William de Warenne, Simon of Senlis, Gilbert of Hertford, William of Aumale, Alan of Richmond and Hugh Bigod, but he was markedly short of cavalry.[22] Orderic says that some of the magnates committed gross treason by serving the king with only a few men, while sending a host of their vassals to support the enemy,[23] and in this connection one might particularly suspect Alan of Richmond and Hugh Bigod. But all chroniclers considered it a scandal that as soon as the battle was joined, the magnates took advantage of the fact that they were mounted and fled, deserting the king who had decided to fight on foot with the lesser barons. There he performed extraordinary feats of valour. Even when surrounded, he lay about him with a two-headed axe presented to him by a citizen of Lincoln, and when it broke under the wealth of blows, he used his sword until that was broken too. Finally, struck down by a stone, he was captured by William de Cahaignes, a vassal of the earl of Gloucester, who was heard shouting: 'Here, everyone, here! I've got the King.'[24]

With the king were captured Baldwin fitz Gilbert (who had delivered the battle speech because the king's voice was too soft),[25] Bernard de Balliol, Roger de Mowbray, Richard de Courcy, William Peverel of Nottingham, Gilbert de Gant (who was little more than a boy), Ingelram de Say, Ilbert de Lacy, and Richard fitz Urse, all men of respected baronial families.[26] It was only the earls and magnates who had fled. That was one of the lessons that Stephen learnt on that day. He regarded the battle as a judgment of God not only (as the popular opinion had it) for having offended the Church by his arrest of the bishops, but also for having thought that he could base an effective government on the magnates whom he had made earls. That is why the *Gesta Stephani* so poignantly tells us that after his capture Stephen was at one moment humbly confessing that defeat had come upon him as God's vengeance for his misdeeds, and at the next complaining that:

---

21 Excepting for *G.S.* 110, the chronicles are silent about Miles of Gloucester, but *Reg.* iii. 393 implies that he took part in the battle.

22 The best and fullest account of the battle is in *Henry of Huntingdon* (R.S.) 268–74, from which these and other details are taken. Gilbert de Clare's presence is noted in *OV* vi. 542.

23 Orderic, *OV* vi. 542.

24 *Henry of Huntingdon* (R.S.) 274.

25 'Quia rex Stephanus festiva voce carebat', *ibid.* 271.

26 The list is compiled from John of Hexham in *Symeon of Durham* (R.S.) ii. 307–8, with addition from *Henry of Huntingdon* (R.S.) 274 and *OV* vi. 542–4.

none the less those men were guilty of the greatest possible crime; they had broken their faith, spurned their oath, thought nothing of the homage they had done him, and had rebelled most wickedly and abominably against him,—him whom they had taken of their own free will as king and lord.[27]

After the battle the earl of Gloucester's troops sacked the city of Lincoln—they deserved it, said William of Malmesbury, for it was they who had instigated the king's whole expedition—but Stephen himself was treated with respect.[28] He was taken to the empress at Gloucester, arriving there on Quinquagesima Sunday (9 February). Four days later he was taken to Bristol where he was imprisoned in the earl of Gloucester's castle, at first being given a certain amount of liberty, but subsequently put in chains.[29] As the news of his defeat and captivity spread, his party began to disintegrate. Earl Alan of Richmond lost his northern castles to the earl of Chester, and his earldom of Cornwall to Reginald fitz Roy. Hugh Pauper lost Bedford to Miles de Beauchamp. Hervey Brito lost Devizes to a mob of rustics, abandoned Wiltshire and retired to Brittany. The earl of Warwick and Robert d'Oilli, castellan of Oxford, went over to the empress voluntarily.[30] In Normandy the magnates assembled at Mortagne and offered the kingdom and duchy to Stephen's brother, Theobald Count of Blois. He refused, but hoped that Geoffrey of Anjou would reward his altruism by giving him the city of Tours, releasing Stephen from prison, and restoring to him the lands which he had held before he was king. Geoffrey of Anjou was too much of a realist to bother about such terms. Castle after castle was surrendering to him, and his power soon extended up to the left bank of the Seine.[31] It seemed that nothing could now prevent his triumph or that of his wife.

27 *G.S.* 112–14.
28 *Hist. Nov.* para. 489.
29 *Ibid.* para. 490. Continuation of *Florence of Worcester*, ed. Thorpe, ii. 129.
30 *G.S.* 116–18.
31 *OV* vi. 548–50.

CHAPTER SIX
Recovery, 1141

With the king in custody at Bristol, it might have seemed an easy matter for the empress to secure the throne, but, taken by surprise at the extent of her victory, she moved with the utmost caution. It was not until 17 February that she left Gloucester for Cirencester, and then, having been advised above all to win the support of Henry of Blois (who was Stephen's brother, papal legate, and bishop of Winchester), she lost several more days in negotiating a meeting with him. They met eventually on 2 March at Wherwell near Winchester, and came to a formal agreement whereby the empress took an oath to the bishop, promising that all matters of importance in England, and particularly appointments to bishoprics and abbeys, should be decided according to his will, and that he for his part should receive her formally in the Church as Lady, and be faithful to her for ever. Though Henry was papal legate, this agreement was essentially personal. It did not bind the whole Church. What it meant was that Henry submitted the city of Winchester to her control—it included the royal treasury in which was the royal crown—and publicized his own change of allegiance by receiving her in his cathedral with all the honours due to a queen. This 'reception' took place on the following day (3 March). Sharing in the ceremony and associating themselves with the legate were six other bishops, Bernard of St David's (who was given precedence next to the legate), Alexander of Lincoln and Nigel of Ely (the two survivors of the trio whom Stephen had arrested), Robert of Hereford, Robert of Bath, and probably Seffrid of Chichester.[1] Archbishop Theobald was not there but arrived a few days later, doing his best to assert his

---

1 Most of the names are from *Hist. Nov.* para. 491, but Seffrid of Chichester has been added because he witnessed *Reg.* iii. 343 for the empress at Wherwell.

archiepiscopal powers in spite of the legatine authority wielded by his suffragan. He scored a point off Henry when he declared that he would have to delay swearing fealty to the empress as Lady, because 'he thought it unbefitting his reputation and position to transfer his allegiance without consulting the king'.[2] He was given permission to take most of the bishops on to Bristol where, having received Stephen's gracious permission to move with the times, they fell in with the legate's policy.

This was to summon to Winchester on 7 April a legatine council of the English Church, which in the best Hildebrandine manner would proclaim that Stephen had been cast down by the judgment of God, elect Matilda as Lady, and proceed to London to consecrate her as queen in Westminster Abbey. The purpose of the council being legatine was not simply that its president would be Bishop Henry instead of Archbishop Theobald, but more particularly that it should exercise the authority of the pope and include clergy from both provinces of the English Church. In fact the attendance seems to have been disappointing, for William of Malmesbury, who has left us an eye-witness account, refers particularly to the apologies for absence which were read aloud at the opening ceremony; and when, on the second day, the council had formally chosen the empress as Lady, it emerged that it could not proceed to consecrate her at once, because it was denied access to London and Westminster.

The legate's plan had apparently been to confront the Londoners with the council's decision, in the hope that they would respond by inviting the empress to their city in order that she might be anointed at Westminster. He had accordingly arranged for them to send delegates to Winchester, to be introduced to the council on the third day. They duly arrived, but their attitude was most disappointing. They said that their instructions were to demand the release of the king; and though they listened to the decree of the council and promised to report it to their fellow-citizens, they made it clear that without further instructions they could not change their position. A clerk of Stephen's queen then seized the opportunity to read a letter from her. She begged the clergy to restore the king, reminded the legate that the king was his brother, and insisted that those who had put the king in chains had previously done him homage and were therefore perjurors. The council was now getting out of hand, so the legate brought it to an end on the fourth day by excommunicating many of the king's adherents, particularly William Martel, the king's steward, presumably because he

2 *Hist. Nov.* para. 491.

was still holding Bishop Roger's castle at Sherborne in the name of the king.[3]

So far from having proved the strength of the empress, the council had demonstrated the pertinacity of those who, in spite of the captivity of the king, had remained loyal to Stephen's queen. Of these the chief, according to Henry of Huntingdon, was William of Ypres, Stephen's mercenary captain.[4] He held Kent and would therefore have been able to keep in contact with the queen's county of Boulogne, and obtain additional mercenary forces from Flanders at will. Other prominent supporters, according to Orderic, were Waleran of Meulan Earl of Worcester, William de Warenne Earl of Surrey, and Simon of Senlis Earl of Northampton,[5] while the legate's 'many' excommunications at Winchester suggest that there may have been others besides William Martel who held particular castles or districts for the king.[6] Stephen's supporters were still a force to be reckoned with, especially as they included the Londoners to whom he had apparently granted a commune.

A town was called a commune when its citizens had taken an oath to unite into a single corporation, and the king or overlord had recognized it and given it privileges equivalent to those of a baron or tenant-in-chief. Most feudal lords regarded communes with horror; at the end of the twelfth century an English monk described them as 'a tumult of the people, the terror of the realm, and the tepidity of the priesthood', and said that King Henry II would not have allowed one for a million silver marks;[7] but everything goes to suggest that in 1141 London was a commune, and that it was because Stephen had recognized it and given it special liberties that it was loyal to him. William of Malmesbury and the *Gesta Stephani* both refer to the commune explicitly;[8] the *Gesta Stephani* and the *Liber Eliensis* call the city the capital of the kingdom (*caput regni*);[9] Henry of Blois is

---

3 *Hist. Nov.* para. 496. 'Iste [Willelmus] immaniter exulceraverat legati animum, multis rebus eius interceptis et surreptis.' Sherborne castle belonged to the see of Salisbury, which Bishop Henry was administering during the vacancy, but was held by William Martel at any rate in 1142 (G. S. 148).

4 Henry of Huntingdon (R. S.) 275.

5 *OV* vi. 546.

6 The earls of Sussex, Hertford, Derby and York seem not to have joined the empress, since they did not witness any of her charters. The earl of Leicester seems to have been loyal to Stephen in Normandy. William of Malmesbury's silence about Simon Bishop of Worcester, coupled with the fact that he never witnessed for the empress, suggests that he may have followed his earl in not recognizing her.

7 Richard of Devizes (ed. J. T. Appleby), 49.

8 *Hist. Nov.* para. 495; *G.S.* 6

9 *G.S.* 12; cf. 'regionis reginam metropolis', *ibid.* 4; *Liber Eliensis* (ed. Blake), 324.

reported to have called the Londoners 'more or less nobles on account of the greatness of their city in England';[10] and the archbishop of Rouen, writing to thank them for their loyalty to Stephen, addressed his letter to 'the glorious senators, honoured citizens, and all of the Communal Concord (*commune concordie*) of London'.[11]

They were certainly a force to be reckoned with, and their attitude to the empress proved to be one of the decisive factors in the civil war. At this juncture they gave Stephen's supporters a valuable breathing-space by making the progress of the empress extremely slow. By 7 May she had advanced no further than Reading from where, checked (it would seem) by a hostile garrison at Windsor, she worked her way round to St Albans; and it was only a few days before 24 June that she persuaded the Londoners to admit her to their city. She apparently owed that success to the fact that she had purchased the support of the castellan of the Tower of London, Geoffrey de Mandeville. (See Appendix VI.)

Geoffrey was an important baron. His father had been castellan of the Tower before him, and so probably had his grandfather who had been the first Norman sheriff of London and Middlesex, but his ambitions were not confined to London. He had also inherited considerable lands in Essex (another county of which his grandfather had once been sheriff), and he had castles at Pleshy and Saffron Walden. In 1140 Stephen had made him earl of Essex. Now the empress was prepared to grant him unlimited powers in that county if he would win it for her cause. Essex was essential for the security of London, not only because it was so close, but also because its harbours could shelter a hostile fleet (such as that of Boulogne) and blockade the Thames estuary. The danger was particularly pressing because the county was dominated by the queen's Honour of Boulogne, and her tenants could be expected to be loyal to her, her husband and her son. If the empress was to secure control of the county, it would be necessary for her to eject (i.e. disinherit) the queen and all her tenants, and this could only be done by force. That was why the empress not only confirmed Geoffrey in his earldom, but also made him hereditary sheriff and justiciar of the county. He was to have plenary powers in order that he could conquer the Honour of Boulogne.[12]

---

10 *Hist. Nov.* para. 494, 'quasi optimates'; cf. para. 495 'sicut proceres'.
11 *G. de M.* 116.
12 The charter (*Reg.* iii. 274) is printed and discussed by Round in *G. de M.*, ch. iv, and he notes that it states specifically that Stephen's brother Theobald had already been disinherited (pp. 91, 102). To my mind he laid too little stress on the Honour of Boulogne; it was based on Colchester and enabled the queen to control most of the county, while

The intentions of the empress seem to have been no secret. They could be deduced from the terms of the charter which she gave to Geoffrey de Mandeville, and they were sufficiently well known to be mentioned by both William of Malmesbury and the author of the *Gesta Stephani*.[13] The latter tells us how the queen sent envoys to the empress entreating, besides the release of her husband, that her son be granted the Honour of Boulogne which was his hereditary right. The empress refused in 'harsh and insulting language', and according to William of Malmesbury she had already promised the land to others. In consequence she lost one of her most important allies, Henry of Blois. He, as we have already seen, had been attempting to negotiate a peace since 1140, and everything goes to suggest that the basis of his proposals had been the recognition of hereditary rights in land. At this juncture he certainly urged the empress to bestow the Honour of Boulogne on Stephen's son Eustace, and his motive seems to have been not only affection for his nephew, but also the realization that no lasting peace would ever be possible so long as there was a large class of 'disinherited', with everything to gain and nothing to lose by a prolongation of the war. The empress, however, did not listen to his advice. In spite of the pact she had made with him in March, she paid no attention to his views, and forgot how important it was to retain his good will.[14]

He was not the only person whose advice she spurned or whose good will she lost. All chroniclers agree that in her hour of victory she displayed an intolerable pride and wilfulness, refusing to take advice even from her oldest and noblest supporters. It is possible that this was due to the manners she had learnt at the court of her first husband, the Emperor Henry V, but there is no doubt that by English or French standards her conduct was intolerable. It was reported that she did not even rise to greet her uncle King David, her brother Earl Robert, and Henry Bishop of Winchester, but while they knelt before her with a request, bawled out a furious dismissal.[15] She was similarly imperious with the Londoners and demanded from them a large sum of money,

---

Geoffrey's castles and lands were mainly at its western extremity. In July the empress optimistically granted Colchester castle to Aubrey de Vere *quam citius ei deliberare potero* (Reg. iii. 634).

13 *Hist. Nov.* para. 498; *G.S.* 122

14 A paragraph from the first edition has been deleted here, see Epilogue to this Chapter.

15 *G.S.* 120; cf. *Hist. Nov.* para. 498; Henry of Huntingdon (R. S.) 275; John of Hexham in *Symeon of Durham* (R.S.) ii. 309; Newburgh, 63. Karl Schnitt 'Regni et pacis inquietatrix: Zur Rolle der Kaiserin Mathilde in der Anarchie', *Journ. Med. Hist.* 2 (1976), 135–57 shows that the divisions which emerged in her party at this juncture had much to do with the unwillingness of the Anglo-Normans to accept a woman as a ruler.

presumably as a tallage. When they pleaded their losses in the war and begged her to limit her demands,

> She, with a grim look, her forehead wrinkled into a frown, every trace of a woman's gentleness removed from her face, blazed into unbearable fury, saying that many times the people of London had made very large contributions to the king, that they had lavished their wealth on strengthening him and weakening her, that they had long since conspired with her enemies for her hurt, and therefore it was not just to spare them in any respect or make the smallest deduction from the money demanded.[16]

This was the height of folly on the part of the empress. Even if she was desperate for money, and even if she could find precedents for tallaging the city in her father's reign, she should have remembered that she had not yet been anointed queen. Until she had received divine authority for her government, it was no time for threats but only for promises; and Stephen's queen was determined that the empress should not receive it. She brought up an army—most probably Flemish mercenaries—from Kent to the south bank of the Thames, and proceeded to devastate the district opposite London and Westminster, thus demonstrating to the citizens that the empress, for all her threats and demands, was incapable of protecting their property. They regretted their desertion of King Stephen, made a pact with her to restore him, and set their bells ringing which (as in the communes of Flanders and Italy) was the call to arms. Then they opened their gates and made a mass attack on Westminster.[17] There the empress had prepared a pre-coronation banquet, but as soon as she received warning of the attack, she and her supporters took to their horses and fled, leaving the Londoners to plunder their deserted lodgings. William of Malmesbury claimed that there was some sort of order in the retreat, but the *Gesta Stephani* was confident that it was a rout.

When the empress eventually rallied her supporters at Oxford, she had to reorganize her forces and make new plans for the future. It was apparently her policy, as it had been Stephen's before the battle of Lincoln, to put particular districts in charge of earls. Of these the chief were her uncle King David who was earl of Huntingdon (though the extent of the earldom was a matter of dispute), and her half-brother Robert Earl of Gloucester, but she had also made another half-brother, Reginald Earl of Cornwall, Baldwin de Redvers Earl of Devon, William

---

16 *G.S.* 122.
17 That she was not in London but at Westminster is shown by the fact that the citizens had to open the city gates in order to advance against her (*G.S.* 124), and by three charters which she dated at Westminster (*Reg.* iii. 274, 316, 911).

de Mohun Earl of Somerset, and Hugh Bigod Earl of Norfolk.[18] On 25 July she made Miles of Gloucester Earl of Hereford, and within the following week she made Aubrey de Vere Earl of Oxford,[19] and confirmed Geoffrey de Mandeville as earl of Essex in a solemn pact which revealed her plans for the reconquest of London. His plenary powers over Essex were extended to London, Middlesex and Hertfordshire by the grant of the shrievalty and justiciarship of those counties also; and to facilitate an advance on London from the north, the empress promised him the castle of Bishop's Stortford (which was not hers but the bishop of London's), permitted him to keep the new castle he had built on the River Lea, and allowed him to build one other wherever he liked.[20]

No doubt these grants were intended as an inducement for Geoffrey's continued loyalty, but since they were all in counties in which the empress's party was either hard-pressed or defeated, they could none of them be effective unless Geoffrey first recovered those counties by force; and so far was he from being able to do that, that he was in real danger of losing the lands which he already held in them. He therefore decided to ignore the empress's grant and return to the king's allegiance if he possibly could. This was less easy for him than it had been for the Londoners, since he had betrayed the queen in a very notable way. When Stephen had gone to Lincoln he had apparently left his queen and his daughter-in-law, Constance of France, in Geoffrey's safe keeping at the Tower of London.[21] Subsequently, when London became unsafe and the queen retreated to Kent, Geoffrey had prevented her from taking Constance with her, and kept the princess in his own custody in the Tower. Now he would have to find a plausible defence of his conduct. It cannot have been easy, but the queen needed his support so badly that she pretended to accept his excuses with a good grace, and Geoffrey was able to think he had been clever in returning to his allegiance before it was too late.[22]

18 For him, as for all the earls, see Appendix I, esp. pp. 138–9
19 She had intended to give him Cambridgeshire, but King David claimed that that country was part of his earldom of Huntingdon. See Appendix I, pp. 135 and 137–8.
20 *Reg.* iii. 275. It was printed and discussed by Round in *G. de M.*, ch. viii, as 'the second charter of the empress'. He dated it between Christmas 1141 and June 1142. I have explained why this date is unacceptable and why 25 July–1 August 1141 is to be preferred, in *E.H.R.* lxxix (1964), 302–7. See below, Appendix VI
21 Newburgh, BK i, ch. xi. Round dated the incident to 1140 (*G. de M.* 47–8), but I have shown why 1141 is more likely in *E.H.R.* lxxix (1964), 302. The queen was certainly in London on 9 Feb. 1141 (*Reg.* iii. 24) and we know that she had regained her liberty before 7 April 1141, when she wrote to the Council of Winchester (above, p. 53).
22 Round thought that she purchased his support with a charter containing yet additional grants of land (*G. de M.*, ch. v), but the references to charters by the queen

As a matter of fact, his support came to the queen at a crucial moment, when an appeal for help had reached her from Henry Bishop of Winchester. He, as we have already seen, had quarrelled with the empress on both secular and ecclesiastical grounds, and after the revolt of the Londoners (in which some said he had had a hand) he had withdrawn from her court. He made no secret of his opinion that the empress had disregarded everything she had sworn to him. He met the queen at Guildford, came to an understanding with her, and released Stephen's supporters from the excommunication laid upon them at the council of Winchester. Though he did not actually revolt, he was obviously contumacious, so the empress went to Winchester with a large force, and as soon as she was admitted to the royal castle, summoned him to attend on her. He, realizing that the summons could only be a prelude to his arrest, told the messenger to wait so that he could 'get himself ready', and while he was waiting, fled from the city, and got himself ready for war.[23] He had left a garrison in his own castle (Wolvesey) in the south-east corner of the city,[24] and while the empress set siege to that, he appealed to the queen and all her supporters to come to his rescue.

The queen responded with alacrity. In command of her army was William of Ypres, but there were also present William de Warenne Earl of Surrey, Simon de Senlis Earl of Northampton, Gilbert de Clare Earl of Hertford, the Londoners and—recruited in the nick of time—Geoffrey de Mandeville Earl of Essex. This force does not seem to have been any larger than that of the empress who had with her, under the command of Robert Earl of Gloucester, the King of Scotland and six other earls,[25] but William of Ypres and his Flemings were professionals and knew their business. While the earl was blindly besieging the bishop's castle in the town, they began to surround him; and when they had captured

---

most probably refer to grants made from her Honour of Boulogne and need not be dated 1141. The charter which he quotes as a parallel on p. 120 concerns land in Gamlingay which belonged to the Honour of Boulogne and is probably subsequent to 1143. For other honorial charters given by the queen and confirmed by Stephen as king, see *Reg.* iii. 503–4, 509–10, 539–42, 548–9, 553–5.

23 *Hist. Nov.* paras. 498–9.

24 *G.S.* 126 says that the bishop had two castles in the town, one in the centre, which would have been the Palace of William the Conqueror, and another *domum. ad instar castalli* which was presumably Wolvesey.

25 *G. S.* 128 names the earls of Cornwall, Devon, Somerset, Hereford, Warwick and Chester, though this last was 'late and ineffectual' according to *Hist. Nov.* para. 499. According to John of Hexham (p. 310) Ranulf rallied at first to the queen, but her army, fearing that he was not acting in good faith, murmured against him to such effect that he fled to the empress.

Wherwell on the road to Andover, they had his army completely enclosed. Realizing at last that he was caught in a trap, Earl Robert prepared to fight his way out of the city on Sunday 14 September, the Feast of the Exaltation of the Holy Cross. Being a man of honour, he arranged to take the brunt of the fighting himself, while Brien fitz Count and Reginald Earl of Cornwall got the empress to safety, reaching Ludgershall on the first night and Devizes on the next. Others of the nobles fought and fled as best they could. King David was captured three times, and three times purchased his release. Miles of Gloucester 'discarded his armour and all his accoutrements and, glad to escape with his life, fled in ignominy, reaching Gloucester weary, half-naked and alone'.[26] Earl Robert himself insisted on delaying the pursuit to the last possible moment, and was surrounded and captured at the ford of Stockbridge.

With the capture of the earl, the Rout of Winchester became the perfect counterpart of the battle of Lincoln, undoing almost everything that the earlier battle had done. Henry of Blois as usual had hopes of a negotiated peace, the suggestion this time being that if Earl Robert would abandon the empress (which he would not), he should have the lordship of the whole land and be second only to the king.[27] All that could be agreed was that the two sides should exchange their royal captives, the king and the earl. The arrangements made were complicated but prudent. On 1 November the king left Bristol, leaving his queen, his son and two magnates as sureties for the release of the earl. When he reached Winchester (3 November) the earl was released, and he, leaving his son as surety for the return of the queen, set out for Bristol. Finally when the queen and her companions were safely back at Winchester, the earl's son was released and the whole operation complete. [28] The war could continue almost as if the thirty-two weeks between the two battles had never existed.

POSTSCRIPT: THE EMPRESS MATILDA AND THE CHURCH

I have deleted the paragraph which appeared on pp. 60–1 of earlier editions of this book, because Dr Chibnall's paper on 'The Empress Matilda and the Church' (*TRHS* 5th series 38 (1988), 107–33) has

---

26 Continuation of *Florence of Worcester*, ed. Thorpe, ii. 135.*G.S.* 134 also alludes slyly to his sorry plight, but without naming him.

27 *Hist. Nov.* para. 508.

28 *Ibid.* para. 500; cf. 511–14.

convinced me that its general tenor was mistaken. I was following a near-contemporary narrative from Durham, but I had not recognized how much of it belonged to the literature of propaganda–warfare rather than history.

As explained in Chapter IX below, church affairs were highly politicized, especially in the north of England. For both Stephen and Matilda control of the bishopric of Durham was important because of its position close to, if not actually on, the Scottish border. But when a disputed election occurred, it was prudent for the opposing parties to accuse each other, not of political or national bias, but of uncanonical behaviour. The main source for the disputed election of 1141 certainly takes this line. It is the First Continuation of Symeon of Durham's History of the Church of Durham (*Symeonis Monachi Opera Omnia*), ed. Thomas Arnold (R. S., 2 vols, 1882–5), i. 143–60 which was evidently written soon after the enthronement of Bishop William of Sainte Barbe in October 1144. At that date the dispute over the York election (where William of Sainte Barbe had previously been dean) was at its height, and St Bernard was publishing vehement letters in which he castigated both King Stephen and Henry of Blois as oppressors of the Church and enemies of the reforming papacy. Not unnaturally Stephen's party retaliated by doing its best to blacken the reputation of Matilda, making much use of her title of 'Empress' so as to suggest that it would be in her nature to behave in an imperial or anti-papal way. Hence the accusation that she *would have been* prepared to bestow the bishopric of Durham on William Cumin by lay investiture, and he to receive it at her hands. Accusation of an unfulfilled intention can never be proven, but it often has an emotive success, as it did in this case. It should be noted, however, that the Durham writer (p. 145) made his case less than convincing by admitting that when the delegation from Durham first came to the empress's court, she refused to consider their request until the papal legate (Henry of Blois) had arrived.

Dr Chibnall has shown that over the course of her career the Empress earned a reputation for fair-dealing with the Church. Her conduct in filling the see of London, which was vacant in 1141, was correct, and her attachment to St Bernard and the Cistercian Order seems to have been genuine. Critics have claimed that the way in which she took over the Cistercian abbeys founded by Waleran of Meulan— Bordesley and Le Valasse—was both high-handed and cynical, but Dr Chibnall points out that Waleran's claim to the site of both abbeys was disputed, that of Bordesley being royal demesne granted to Waleran by Stephen whose right the empress could not recognize, and that of Le Valasse being claimed by two other abbeys, Bernay and Mortemer. The empress made several foundations of her own, and was a notable friend and benefactor of the abbey of Bec.

Though insistent on the prerogatives of the Crown, the Empress was able to see the papal point of view. She had a moderating influence on both her husband, Geoffrey of Anjou, and her son King Henry II. In part this may have been because she was aware how much she herself owed to the Papacy. Though Pope Innocent II had recognized Stephen as king, Matilda had worked hard to get that recognition reversed, had taken her case to the Lateran Council (1139) and made every effort to influence the cardinals, especially Guy Cardinal Priest of St Mark who in 1143 succeeded Innocent as Pope Celestine II. His pontificate, even though it lasted no more than five months, was decisive for her because he reversed the policy of his predecessor toward England, writing to Archbishop Theobald 'forbidding him to allow any change to be made in the position of the English crown, since the transfer of it had been justly denounced, and the matter was still under dispute' (*The Historia Pontificalis of John of Salisbury*, ed. Marjorie Chibnall (Nelson's Medieval Texts, 1956), 85–6). This instruction became the basis of Archbishop Theobald's policy, leading to his refusal to crown Stephen's son Eustace in 1152 (below, p. 114), to the Treaty of Westminster and the accession of King Henry II. It is hard to believe that the papacy would have swung its support over to her in 1143 if her reputation was really as black as the Durham writer would have had us suppose, or if she had ever attempted to re-impose lay investiture.

CHAPTER SEVEN
A Second Start, 1142–1143

In one sense very little had been achieved by the events of 1141, but emotionally the significance of the events was without parallel. Everyone had had to declare his loyalty in defeat as well as in victory, and those who had proved constant to either the king or the empress exhibited a new self-confidence and *esprit de corps*. The situation was easier for Stephen's men than Matilda's, not only because he had eventually won, but also because he had behaved with dignity in his captivity, and while never forgetting that he was still king, had made no unreasonable demands on his subjects. Nothing, for example, could have been more tolerant, than the way in which he had allowed the Church to 'move with the times' in April, and subsequently permitted it to return to his allegiance at a legatine council held by Henry of Blois at Westminster on 7 December 1141. He did not allow it to restore or reconsecrate him, for he was insistent that he had never been deposed (and for this reason would not even change his seal), but he came to the council and addressed it personally, in order to lay his complaint against those who had held him captive although he had never denied them justice. He then permitted his brother to explain away as best he could the proceedings of the council which he had held at Winchester in April, and to call upon the clergy to support him as a king who had been 'annointed with the good will of the people and the approval of the Apostolic See'. It was a splendid combination of firmness and moderation. [1]

The empress, on the other hand, had been unbearable. Arrogant, domineering and completely lacking in political sense, she had

---

1 *Hist. Nov.* paras. 501–2. Though Stephen was not reconsecrated, he was recrowned in a ceremony which was taken as a precedent by Richard I after his release from captivity (Gervase of Canterbury) (R.S., i. 524).

antagonized almost all the waverers who might have been won for her cause, and made it unlikely that she would win any more in the future. Her most devoted supporters insisted not on her personal merits but on her ancestry, and that the sole justification for what they had done was the oath which they had taken to King Henry I. Their attitude is well illustrated in a letter written (*c.* 1142–4) by Brien fitz Count to Henry Bishop of Winchester. Henry had complained that Brien had broken his word by plundering merchants on their way to the fair at Winchester, in spite of his promise to the contrary. Who, asked Brien, was Bishop Henry to complain about broken promises?

> For even you yourself who are a prelate of the Holy Church, have ordered me to adhere to the daughter of King Henry your uncle, and to help her to acquire that which is hers by right but has been taken from her by force, and to retain what she already has . . . . King Henry gave me land, but it has been taken away from me and my men because I am doing what you ordered me to do; and as a result I am in extreme straits and am not harvesting one acre of corn from the land which he gave me. It is not surprising that I take things from other people in order to sustain my life and the lives of my men, and in order to do what you commanded of me. Nor have I taken anything from anyone who has left my own possessions alone. You should know that neither I nor my men are doing this for money or fief or land, either promised or given, but only because of your command (in 1141) and the lawfulness of myself and my men.[2]

Brien fitz Count was one of the few magnates who ruined his fortune in the service of either empress or king. Most of the others, however devoted their service, contrived to combine it with their own interests; and it was universally conceded that though a man ought in theory to be loyal to his lord in all circumstances, his loyalty was bound to become precarious if it involved him in the loss of his patrimony. To lose lands which one had acquired or been given oneself (as Brien fitz Count had been given the Honour of Wallingford) was perhaps a thing which could be tolerated, but the lands which one had inherited from one's ancestors were a different matter. They had to be defended at all costs because, in an age which believed that everything sacred should be given a tangible form, they *were* a man's ancestry, and served to identify him, no matter how many other lands he might acquire. To preserve them was more than an act of *pietas*. To lose them was almost betrayal of oneself. Waleran of Meulan, for example, had been made earl of Worcester, but no one spoke or thought of him as 'Waleran of Worcester'; if ever he lost

2 For the full text, see H. W. C. Davis in *E.H.R.* xxv (1910), 297–303.

Meulan and had to change his name, hardly anyone would know who he was. That was why he finally defected to the Angevins. Though he had been Stephen's chief adviser and had been betrothed to his daughter, he could not bring himself to renounce his patrimony, since that would have been tantamount to changing his identity.

It was in the second half of 1141 that he deserted. Though he had fled from the battle of Lincoln, he had not gone over to the empress then, but had remained faithful to Stephen and supported his queen in Kent. There he must have been joined by his twin brother, Robert Earl of Leicester, who held the English lands of the family, but had been acting as Stephen's principal lieutenant in Normandy, though he had been unable to prevent Geoffrey of Anjou from overruning all the territory south of the Seine and east of the Risle. By the end of March he had secured from Geoffrey a truce for his brother and himself while he went to England for consultations.[3] This was a regular procedure for a man who knew he would have to surrender unless he could get substantial assistance, but in the early months of 1141 no reinforcements could be expected since the king was in captivity, and the queen needed every available man in England. The only hope of relief was that Louis VII would abide by the treaty he had made with Stephen, and send an army to Normandy to oppose the Angevins; but that hope vanished when on 24 June Louis led his army to the south of France for an expedition against Toulouse. Waleran had then to choose between saving his patrimony in Normandy or serving his king in England. He crossed over to Normandy and came to terms with Geoffrey of Anjou before the autumn.[4] He managed to avoid taking part in very much warfare against his former lord, the only action in which he is known to have fought being the siege of Rouen castle in 1144, but the fact remained that he had deserted.

So far as Stephen was concerned, the moral to be drawn must have been clear. It was the same as at the battle of Lincoln, that nobles with vast patrimonies would always have their own safety to consider as well as the king's. When, after his release from captivity, he made a second start as king, he was careful not to repeat the 'aristocratic' policy of the first six years of his reign. He could not refuse to confirm existing earls

---

3 *OV* vi. 548.

4 G. H. White, 'The Career of Waleran Count of Meulan and Earl of Worcester (1104–66)', *T.R.H.S.*, 4th series, xvii (1934), 19–48; cf. Orderic, v. 132–3. Robert Earl of Leicester and Waleran of Meulan were twin brothers and had consequently shared their patrimony, Waleran having the Norman and Robert the English lands. Therefore when Waleran went to Normandy and deserted, Robert remained in England and was loyal to Stephen till 1153, though he also avoided as much action as possible. See David Crouch, *The Beaumont Twins* (Cambridge, 1986) and Appendix V below.

who had fought for him at Winchester—and thus even Geoffrey de Mandeville had his lands and offices confirmed—but he could fill every possible vacancy with 'new' men. It was not only that he had the example of Henry I before him. After 1141 he had also his own experience, for he could not have been in any doubt that in that year his cause was saved by the most prominent of his 'new' men.

This was William of Ypres. Though he made his fame as the leader of Stephen's Flemish mercenaries, he was of noble birth, being the illegitimate son of Philip of Loo and consequently the grandson of Robert the Frisian Count of Flanders (1071–93).[5] He had in fact claimed the County of Flanders after the murder of his cousin Charles the Good in 1127, and might well have made his claim good if it had not been for the suspicion that he had been cognizant of the murder plot.[6] As it was, after many vicissitudes, he was driven out of Flanders in 1133, and seeking a refuge found one with Stephen, then only Count of Boulogne; and with Stephen he decided to make a new career. It was presumably he who provided the mercenaries for Stephen's Scottish campaign in 1136, and certainly he who commanded Stephen's Flemish force in Normandy in 1137, and captured Devizes castle from Roger of Salisbury in 1139. Stephen rewarded him handsomely. He did not make him an earl (comes) perhaps because he did not want to revive his title to the county of Flanders, but he gave him vast estates and put him in virtual control of Kent.[7] The Norman nobles hated him because he was not one of themselves (see p. 25), and pointed out that he also had fled from the battle of Lincoln, but when Stephen was in captivity it was William who made himself responsible for the safety of the queen, William who organized a new army, and William who led it to victory at Winchester.

Though William of Ypres had been the most prominent and successful of the 'new' men, there were several others who had been equally unswerving in their loyalty and now received their reward. To judge from the witness-lists of Stephen's charters, he only occasionally had earls in his entourage in the later part of his reign, but was scarcely ever separated from men like William Martel, Richard de Lucy or

---

5 His mother was a wool-carder, apparently from Ypres.

6 Such was the opinion of Galbert of Bruges, trs. J. B. Ross, 144.

7 See Appendix I, p. 140. We know that besides the revenues which he drew from the royal demesne he had lands in Kent, since he was able to found Boxley Abbey (c. 1144–6), and give the churches of Throwley and Chilham to the abbey of St Bertin. His possession of Chilham suggests that Stephen had given him the lands of Hugh of Dover (Letters of John of Salisbury, ed. Millor, Butler, and Brooke, i. 37–40 and 258–60). He also gave 100s. a year to Holy Trinity Aldgate from his property at Queenhithe (Saltman, Theobald, nos. 162–3).

Robert de Vere, not to mention the less important 'new' men such as William Chesney, Richard de Camville, Warner de Lusors or Henry of Essex.[8] It did not matter whether they were of high birth or low, so long as they owed their lands to the king's favour and realized that they would inevitably lose them if he was overthrown. If the lands bestowed were from the royal demesne, the recipients might have to be reminded that the empress claimed the demesne as hers. If the lands were estates which had been forfeited from the empress's supporters, the recipients would need no reminder at all; Simon de Senlis Earl of Northampton, for example, was noticeably loyal throughout the reign, because he knew that if the empress triumphed, his earldom would be absorbed into that of King David of Scotland. 'New' men, even when they came from ancient families, could not afford to desert the king who had 'made' them.

As it happened, no decisive action could be taken for more than eight months after Stephen had regained his liberty. He celebrated his Christmas court at Canterbury,[9] a polite compliment to William of Ypres and his Kentish vassals, and as soon as Lent was over marched northwards with a large army. His intention was 'to restore the kingdom to its ancient dignity and entirety', and it is most probable that he intended to wipe out the last traces of his defeat by recovering the city and castle of Lincoln. As matters turned out, however, he had first to go to York to prevent a tournament (which could easily have become a war) between William d'Aumâle Earl of York and Count Alan of Brittany, and then he was taken seriously ill at Northampton with the result that he was out of action for the whole of May and the early part of June.[10]

To the supporters of the empress the news of the king's illness came as a godsend. Since the Rout of Winchester their morale had been extremely low. Realizing that the only way to stave off complete defeat would be to get substantial aid from Geoffrey of Anjou, they sent him envoys imploring him to come to the assistance of his wife, but

8 Of these men, William Martel witnessed 181 charters for Stephen, Robert de Vere 142, and Richard de Lucy 135. Richard de Camville (who witnessed 63 charters) was given the lands of John de St John; and William de Chesney (who witnessed 22 charters) was given those of Robert d'Oilli; Henry of Essex's estates were disputed by Robert de Montfort who got his revenge by accusing Henry of cowardice as constable, and proving his case in trial by battle in 1163 (Eyton, *Court, Household and Itinerary of King Henry II,* 61); he witnessed 37 times.

9 Gervase of Canterbury (i. 527) states that the king stood before the archbishop's throne and the queen opposite him, and that the archbishop crowned (*imposuit coronam*) them both. The ceremony was considered a precedent for Richard I after his release from captivity.

10 John of Hexham in *Symeon of Durham* ii. 312. *Hist. Nov.* para. 516.

though the envoys had left England in March they were detained in Normandy and did not return for three months. During the period of waiting, the empress's adherents were able to encourage themselves with rumours that the king was dead or dying, and they probably had no idea that he had already recovered when their envoys returned and delivered Count Geoffrey's reply at Devizes on 14 June. According to William of Malmesbury, the message was,

> That the Count of Anjou was to some extent in favour of some of the things proposed by the nobles, but the only one of them whom he actually knew was the earl of Gloucester whose prudence, loyalty, high-mindedness and proved diligence he had long cherished. If he would cross the sea and come to see him, he would do his best not to neglect his wishes; but for anyone else to make the journey would be labour in vain.[11]

The truth of the matter was that while Geoffrey had no intention of crossing to England, he needed Earl Robert's presence in order to give a respectably Norman appearance to his Angevin army, and to make it easier for the barons of western Normandy to surrender to him. But neither the empress nor the majority of her advisers realized this. They urged Earl Robert to go, and left themselves leaderless at the very moment when Stephen had recovered from his illness and was ready to attack them.

Stephen saw his chance and took it. He marched on Wareham, the port from which Earl Robert had just sailed, captured it, and put a garrison in the castle to prevent his return. Then he turned his attention to the empress. She was at Oxford, where Earl Robert had left her with all the magnates sworn to remain by her side, but they (despite the hostages which they had given in earnest of their good intentions) were more anxious for the security of their patrimonies than for the safety of the empress, and were lured from Oxford by a diversion in the direction of Bristol, Devizes and Gloucester.[12] After capturing Wareham, Stephen had marched north-westwards, presumably by way of Sherborne and Bath, captured Cirencester while its garrison was absent, burnt the town, and created alarm throughout Gloucestershire and Wiltshire. Then making no attempt to hold Cirencester himself, he turned eastwards and marched rapidly on Oxford. By capturing small castles at Bampton and Radcot, he was able to cross to the south side of the Thames and reach Oxford while

---

11 *Hist. Nov.* para. 517.
12 *Ibid.* para. 520 says he went from Wareham to Oxford, and *G.S.* 92 that he took Cirencester, Bampton and Radcot before reaching Oxford. I have here combined the

it was still unprepared. Fording the river, he took the city by storm (16 September) and besieged the empress in the castle. Her supporters returned in haste and offered battle outside the city, but Stephen had learnt his lesson at Lincoln, and went firmly on with the siege. There should be no escape for the empress.

When the news reached the earl of Gloucester in Normandy, he was furious with the magnates who had left Oxford, and furious with Geoffrey of Anjou who was simply making use of his presence in Normandy, and always had a fresh excuse for not joining his wife in England. [13] Even when Earl Robert had helped him to capture ten castles—Tinchebray, St Hilaire d'Harcouet, Briquesard (near Caumont l'Evente), Aunay-sur-Odon, Bastonborg, Trévières, Vire, Plessis-Grimoult, Villers-Bocage, and Mortain[14]—he still found reasons for not leaving Normandy, and on hearing of his wife's danger he apparently thought it sufficient to let his nine-year-old son, Henry fitz Empress, accompany Earl Robert on his journey back to England. The earl, knowing that he would have to force a landing, sailed with fifty-two ships and a force of more than 300 knights. He made boldly for Wareham, captured the harbour and town, and vigorously besieged the castle in the hope of distracting Stephen's attention; but Stephen did not repeat his mistakes of 1139 and 1140, and dash away from Oxford in order to relieve Wareham. Determined to capture the empress he allowed the castle at Wareham to surrender and remained at Oxford with all his army.

In spite of his good intentions he was unsuccessful. Early in December the empress escaped from Oxford. There was snow on the ground, so she and the four knights who accompanied her camouflaged themselves in white cloaks, crossed the frozen river on foot, and made their way to Abingdon and Wallingford.

> Unhindered and unharmed, as has been said, she left the castle and passed through the king's pickets which everywhere were breaking the silence of the night, here with the blare of trumpets, there with the clamour of men shouting out loud, but no one any the wiser except for

---

two accounts, and assume that he went by way of Sherborne, Castle Cary. Bath and Malmesbury (which were all held by his supporters), in order to avoid Salisbury, Marlborough, Devizes and Trowbridge (which were held for the empress). G.S. implies that he made no attempt to hold Cirencester, and *Hist. Nov.* para. 523 says that Earl Robert assembled his army there for his intended relief of Oxford.

13 William of Malmesbury, from whom all the following details are taken (*Hist. Nov.* paras. 518–23) reflects the fury of the earl, from whom he learnt his facts.

14 These castles are nearly all in the *bocage* of S. W. Normandy, roughly speaking in the triangle formed by Caen, Falaise and Avranches.

those who were with her, and one man on the king's side who knew of her escape and was the only betrayer of it.[15]

Whether the failure to apprehend her was due to carelessness or treachery, Stephen had clearly lost his opportunity of winning the war at a single blow. Contemporaries interpreted it as the will of God, and even a less superstitious age might have thought that a man who let such chances slip did not deserve to be victorious.

The only consolation was to be found in the fact that Stephen had at any rate captured the castle of Oxford, for in the prevailing conditions castles were extremely important. In disputed districts such as Berkshire, Wiltshire and Dorset, neither side was capable of controlling large expanses of territory. The only firmly held points were the castles, and as they could only exercise a continuous control over the area which could actually be seen from their towers, the rival forces could move between them as easily as if they were fleets at sea, secure so long as they were not sighted from particular islands. That was why both King Stephen and Earl Robert were able to march from Wareham to Cirencester within two months of each other, and why a castle which was not closely besieged could maintain itself almost indefinitely among hostile neighbours, provided that it was strong enough to protect the crops of one or two villages around it. What the castles did was to block particular roads, cross-roads or river-crossings; and Oxford was particularly important because it was situated at the intersection of the main routes from London to Gloucester and from Northampton to Winchester and Southampton, at a point where both routes had to cross rivers. From Stephen's point of view, it assured him of the safety of London and the midlands, and gave him a base from which to launch raids into both Gloucestershire and Wiltshire.

The strategic position of the two parties was now dominated by the fact that owing to their concentration on castles, both of them found themselves with dangerous salients which their enemies were trying to cut off. The empress had a salient which stretched south-east from Gloucester and Bristol to Wallingford and Salisbury. Within it the principal castles held for her were Trowbridge, Devizes, Marlborough and Ludgershall, but it also included near its 'neck' the castle of Malmesbury which was held for the king, and which could apparently maintain communications of a sort with Oxford on the one hand and Bath on the other. Bath was in the king's salient which stretched from

15 *G.S.* 142; cf. *Hist. Nov.* para. 524. The Latin of *G.S.* is ambiguous and one cannot be sure whether he meant that there was one traitor in Stephen's army, or that one man raised the alarm.

1. Castles held for Stephen and the Empress, 1142–3

▲ Held for Stephen
● Held for the Empress
   The italicised towns were forced to surrender to the Empress

Framlingham
Eye
Bungay
Norwich
Colchester
Hedingham
Castle
St. Edmunds
Bury
Peterborough
Ely
Ramsey
Pleshey
Huntingdon
Hertford
St Albans
Cambridge
Saffron Walden
LONDON
Stamford
Canterbury
Dover
Rochester
Tonbridge
Lincoln
Nottingham
Leicester
Oxford
Wallingford
Windsor
Guildford
Arundel
Northampton
Reading
Farnham
Ludgershall
Southampton
Portchester
Derby
Salisbury
Winchester
Dudley
Tamworth
Worcester
Gloucester
Radcot
Bampton
Marlborough
Wilton
Stafford
Cirencester
Devizes
Trowbridge
Downton
Chester
Malmesbury
Bristol
Sherborne
Lulworth
Bath
Glastonbury
Castle Cary
Wells
Wareham
Hereford
Abergavenny
Monmouth
Dunster
Taunton
Cardiff
Barnstaple
Exeter

71

Winchester and Southampton to Sherborne, Castle Cary and (probably) Dunster and Barnstaple.[16] The point at which it could most easily be cut off was between Salisbury and Wareham. Wareham, therefore, which Earl Robert had recaptured at the end of 1142, had a strategic significance very comparable to that of Oxford.[17] It gave the empress good communications with Normandy, and threatened Stephen's communications with his castles in Somerset, Dorset and North Devon.

Stephen obviously had to take notice of it, and he explored the situation in the spring of 1143 with a small mobile force, composed apparently of Flemish mercenaries.[18] The advantage of having a small force was that it could move quickly and undetected between enemy castles, whenever possible burning the crops on which the enemy garrisons depended, and always hoping to take some castle by surprise, as Stephen had surprised Cirencester in the previous year while its garrison was away on a mission of its own. The disadvantage of a mobile task force, however, was that it could never carry out a full-scale siege without exposing itself to attack by a large relieving army, as had happened at Lincoln. When, therefore, Stephen found that Wareham was strongly garrisoned, he made no attempt to besiege the place, but moved northwards to explore the situation at Salisbury on the northern flank of his salient. There, since he was only twenty-four miles from his base at Winchester, he could safely summon the full feudal army and undertake a regular siege. Acting as an advance party, he and his brother, Henry Bishop of Winchester (now giving military as well as ecclesiastical advice), fortified a castle at Wilton in order to block the route from the west, but in doing so they made a serious mistake. They had only a task force with them until the great army arrived, but by occupying Wilton they made themselves stationary, and therefore liable to attack by a superior force. The earl of Gloucester seized the opportunity and won a victory which was almost a repetition of the battle of Lincoln (1 July).[19] The one important difference was that this

16 Sherborne and Castle Cary are clear from *G.S.* 148–50, since Castle Cary was Henry de Lacy's main castle. Barnstaple also belonged to him, at any rate in 1139 (*G.S.* 82), and Dunster belonged to William de Mohun who had almost certainly deserted the empress by now (see Appendix I, p. 138).

17 It is tempting to think that when the chronicles refer to the castle, as opposed to the town, of Wareham, they are referring to Corfe Castle four miles to the south. But there was a castle at Wareham itself, even though it was much smaller than Corfe Castle, and I have therefore not attempted to amend the language of the chronicles.

18 For the following details, see *G.S.* 144–6, and *Gervase of Canterbury* (R.S.) i. 125–6.

19 The date is from Gervase of Canterbury (i. 125), but *G.S.* 145 puts it 'pauco dilapso tempore' after the siege of Oxford.

time the king escaped, while his steward William Martel fought a dogged rearguard action until surrounded and taken prisoner.

Was Stephen's flight from Wilton to be compared with that of his father from Antioch? The question was probably on everyone's mind, and Stephen could not afford to have it answered in the affirmative. He had to make it absolutely clear that, no matter what his father had done, he himself would not leave his friends in the lurch. Since William Martel had allowed himself to be captured in order that the king might escape, it would be a point of honour for the king to procure his release, no matter what the cost might be; and when Robert Earl of Gloucester demanded Sherborne castle as his ransom, Stephen agreed to it. It was a very heavy price to pay for the release of one man, for Sherborne was the key to the whole of Stephen's western salient.[20] One of Stephen's 'new men', Henry de Tracy, resisted for a while in the region of Castle Cary and Barnstaple,[21] but when he was eventually forced to make a truce, Somerset, Dorset and the whole district between the Bristol and English channels came under the control of the earl of Gloucester.

> This lordship of his the earl very greatly adorned by restoring peace and quietness everywhere, except that he exacted forced labour from all for the building of his castles, and when he had to fight the enemy, demanded everyone's aid either by sending knights or by paying money. And there was indeed in those regions a shadow of peace, but not perfect peace, because nothing more vexed the people of that district than working not for themselves but for others, and in some sort increasing of their own efforts the sinews of strife and war.[22]

It must have seemed as if Stephen's second start was going to end in a second disaster, but the empress had neither the men nor the leaders to exploit her success. Her remaining supporters were too widely scattered, and too preoccupied with the defence of their own lands, to concentrate their forces where victory could be won. As a result she was unable to recapture Winchester even when William Pont de l'Arche, who held the royal castle and treasury, quarrelled with Bishop Henry and appealed to her for help. The only troops she could send him were those of a mercenary called Robert fitz Hildebrand who proved as treacherous as Robert fitz Hubert at Devizes (p. 42); as soon

20 *G.S.* 20. William Martel had held Sherborne castle for the king even (it seems) during 1141 (*supra*, p. 54). The castle was one of those which had been built by Roger of Salisbury but had been surrendered to the king in 1139.
21 *G.S.* 150. Since his lands and castles were those which Stephen had seized from Robert of Bampton in 1136, he had every reason to continue resistance.
22 *G.S.* 150. The implication would be that Robert's authority as earl had been extended from Gloucestershire to include Somerset and Dorset.

as he had been admitted to the castle, he put William Pont de l'Arche in fetters, seduced his wife, and came to terms with Bishop Henry and the king. We are told that God avenged his treachery and lasciviousness by causing his death through a worm which 'crept through his vitals and devoured his entrails',[23] but the fact that for such an important mission the empress could find no one more suitable than him shows how desperately short she was of reliable supporters. Brien fitz Count was shut up in Wallingford, Miles of Gloucester, Earl of Hereford, was killed in a hunting accident on Christmas Eve 1143, and Robert Earl of Gloucester could not be everywhere at once. If Stephen's second start had failed to fulfil its early promise, the empress was still a long way from victory.

23 G.S. 23.

CHAPTER EIGHT
Stalemate, 1143–1147

The history of the years 1143–47 is singularly confusing, and can easily seem pointless, with manœuvre after manœuvre and siege after siege, but no great change in the general situation. The reason for this is that though the chroniclers found it easy to dilate on the dramatic events which occurred in England, they had little to say about the one fact of real significance, the conquest of Normandy by Geoffrey of Anjou. Geoffrey might be the husband of the empress and the father of King Henry II, but he was a foreigner none the less, and no Norman or Anglo-Norman had any desire to glorify his exploits. In consequence the chroniclers tell us no more than the bare outlines of the campaigns by which he subdued the duchy. In 1142 he won Avranches, Coutances and the greater part of the Cotentin, and in 1143 Cherbourg, Verneuil and Le Vaudreuil.[1] In 1144 he crossed the Seine at Vernon and advanced to Rouen where the citizens opened their gates to him on 20 January, though the king's castle, garrisoned by the earl of Warenne's men, held out for another three months.[2] When it eventually surrendered (23 April), Geoffrey was solemnly invested as duke of Normandy in Rouen cathedral. Soon afterward he purchased the good will of King Louis of France with the cession of Gisors and the Norman Vexin, and was officially recognized by him as duke.[3] By the end of 1144

1 Robert de Torigni, in *Chronicles* iv. 143, 145.

2 *Ibid.* 148. Either now or soon after he rewarded the citizens with a generous charter of liberties whose text is preserved in the subsequent charter of Duke Henry (*Reg.* iii. 729).

3 'Historia Gaufredi Ducis' in *Chroniques des Comtes d'Anjou*, ed. L. Halphen and R. Poupardin (Paris, 1913), 215; Robert de Torigni in *Chronicles* iv. 148–9 and 169. The precise date at which Geoffrey assumed the ducal title has been disputed, but 23 April is generally favoured; see Haskins, *Norman Institutions*, 130, n. 25. On the cession of the Vexin, see J. F. Lemarignier, *Recherches sur l'hommage en marche et les frontières féodales* (Lille, 1945), 33 ff. and 45 n. 53.

Arques was the only castle which remained to Stephen in the whole duchy, and when it capitulated in the following year, the Angevin conquest of Normandy was complete.

It was the completeness of the conquest which was decisive. It left Stephen no serious prospect of reconquering the duchy, and his supporters no hope of recovering their lands unless they followed the example of Waleran of Meulan and deserted to the Angevins (pp. 64–5). The empress's supporters, on the other hand, were fortified in their loyalty. With Duke Geoffrey's government firmly established in Normandy, they could not fail to realize that if they deserted to Stephen, the forfeiture of their Norman lands would be swift and inevitable; while any losses which they suffered for her cause in England could hardly be regarded as final so long as the empress retained a foothold in that country. As a result, the only baron with extensive Norman lands to desert the empress after 1144 was Ranulf Earl of Chester, and his defection was only of short duration (1146). The vast majority understood where their own self-interest lay. Even if they lost the greater part of their English possessions, they could expect some form of compensation in Normandy; Reginald de St Valéry, for example, was given the revenues of the port of Dieppe until he could recover his rightful inheritance (*hereditarium jus*) in England.[4]

The loss of Normandy was a major disaster for Stephen. The only way in which he could hope to recover from it was by making his control of England as complete as Duke Geoffrey's of Normandy. He tried to do this, but unfortunately for him he lacked his rival's methodical nature. He had more energy than judgment, and lacking the patience to concentrate on one central objective, could always be diverted by the lure of easy prizes.[5] As a result he had no overall strategy, and any account of his battles and sieges is bound to seem confused and repetitive. The best that can be done is to distinguish two main cycles of events, separating them from each other by a general account of the state of the country. In each of the two cycles the central issue was determined by a sort of love-hate relationship between Stephen and one of his greater barons. In the first it was Geoffrey de Mandeville (1143–44), and in the second Ranulf Earl of Chester (1145–47). In each case the need for an alliance was clear, since Stephen could not possibly be victorious unless he secured the support of some powerful magnate who had previously opposed him, and in each case Stephen's courage

---

4. *Reg.* ii. 329; cf. *C.D.F.* 1057–8. His English lands had been forfeited by Stephen and given to John de St John (*Historia de Fundatione de Kingswood in Monast.* v. 425).

5 *Hist. Nov.* para. 461.

failed him when he was on the brink of success. He had the weak man's terror of being dominated by a character stronger than his own. In the past, nervousness and jealousy had caused him to trip his brother, Henry of Blois (p. 27) and to ruin Roger of Salisbury (pp. 28–9). Now these same qualities were to determine his relations with two of the most important barons in England.

Geoffrey de Mandeville

According to William of Newburgh, Stephen had determined to ruin Geoffrey de Mandeville ever since he had imprisoned his daughter-in-law, Constance of France, in the Tower of London (p. 58). That would have been in 1141, and he had concealed his 'legitimate rage' until 1143, simply because the supporters of the empress were so strong in the eastern counties, that he could not afford to make an enemy of Geoffrey as well. Earl Hugh Bigod controlled much of East Suffolk from his castles of Bungay, Framlingham and Walton. Nigel Bishop of Ely, whom the empress had restored to his see in 1141, held the Isle of Ely and the castle of Aldreth.[6] Miles de Beauchamp held Bedford, which he had recaptured in 1141,[7] and Ranulf Earl of Chester held the city and castle of Lincoln, and with his half-brother William de Roumare controlled much of the county. If Prince Henry of Scotland had been able to retain control of his earldom of Huntingdon, his lands would have united those of the other rebels, so as to form an almost continuous belt of territory stretching from Lincolnshire to East Suffolk; but fortunately Stephen had been able to dispossess him, bestowing his earldom and lands on Simon de Senlis, who had a rival claim to them. In this respect the only difficulty had been with the former vassals of the Scottish prince; they seem to have retreated to the fens, and to have found a refuge at Ramsey, where the abbot had made a formal alliance with the bishop of Ely.[8]

It was the bishop of Ely who offered the most immediate threat to Stephen's security, for if he could effect a firm junction with Hugh Bigod in Suffolk, he might succeed in cutting Stephen's com-

6 Nigel's history is complicated. He escaped arrest at Oxford in June 1139 and fortified Devizes against the king, but was soon forced to surrender. He was allowed to return to Ely but revolted again after the death of his uncle, Roger Bishop of Salisbury (4/11 December 1139). Stephen then besieged him in Ely and, with the help of Daniel the monk of Ramsey, captured the isle and forced him to flee to the empress at Gloucester. The empress reinstated him in 1141 (*G.S.*98–100; *Lib. Eliensis* (ed. Blake), 314–15 and 433–6).

7 *G.S.* 106. He had captured it from Hugh Pauper in 1141. Cf. p. 28 above.

8 See pp. 79–80 and n. 15.

munication between London and Norfolk. Stephen was alive to this danger, and it is probable that the main reason why he did not break with Geoffrey de Mandeville until 1143 was that in 1142 he was relying on him for the military containment of the Isle of Ely. At the same time he realized that if he was not to repeat the mistakes of 1139, it was important not to attack the bishop openly, but to embroil him in the meshes of canon law. He was therefore fortunate to have the assistance of his brother, Henry of Blois, who presided as papal legate over a mid-Lent council in 1143, at which various charges were preferred against Nigel—he was accused of uncanonically depriving a priest of his church, of inciting sedition in the realm, and of giving church property to his knights.[9] To defend himself against these charges Nigel had to go to Rome, and in the event his enemies saw to it that his journey was made difficult. When he arrived at Wareham—he was using that port because he had visited the empress on the way—he encountered a force of Stephen's men (presumably the one which had just failed to capture the town (p. 72)), was stripped of his valuable, and forced to return to Ely for a fresh supply of funds.[10] As a result he did not reach Rome until 1144,[11] and owing to the slow process of canon law, which Henry of Blois may well have prolonged, he was away from his diocese for the best part of two years (1143–45).

With the bishop of Ely no longer a danger, Stephen was able to turn his attention to Geoffrey de Mandeville. It was not in the least surprising that he wanted to punish Geoffrey's conduct towards Constance of France, for that was an injury to his kindred which any twelfth-century baron would have thought it necessary to avenge. What was remarkable was the cunning with which he dissimulated for almost two years, behaving as if he had no feud with Geoffrey, and trusting him with such honour that 'everywhere in the kingdom he took the king's place, his advice being sought more eagerly than that of the king, and his orders more strictly obeyed'.[12] It was an elaborate deception on Stephen's part, calculated to tide him over a difficult period when he was desperately short of allies in Eastern England. But it was also dangerous, for it must have been obvious that if Geoffrey suspected that he was not trusted completely, he would attempt to

9 *Liber Eliensis* (ed. Blake), 324.

10 The treasure included three albs with cloaks, two stoles, two tunics, two dalmatics, two copes, a green chasuble, a thurible, and two silver vessels, a chalice, a precious gospel-book, 'a privilege (charter) for which the church subsequently paid 52 marks', and an altar cloth. Nigel persuaded the monks to give him a further supply of their treasures by promising to give them back their manor of Hadstock (*ibid.* 324–5).

11 The letters he obtained from Pope Lucius II were dated 24 May 1144 (*ibid.* 326–7).

12 *G.S.* 160.

desert to the empress again. He had to be left in a position of unquestioned authority, until the day came when he could be taken unawares and deprived of all his powers at one stroke. This was the sort of situation in which Stephen specialized, since it required secrecy, deception and surprise. About Michaelmas 1143 he assembled his court at St Albans and welcomed Geoffrey with the other magnates, but when the business of the court was done and everyone else was leaving, Geoffrey found himself arrested by the guards at the door and told that he would not be set free unless he surrendered all his castles, including the Tower of London, to the king.[13] From the technical point of view the affair had been very neatly managed, for Geoffrey was taken completely unawares and, indignant though he was, surrendered his castles. In the long run, however, it had unfortunate consequences since the arrest was, as Henry of Huntingdon put it, 'more in accord with the wickedness of the earl than with the law of nations, and more in accord with necessity than honest-dealing'.[14] It was a sly trick rather than a kingly act, and served to emphasize the strand of shiftiness in Stephen's character.

Geoffrey himself was so enraged by the treatment which he had received, that he revolted as soon as the king released him. No longer having any castles of his own, he made for the fenlands, where chance presented him with a perfect base. In November Stephen had gone north to ensure the peace of Huntingdonshire, and in the course of his operations had forced Abbot Walter of Ramsey, who sympathized with the empress, to resign in favour of a monk called Daniel who had proved his loyalty by guiding the royal army across the fens to Ely in 1140.[15] Stephen's action was both uncanonical and unpopular. Abbot

---

13 I have followed the account in the chronicle of Walden Abbey, of which Geoffrey was founder (*Monast*. iv. 142). *G.S.* 106–8 makes the arrest follow from a quarrel at court, framed in the same way as that which led to the arrest of the bishops. J. H. Round considered that Geoffrey had actually formed an alliance with the empress, but in *E.H.R.* lxxix (1964), 299–307, I have shown why I think his theory untenable. See below, Appendix III.

14 Henry of Huntingdon (R. S) 276; cf. the defensive attitude of the *G.S.* 107, 'ne regia maiestas turpi proditionis opprobrio infamaretur'.

15 *Chron. Abb. Rames.* 325–34. The reasons for thinking Abbot Walter a sympathizer of the empress are (*a*) that he had made a formal treaty with Bishop Nigel in 1141 (*Chron. Abb. Rames.* 307); (*b*) Stephen found it necessary personally to force his resignation and personally to install Daniel in his place (*ibid.* 328–9); (*c*) Walter was supported not only by the monks but also by 'the barons, knights, and freemen of almost the whole abbey' (*ibid.* 328), and these would have included Robert Foliot who had formerly been King David's steward in the honour of Huntingdon (*ibid.* 255, 276, 306, 312). For Daniel's assistance to Stephen at the siege of Ely, see *G.S.* 100. Round (*G.de M.* 210), following the Walden Chronicle, thought that Daniel was in alliance with Geoffrey, but the earlier and more detailed account of the Ramsey Chronicle must be preferred.

Walter appealed to Rome, the monks and the abbey's tenants were in a state of near mutiny and finally, eighteen days after Daniel's installation, Geoffrey de Mandeville appeared on the scene. At first everyone seems to have assumed that the sole object of his coming was to drive out Daniel and restore Walter, and consequently he was welcomed. There was general consternation when he seized the abbey's treasure, dispersed the monks, turned the whole place into a fortress, and terrorized the surrounding countryside.

A vivid, if generalized, picture of the sort of conditions which ensued is given in the *Anglo-Saxon Chronicle* which was written at Peterborough.

> For every man built him castles and held them against the king; and they
> filled the whole land with these castles. They sorely burdened the
> unhappy people of the country with forced labour on the castles; and
> when the castles were built they filled them with devils and wicked men.
> By night and by day they seized those whom they believed to have any
> wealth, whether they were men or women; and in order to get their gold
> and silver, they put them into prison and tortured them with
> unspeakable tortures, for never were martyrs tortured as they were. . . .
> At regular intervals they levied a tax called 'tenserie' upon the villages.
> When the wretched people had no more to give, they plundered and
> burnt all the villages, so that you could easily go a day's journey without
> ever finding a village inhabited or field cultivated. . . . If two or three
> men came riding towards a village, all the villagers fled before them,
> believing that they were robbers. The bishops and clergy were for ever
> cursing them, but that was nothing to them, for they were all
> excommunicated and forsworn and lost. Wherever the ground was
> tilled the earth bore no corn, for the land was ruined by such doings; and
> men said openly that Christ and his saints slept.[16]

The district which Geoffrey thus ravaged was large. We know that to the south-west of Ramsey he held Wood Walton (Hunts) and to the north-east Benwick and Chatteris (Cambs) through which he communicated with Ely. He is known to have sacked Cambridge, fortified Fordham (Cambs) and held Mildenhall in Suffolk.[17] He was also in alliance with Earl Hugh Bigod, and seems to have kept in touch with his castles in East Suffolk; and in this connection it is probably relevant that the abbot of Bury St Edmunds, who was loyal to Stephen, is known to have been troubled by hostile castles at Milden and Lindsey,

---

16 *The Anglo-Saxon Chronicle*, trans. G. N. Garmonsway (London, 1953), 264–5. Geoffrey is not mentioned by name, but the chronicle was written at Peterborough, only thirteen miles from Ramsey. The word 'tenserie' has been much discussed (e.g. in *G. de M.* 414–16), but since c and t are indistinguishable in most MSS, it seems likely that the word should be 'censerie', a French variation of the Latin 'census' meaning tax or rent.
17 *Chron. Abb. Rames.* 332; *Liber Eliensis*, 328; *G.S.* 164–6.

near Lavenham (Suffolk).[18] The seriousness of the revolt was therefore self-evident, and Stephen hurried to East Anglia in order to put it down. The difficulty was that, like Miles of Gloucester before him, Geoffrey de Mandeville was a past master at refusing battle. Whenever an army was sent against him, he retreated into the fens and transferred his attacks to another district. As it was impossible to catch him, Stephen had no option but to build castles all round the fenland in an attempt to hem him in; and as the castles all needed garrisons, the supporters of the empress thought that Stephen's army was immobilized in East Anglia and that it would now be safe to revolt elsewhere. They harried the district round Oxford, besieged Malmesbury, threatened Coventry, and attacked the king's men wherever they could.

In many ways it must have looked like a repetition of the events of 1140. Anxious to demonstrate that he was not immobilized by the fenland revolt, Stephen made lightning advances in this direction and that, hoping to find some of his enemies off their guard, but unable to fight a general engagement because his mobile force was necessarily small. He marched against Lincoln, probably in May (1141), attempted a siege of the city, and withdrew when he had no rapid success. He succeeded in relieving Malmesbury, but when he himself attempted to capture Tetbury (Glos), he had to retreat in a hurry because the earl of Gloucester offered battle. In the course of his retreat he captured a castle at Winchcombe (Glos), but his military measures were just beginning to look ineffective when he suddenly found himself unexpectedly victorious. In August Geoffrey de Mandeville was fatally wounded while attacking a castle at Burwell (Cambs), and on his death (16 September 1141) the whole fenland revolt collapsed.

The moral effect of Stephen's success was greatly heightened by the fact that Geoffrey de Mandeville died an unabsolved excommunicate. In the last resort this was due to the efforts of Henry of Blois who had remained papal legate till near the end of 1143 and had made every effort to realize his Cluniac ideal of a brotherly alliance between Church and King. At his mid-Lent council of 1143, which Stephen himself had attended, he had not only favoured the accusations against Nigel of Ely, but had also urged bishops to make good use of their powers of excommunication, 'not cowering in dastardly fear like a reed shaken by the wind', but 'meeting men wise in the flesh with the sword of God's Word which devours the flesh'.[19] As a result the council had

---

18 *G.S.* 110. *The Chronicle of Jocelin of Brakelond*, ed. H. E. Butler (Nelson's Medieval Texts, London, 1949), 138.
19 *G.S.* 154.

decreed that 'no one who laid violent hands on a cleric could be absolved by anyone except the pope and in the pope's own presence';[20] and since Geoffrey de Mandeville had been excommunicated for the violence which he had done to the monks of Ramsey, it followed that he could only be absolved if he went to Rome. Once he had been fatally wounded, this was impossible. While he lay unconscious his officials did their best to appease the wrath of God by issuing charters in his name for the restoration of church property which he had seized, but it was all to no avail.[21] His body was refused Christian burial, his earldom was abolished, his lands and offices forfeited and his family disinherited.[22] Saffron Walden castle and other lands in the district were retained in the royal demesne,[23] and Geoffrey's offices were distributed among the king's 'new' men, the justiciarship of London being given to Gervase of Cornhill,[24] and the justiciarship and shrievalty of Essex to Richard de Lucy.[25]

The State of the Country

It has sometimes been claimed that the revolt of Geoffrey de Mandeville was an isolated event, and that all the horrors of the so-called Anarchy should be referred to this one time and place, but the evidence to the contrary is far too strong to be ignored. The *Gesta Stephani*, for example, was primarily concerned with West Country, but it is loud in its complaints at the conditions endured at all periods of the reign. One passage which refers to 1143 may be quoted in full:

> At this time England began to be troubled in many different ways; on the one hand to be very hard pressed by the king and his supporters, on the other to be most violently afflicted by the earl of Gloucester, sometimes to endure the furious attacks of one party, sometimes the unbridled rage of the other; but always and everywhere to be in a turmoil and to be reduced to a desert. . . . You could see villages with

20 Henry of Huntingdon (R.S.) 276; *Liber Eliensis*, 324.

21 *Chron. Abb. Rames.* 332. Besides restoring Ramsey to Abbot Walter (who survived till 1160), he restored property to Holy Trinity Aldgate (Round, *Commune of London*, 101) and St Martin le Grand of London (Howlett, in *Chronicles* iii. p. xxxvii).

22 He had three sons. The eldest, Ernulf, shared in his rebellion and excommunication, was captured by Stephen and exiled; though he reappears in Henry II's reign he was excluded from the main inheritance. A younger son, Geoffrey, was with the empress and recognized by her as earl of Essex *c.* 1144–7; Henry II restored the Mandeville inheritance to him in 1156 (*G. de M.*, ch. x.).

23 The castellan whom he appointed, Turgis of Avranches, revolted in 1145 in an abortive attempt to make the castle his own (*G.S.* 174–6). Geoffrey's manor at Bonhunt (Ess.) was apparently given to Gilbert de Clare (*Reg.* iii. 307).

24 A wealthy citizen of London. For his family see *G. de M.* 304–12.

25 After serving Stephen loyally, he became Henry II's chief justiciar.

famous names standing solitary and almost empty, because the peasants
of both sexes and all ages were dead, fields whitening with a magnificent
harvest (for autumn was at hand) but their cultivators taken away by the
agency of a devastating famine, and all England wearing a look of grief
and calamity, an aspect of wretchedness and oppression. To crown all
these evils, England was swamped by a bestial horde of barbarians who
had come together simply for the sake of fighting. In the face of so
much suffering they had neither bowels of compassion nor feelings of
human pity, but everywhere in castles they conspired with one accord to
commit crime and outrage, spent their time insatiably pillaging the
goods of the poor, and devoted all the zeal of their evil hearts to
encouraging hostilities on both sides and to slaughter everywhere.[26]

In the case of some districts it must be admitted that we have no literary
evidence at all, but it cannot be assumed that because a county had no
chronicler it did not suffer in the war.

Numerous attempts have been made to wring information about
Stephen's reign from the earliest Pipe Rolls of King Henry II. At first
attention centred on the amounts of danegeld excused because of
'waste' (63% in Warwickshire, 52% in Nottingham–Derbyshire and
51% in Leicestershire) on the assumption that 'waste' meant
devastation.[27] Plausibility was given to these figures by the fact that
they accorded well enough with Duke Henry's campaign of 1153, but it
has since been shown that so far as the Exchequer was concerned
'waste' was a technical term indicating that no tax was forthcoming
from a particular property, whatever the reason might be. A
particularly common reason could well have been the administrative
confusion caused by outdated claims to exemption or by disputes over
the legal ownership of lands which had changed hands in the course of
the war.[28] But though 'waste' did not necessarily mean devastation it
could include it, and the suggestion has been made that the 'waste'
allowed to boroughs might more probably indicate war-damage
because the sums involved are 'always lump sums in round figures'. In
this case the boroughs most devastated would have been Winchcombe
88 per cent, Hertford 60 per cent, and Cambridge, Huntingdon,
Nottingham–Derby and Shrewsbury all at 50 percent. The same
scholar has pointed out that 'defaults of manors' on the royal demesne
in 1154–55 were highest in Northamptonshire (£86, 2s. 3d.), Lincolnshire
(£61, 1s. 8d.) and Leicestershire (£30, 12s. 5d.), while in the following year

26 *G.S.* 152–4. Cf. *Hist. Nov.* para 483.
27 H. W. C. Davis, 'The Anarchy of Stephen's Reign', *E.H.R.* xvii (1903), 630–41 and
criticism of it in A. L. Poole, *From Domesday Book to Magna Carta* (Oxford, 1951), 151.
28 Edmund King, 'The Anarchy of King Stephen's Reign', *T.R.H.S.* 5th series, 34
(1984), 133–53, esp. 143.

the largest amounts spent in restocking the royal manors were in Nottinghamshire–Derbyshire (£180 1*s.* 2*d.*), Shropshire (£145 8*s.* 8*d.*) and Northamptonshire (£132 12*s.* 8*d.*).[29] However fragile these calculations may be in detail, there can be no denying that taken together they point unmistakably to the North Midlands, and concentrate the attention on districts which were largely ignored by the narratives of William of Malmesbury and the *Gesta Stephani*.

In addition to the destruction of war there was almost certainly a general deterioration of governmental efficiency caused by the inability of the Exchequer to maintain effective control over the local government in the counties. For financial purposes the main official in a county was the sheriff who had to pay an annual 'farm', or fixed money-rent for all the royal dues which he was entitled to collect. This rent could be calculated *blanch* (in which case the coins were assayed and valued by the amount of silver in them) or by *tale* (in which case they were accepted at face value). It has now been shown that while Henry I increased the revenue which he received from these 'farms' by having them all reckoned *blanch*, there was a regression in Stephen's reign since by 1156 only 10 of the county 'farms' were still *blanch*. Of the rest, 8 were paid by tale, while in the remaining 13 cases the method of payment was not mentioned at all. These last cases must have had serious consequences for the Exchequer, since with the sum due from the 'farm' indeterminate, any effective examination of the sheriff's accounts would have been impossible. The countries concerned were Cornwall, Hampshire, Berkshire, Oxfordshire, Buckinghamshire, Hertfordshire, Bedfordshire, Cambridgeshire, Huntingdonshire, Worcestershire, Warwickshire, Northamptonshire and Derbyshire-Nottinghamshire. Plotted on a map they show that, as might have been expected, the efficiency of government deteriorated where a county was remote (as in the case of Cornwall) or in a sort of 'no-man's-land' between the power bases of King Stephen and the empress.[30]

A similar conclusion has been suggested by recent numismatic studies. Broadly speaking, Stephen's coinage circulated widely in the east of the Kingdom, and that of the empress, though never so successful as his, in the west. In between them coins known as Stephen Types III, IV and V were struck at Lincoln, Nottingham, Leicester and Northampton. Though they bore Stephen's name, their dies had not

29 Graeme White, 'Were the Midlands "wasted" during Stephen's reign?', *Midland History* X (1985), 26–41.

30 Kenji Yoshitake, 'The Exchequer in the reign of King Stephen', *E.H.R.* ciii (1988), 950–59.

come from the official die-cutters at London but from local engravers. Consequently these three types are no longer regarded as substantive issues. They are best seen as the products of lords or local communities which professed loyalty to the king but were no longer in regular contact with his government.[31]

The royal chancery (or secretariat) also shows a mixture of good order and ineffectiveness. It produced writs and charters in the same form as in Henry I's reign, and in only slightly smaller numbers overall—an average of 38.2 a year instead of 43—though more refined statistics have suggested that the number was far greater before 1140 than after. Strictly speaking the writs should have been addressed to the relevant sheriff or local justiciar by name, but in fact the names are often missing, and this also is most noticeable after 1140.[32] From 30 counties or combinations of counties we have the names of only 83 sheriffs or justiciars. This must be a long way short of the total for the reign, especially when it is considered that 40 of these 83 individuals are known to have gone over to the empress. One often gets the impression that in those counties which were inconveniently situated, Stephen's chancery officials were no longer familiar with officers in the counties.[33]

As governmental control grew erratic there must have been a temptation for former chancery clerks, whether retired or dismissed, to indulge in a certain amount of free enterprise, issuing writs and charters for their own benefit. The college of St Martin-le-Grand of London, which was closely connected with the royal chancery, had 30 writs or charters from the king, 8 from his queen, one from his son Eustace and one from the empress. Reading Abbey, where Robert de Sigillo, the master of Henry I's scriptorium, was a monk from 1136–41, and Reginald, a former clerk of King Stephen's abbot from 1154, had (apparently) 22 charters from King Stephen, 7 from the empress and 7 from Duke Henry. Since chancery clerks were necessarily well schooled in the correct formulae and styles of handwriting, it is difficult, if not impossible, for a historian to know how many of the documents they produced were genuinely authorized. But the idea

31 Full references in King, 'Anarchy', 147–52.

32 Edward J. Kealey, 'King Stephen: Government and Anarchy', *Albion* 6 (1974) 201–17. Kealey's detailed figures are criticized by Kenji Yoshitake 'The arrest of the bishops in 1139 and its consequences', *Journ. Med. Hist.* 14 (1988), 97–114, on the ground that no allowance is made for the fact that Stephen was in captivity for most of 1141. Yoshitake insists (rightly) that the King's government suffered more from the battle of Lincoln than from the arrest of the bishops.

33 Reg iii, pp. xxiii–xxvi.

that Reading and other abbeys also made use of a forged seal must now be abandoned.[34]

Government did not break down completely in Stephen's reign. In some districts it was more effective than in others, and there must have been spasmodic outbreaks of 'anarchy' in many places, but that did not mean that the traditions of good government and legal practice were forgotten. Richard de Lucy who was one of Henry II's chief justiciars from 1155 to 1179 had received most of his training under Stephen, for whom he acted as Justiciar of London, Middlesex and Essex, and for whom he witnessed as many as 135 charters. But it was one thing to practise justice in the security of London or the king's court, quite another to see that it was observed in those parts which were in, or adjacent to, the war-zone. In the 1140s England was renowned for its wealth and consequently attracted mercenaries of the most predatory type; and if as is probably the case, there were times when neither king nor empress could pay their soldiers' wages, there would have been full opportunity for the unscrupulous activities of men like Robert fitz Hubert or Robert fitz Hildebrand (pp. 42 and 73). The fact that the country had long been used to the rule of law made it particularly defenceless. Everyone had come to rely on the power of the king's sheriffs and justiciars, and when that power became uncertain or ineffectual, the country became a freebooter's paradise.[35]

The resultant miseries coincided with an outburst of religious enthusiasm which, though not confined to England, was exceptional even for the Middle Ages. In 1144 the city of Norwich was in a religious frenzy because the townsmen believed that a miraculous light in the sky had revealed the body of a murdered boy (St William), whom they thought to have been crucified by the Jews.[36] In Hertfordshire an

34 T. A. Heslop in *English Romanesque Art, 1066–1200*, ed. George Zarnecki, Jane Holt and Tristram Holland (London, 1984), p. 303 (no. 332) has shown that in *Reg.* iii, pp. xvi–xvii I was mistaken in thinking that a 'third' seal of King Stephen's was only a forgery of his first seal. I am now persuaded that the differences, though individually trivial, are too many for a forgery, especially since the 'third' seal is almost a quarter of an inch larger in diameter than the first, presumably to make it seem grander. It follows that the documents on which it is used cannot be regarded as forgeries on that ground alone. As Heslop states, it could have been used from 1138 to June 1139, after the first seal and before the second. To avoid the confusion which would be caused by renaming the latter, I follow Heslop in calling the 'new' seal the 'so-called Third'.

35 The extent of freebooting should not be exaggerated. Thomas Callahan Jr, in 'The Impact of Anarchy on English Monasticism, 1135–54' (*Albion* 6 (1974), 218–32) reckons that less than 10% of all religious houses are recorded as having suffered losses in this period, that in many cases the losses were slight, and that in almost half of them some sort of restitution was made. It was only in a few cases that the damage was severe, and the general impression, as with all aspects of law and order in this period, is patchy.

36 *The Life and Miracles of St William of Norwich by Thomas of Monmouth*, ed. and trans. by A. Jessopp and M. R. James. It is the first known allegation of ritual murder against

anchoress called Christina of Markyate displayed remarkable gifts of prophecy and vision.[37] In Somerset an anchorite called Wulfric of Haselbury recited the whole psalter nightly in a cold bath, and converted a robber knight to religion so that he became a monk and eventually abbot of Waverley.[38] Everywhere new religious houses were being founded, the average during the reign being six a year, a rate unequalled in any other period.[39] In 1145 men and women were so enthusiastic for the rebuilding of the Norman abbey of St Pierre-sur-Dives, that they harnessed themselves to the carts transporting stone and timber, as they had also done at Chartres.

> Everywhere there was penitence and forgiveness of sins, everywhere lamentation and grief. You could see men and women hauling loads through deep swamps and being beaten with scourges; and everywhere miracles were done and praises sung to God.[40]

In 1146 a further upsurge of religous feeling was occasioned by the preaching of the Second Crusade. In a famous letter which was addressed, among others, to the English people, St Bernard appealed to Christians to stop fighting among themselves:

> What is this savage craving of yours? Put a stop to it now, for it is not fighting but foolery. Thus to risk both soul and body is not brave but shocking, is not strength but folly. But now, O mighty soldiers, O men of war, you have a cause for which you can fight without danger, a cause in which to conquer is glorious and for which to die is gain.[41]

Coming at a moment when the civil war had begun to seem endless, St Bernard's appeal fell on willing ears. Waleran of Meulan, Earl William de Warenne, Roger de Mowbray, Walter fitz Gilbert of Clare, Philip son of Robert Earl of Gloucester, William Peverel of Dover and Roger Clinton Bishop of Chester all took the cross and set out for the Holy Land. In addition a host of lesser men took part in the maritime crusade which captured Lisbon from the Muslims in 1147, Hervey Glanville leading the men of Norfolk and Suffolk, Simon of Dover the men of Kent, Andrew the Londoners, and William and Ralph Veal the men of Southampton. [42]

---

the Jews. Neither the sheriff nor the bishop seem to have believed it, but they were powerless in face of the popular frenzy.

37 *The Life of Christina of Markyate,* ed. and trans. C. T. Talbot (Oxford, 1959).

38 *Wulfric of Haselbury by John of Ford*, ed. Dom. Maurice Bell (Somerset Record Soc., 47, (1932), esp. 19 and 68 ff.)

39 David Knowles, *The Monastic order in England* (Cambridge, 1940), 711.

40 Robert de Torigni, in *Chronicles* iv. 150–1.

41 *The Letters of St Bernard of Clairvaux*, trans. Bruno Scott James (London, 1953), 462.

42 *De Expugnatione Lyxbonensi: The Conquest of Lisbon,* ed. and trans. C. W. David (Columbia: Records of Civilization Series, 1936), 5–6, 55–7, 101–5.

> You would have thought England was empty and drained of men when
> so many, and of such importance, were everywhere setting out, yet did
> not strife and plunder, the sword and the enemy give any respite in
> England, because as some departed others took their places, the more
> zealous in doing evil the more recently they had come to it.[43]

It is this juxtaposition of religious enthusiasm and the predatory
instincts of war which we must remember, if we are to understand the
sudden shifts with which, in the later part of the civil war, men changed
sides, fought with redoubled fury, or abandoned England completely.

Ranulf Earl of Chester, 1145–47

In order to understand the events centring on the arrest of Ranulf Earl
of Chester, it is necessary to explain the state of the parties in 1145.
During the course of that year Stephen had made his peace with Nigel
Bishop of Ely,[44] so that the only rebel still active in East Anglia was
Hugh Bigod who, though he continued to hold his castles on the
Suffolk coast, could safely be ignored. The focal point of the war had
shifted to the West Midlands, where the empress was making desperate
attempts to capture Malmesbury, which continued to hold out for
Stephen although it was almost surrounded. She soon discovered that
if the place was to be taken, the war had to be fought with the utmost
ruthlessness, and this was only possible so long as men believed in a
quick victory. When the war began to seem endless and brought
disaster to the supporters of both parties in turn, the most enduring
loyalties proved to be those of family and feudal relationships. This was
soon demonstrated by the empress's commanders at Cricklade.

The first, William Peverel of Dover, succeeded in capturing Walter
de Pinkney, who was the king's castellan of Malmesbury, but having
handed him over to the empress, was smitten with remorse for 'the
woes and sufferings which he had pitilessly brought on the people', and
left Cricklade to go on the Second Crusade.[45] Though she had thus lost
her own commander, the empress still had Walter in her power, and it
might have been thought that she would have hanged him as a traitor if
he refused to order his men to surrender Malmesbury, but even she had

43 *G.S.* 192–3

44 He made peace at Ipswich, then held by Stephen, and gave his son Richard fitz
Neal (who was subsequently to write the *Dialogue of the Exchequer*) as a hostage. *Liber
Eliensis*, 332–4; *Reg.* iii. 267. Nigel witnessed at least six charters for Stephen after this date
(*Reg.* iii. 183, 301, 302, 402, 624, 760), and it may even be, as Round suggests, that he was
restored to some position in the central administration.

45 *G.S.* 178.

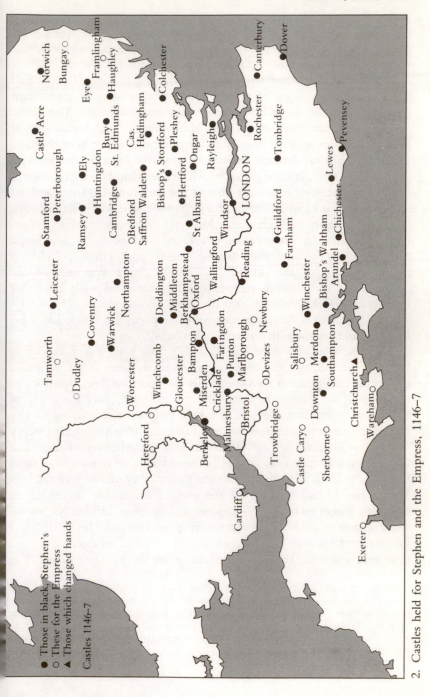

2. Castles held for Stephen and the Empress, 1146–7

Castles 1146–7
● Those in black, Stephen's
○ These for the Empress
▲ Those which changed hands

passed the stage of ruthlessness. She imprisoned him and threatened him, but dared not execute her threats because of Walter's close connection with the earl of Hereford; in little more than a year he had regained his liberty and was fighting her supporters in Dorset.[46]

Her second commander at Cricklade was Philip, son of Robert Earl of Gloucester, and he, after a short period of aggressive warfare, went over to Stephen in rather mysterious circumstances. The *Gesta Stephani* states that Stephen purchased his support with lavish gifts of lands and castles selected presumably from those which his father had forfeited;[47] but his defection seems also to have been connected with the fall of the castle at Faringdon, which had been built by Earl Robert at Philip's own request in order to harass the garrison of Oxford and cut its remaining links with Malmesbury. As soon as it was built, Stephen advanced to besiege it with a large force of Londoners, but Earl Robert made little or no attempt to relieve it, and those in command surrendered to the king after making a secret pact with him 'without the knowledge of the others'.[48] Whether Philip was one of the commanders in question, or whether he quarrelled with his father because of his failure to relieve the place, we have no means of knowing. All that is certain is that he went over to Stephen, put Cricklade at his disposal, and fought with ferocity on his behalf.

The desertion of one of Earl Robert's own sons was a damaging blow to the cause of the empress, particularly since it introduced a disturbing new element into the family ties and feudal relationships of her supporters. Roger de Berkeley, for example, was the uncle of Philip's wife, but it was essential for the empress to retain his loyalty because of the strategic importance of his castle, which was only twenty miles from Malmesbury and dominated the route between Bristol and Gloucester; if Stephen secured it, he would have driven a wedge right through the lands of the empress's supporters. In order to forestall him Walter fitz Miles, brother of the earl of Hereford, succeeded in capturing Roger by trickery—apparently it was not difficult because he was a relative—and in an attempt to make him surrender his castle 'put a halter round his neck and hanged him three times' in front of it, 'the third time loosening the halter and letting him drop to the ground'.[49] In

---

46 *G.S.* 178–80 and 212; cf. *E.H.R.* lxxvii (1962), 211–12.

47 *G.S.* 186. If the lands granted to him would otherwise have been held by his father or elder brother, Stephen would have succeeded in putting him in the position of one of Henry I's 'new' men (cf. p. 9). This in turn would explain Philip's attempt to wreck the peace negotiations by capturing Reginald Earl of Cornwall when on an embassy. *G.S.* 186

48 *G.S.* 182.

49 *G.S.* 190.

the end it all turned out to be pretence. Since Walter was a close kinsman of Roger's he would not kill him, and since Roger realized the fact, he would not surrender his castle. Philip came to the rescue and prepared to ravage the district, but smitten by a mysterious illness he repented of his former actions, took a vow to go on the Second Crusade and disappeared from history.[50]

With many torn by such conflicting loyalties, it was hardly surprising that some thought the time ripe for reopening peace talks. But there was still no basis for agreement; Stephen was so convinced of his strength in England, and the empress of her husband's in Normandy, that neither was prepared to compromise. When a conference was finally arranged, the empress claimed the crown as hers by hereditary right, while Stephen insisted that it was his, and that he would not make 'any concession at all with regard to anything he had got in any way whatsoever'.[51] Ignoring the importance of what had happened in Normandy, he was dazzled by his recent successes and believed that the empress's party would soon disintegrate, particularly since he had just won an impressive new ally in Ranulf Earl of Chester.

Ranulf's defection to Stephen was in some ways surprising, for quite apart from the fact that he had extensive lands in Normandy, he was generally regarded as the arch-rebel against the king, since it was he who had been the cause of the battle of Lincoln, and consequently of the king's captivity. On the other hand the mainspring of all his actions was, as we have already seen (pp. 46–7), his hostility of King David of Scotland from whom he wanted to recover his honour of Carlisle. Since 1141 King David had supported the empress and become her most-favoured friend, and it was therefore not surprising that Ranulf wanted to revert to Stephen's allegiance. It was true that his wife was the daughter of Robert Earl of Gloucester, but in 1145 it was equally relevant that her brother Philip could well have acted as an intermediary with the king. Be that as it may, Ranulf

came to the king [at Stamford] in humility and submission, and, repenting at last of the cruelty and treachery he had shown to him when he stretched forth his hands against his King and lord at the capture of Lincoln, and when he encroached for his own aggrandizement on a very wide extent of the royal possessions, was restored to the favour of their old friendship after the pact between them had been renewed.[52]

50 He was at Rouen at some date in 1147, possibly on the way to the Holy Land (*C.D.F.* no. 98).

51 *G.S.* 186.

52 *G.S.* 184. The date is uncertain, either late 1145 or early 1146. The place is stated in *The Anglo-Saxon Chronicle*, trans. Garmonsway, 267.

The normal procedure in such a pact would have been for each side to give hostages, but in this case there were none; Ranulf was simply allowed to retain Lincoln castle until he could recover his lands in Normandy (an eventuality that might never occur), and demonstrated his good will by helping Stephen to capture Bedford from Miles de Beauchamp, and by bringing 300 knights to assist in a new siege of Wallingford.[53]

Though Ranulf's support was naturally welcome to Stephen, it cannot have been welcome to all his supporters, because he had seized lands from many of them as well as from the king, those particularly mentioned being William de Clerfeith, Gilbert de Gant (whose uncle was Stephen's chancellor), Earl Alan of Richmond, William Peverel of Nottingham, William d'Aubigny *Brito* and John Count of Eu.[54] Besides these there were others who were jealous of the favours suddenly showered on the earl, or who mistrusted him, and were alarmed when they discovered that he wanted the king to take part in a campaign against the Welsh. Ranulf's claim, which others thought to be nothing more than barefaced flattery, was that the Welsh would be subdued more effectively 'by the dread of the king's presence than by the presence of a thousand warriors without the king'. Ranulf's opponents, on the other hand, pointed out that the 'precipitous hills and tangled forests' of Wales were an ideal setting for an ambush, and did not hesitate to suggest that the earl might be planning treachery since he had offered no hostages or security for his good faith.[55]

So far as Stephen was concerned such suspicions never fell on deaf ears; they gave him an opportunity to practise his special technique of the contrived quarrel at court leading to a disingenuously sudden arrest. In this case the court was at Northampton, and the quarrel was provoked by unnamed advisers who told the earl that the king would not assist him unless he restored all the property which he had taken from him, and delivered hostages for his future loyalty. The earl refused the sudden demand, saying that it was not for this that he had come to court, and that he had been given no notice of the matter. In the ensuing quarrel he was accused of treason, arrested and imprisoned in chains,

[53] *G.S.* 184, 192: Henry of Huntingdon (R.S.), 279. It is probable that *Reg.* iii. 178 embodies the terms of the agreement, and it is from this charter that the condition about Lincoln and the Norman lands is taken.

[54] John of Hexham in *Symeon of Durham* (R.S.) ii. 308–9, and *Reg.* iii. 178. Tickhill, which was now promised to him, was part of the honour of Blythe and had previously been granted by Stephen to John Count of Eu as grandson and lawful heir of Beatrix de Busli.

[55] *G.S.* 195–7. See also Appendix VII, below.

until his friends succeeded in coming to terms with the king (28 Aug. 1146)[56]. It was then agreed that the earl should be released provided that he surrendered all the royal lands and castles which he had seized (Lincoln included), gave hostages, and took a solemn oath not to resist the king in future.[57]

For a short while Stephen may have thought the stratagem a great success. He recovered Lincoln and held his Christmas court in triumph there (1146), in order to show that he had at last wiped out the shame of his captivity. Henry of Huntingdon tells us that 'certain superstitions' had prevented other kings from wearing the crown in the city,[58] but Stephen evidently felt that fate could no longer harm him. Having subdued East Anglia and annihilated Geoffrey de Mandeville, he was now supreme in the city which had witnessed his downfall. He was apparently delighted with his own ingenuity in turning the tables on the earl of Chester, and may even have thought that he had shown restraint and justice in demanding from him only those lands which he had unjustly seized, so as to leave him in full possession of his earldom and patrimony. If so, he was living in a fool's paradise. The plain fact was that Ranulf had been arrested while he was in the king's peace and protection, and in contravention of the oath which the king had sworn to him at Stamford.[59] It was not the first time that he had been deceived by the king, for there had been deception in 1141 also (p. 48), and it was not surprising that he revolted as soon as he regained his liberty. He had learnt that it was useless to try and come to terms with a king who would not keep his word.

In the long run Stephen's arrest of Earl Ranulf was a disastrous mistake, for it discouraged further defections from the empress's party, and ruined all hopes of persuading his opponents to abandon the struggle; but in the short run it gave Stephen the military initiative and some cheap successes. When Ranulf made abortive attacks on Lincoln and Coventry, Stephen seized his hostages. The most important of these was Ranulf's nephew, Gilbert fitz Richard de Clare Earl of Hertford, and Stephen refused to release him unless he surrendered his castles. It was the king's invariable device, and Gilbert reacted to it in the inevitable way, handing over the castles but revolting as soon as he was

---

56 *Annales Cestrienses*, ed. R. C. Christie (Rec. Soc. of Lancs. and Cheshire, xiv (1887), 20).

57 *G.S.* 197–9. The date of the earl's arrest was 28 Aug. 1146 (*Annales Cestrienses*, ed. R. C. Christie (*Rec. Soc. of Lancs and Chesh* xiv), 20).

58 Henry of Huntingdon (R.S.), 279.

59 *Ibid.* The fact was also admitted (after 1153) in *G.S.* 236—'cum curiam suam subintrasset de pace sibi indulta securus'; cf. *E.H.R.* lxxvii (1962), 211.

set at liberty. His father's brother, Gilbert Earl of Pembroke, claimed the castles as his rightful inheritance (*jure hereditaris*) as senior member of the house of Clare, and when he was refused withdrew from court.[60] Stephen anticipated his revolt by capturing three of his castles before he had had time to alert them, and besieged him himself in Pevensey. It was a splendid example of what William of Malmesbury would have called 'activity without judgment', for the Clares were not supporters of the empress but simply defending their family's rights.

That would have been towards the end of 1146 or the beginning of 1147, but the chain reaction resulting from Earl Ranulf's arrest was not yet at an end. When the news reached Normandy, the empress's eldest son, Henry, little more than fourteen years old, conceived it his duty to escape from tutelage and rush to the assistance of those whom Stephen was so brutally attacking. He hired a few mercenaries on credit, crossed the channel, landed probably at Wareham and attempted a diversion in Wiltshire. With insufficient force and a complete lack of experience, it was not surprising that he failed to capture either of the places which he attacked—Cricklade or the neighbouring castle of Purton—or that he found himself unable to pay his troops. He appealed to his mother and his uncle, Robert Earl of Gloucester, but they disapproved of his escapade and thought that the easiest way of bringing him to heel was by refusing him money. In this they were mistaken, for with a rare show of effrontery, Henry 'sent envoys in secret to the king as to a kinsman' and succeeded in begging money from him.[61] The story is so astounding that many historians have refused to believe it, but it is consistent with Stephen's display of chivalry in 1139, when he had given the empress free passage from Arundel to Bristol (p. 38), and he may well have persuaded himself that it was worth paying the boy's fare home in order to get him out of the country. At any rate events conspired to give his action the appearance of wisdom. Henry was back in Normandy by 29 May 1147,[62] Robert Earl of Gloucester died on 31 October, and the empress, finding it difficult to maintain herself in

---

60 *G.S.* 200–4. Gilbert's claim was similar to that of the German princes who forced Frederick Barbarossa to agree that the emperor should only hold forfeited lands for a year and a day. Cf. H. Mitteis in G. Barraclough, *Mediaeval Germany, 911–1250* (Oxford, 1938), ii. 259.

61 *G.S.* 204–6. The story was dismissed by J. H. Round (*Feudal England*, 491–6) but rehabilitated by A. L. Poole in *E.H.R.* xlvii (1932), 447–52. *Reg.* iii. 43 should also be dated to this period. See Appendix V, below. There is no good reason for identifying the 'municipium quod Burtona dicitur' with Black Bourton (Oxon). Purton (Wilts) is four miles south of Cricklade.

62 Robert de Torigni, in *Chronicles* iv. 154; cf. *E.H.R.* xlvii (1932), 451–2.

England without him, sailed for Normandy in the first weeks of 1148, never to return.

At that point Stephen may well have thought his victory complete, particularly as the courts which he held in London at this period were better attended than any since 1141,[63] but none the less he was far from secure. What proved to be significant was not that the empress had left England—in some ways her supporters were happier without her—but that she now resided in the security of Normandy. In the duchy the civil war was over, and Duke Geoffrey's authority unquestioned. It was a sure refuge for exiles, an ideal base for invasion, and an absolute guarantee against defeat. Stephen had tried to reduce its importance by winning a comparable supremacy in England, but though he had fought hard and won victories, the men whom he had attacked were not his inveterate enemies but waverers who, if treated in a different way, might have given him their loyal support. He had failed to reduce the hard core of the opposition—King David of the Scots, Brien fitz Count, and the earls of Cornwall, Devon, Gloucester, Wiltshire, Hereford, Worcester and Norfolk—but had merely added the earl of Chester to their number. More important still, he had demonstrated that his word was not to be trusted. He had given his peace to Geoffrey de Mandeville and sworn oaths of friendship with Ranulf Earl of Chester but he had ruined the one and done his worst against the other. Did he imagine that such conduct would encourage others of his opponents to rally to his cause? Or was he so vain as to imagine that he could conquer them all?

---

63 *e.g. Reg.* iii. 402.

CHAPTER NINE
The New Opposition, 1147–1149

In the same year as the empress finally withdrew from England, Stephen found his authority challenged from a new and unexpected quarter, the Church. This was not because of any particular mistake on his part, but because of a change in the climate of religious opinion in the whole of Latin Christendom. When Stephen had won the throne, the most powerful influence had been exercised by the monks of Cluny, with the result that his Cluniac brother had been able to control the Church's policy in England and act as papal legate from 1139 to 1143. Since then the Cluniacs had been eclipsed by the Cistercians in both numbers and influence; in England the number of Cistercian abbeys had increased from five in 1135 to twenty-seven in 1147, and in the Church at large it was their leader, St Bernard, who had become the arbiter of western Christendom. Having spent eight years travelling round much of western Europe in order to heal the papal schism (1130–38) and secure the recognition of Innocent II, Bernard had adopted the role of perpetual pricker of the papal conscience, demanding the condemnation of theological views which he thought to be erroneous, and appealing against episcopal elections of which he disapproved. When, in 1145, one of his own monks was elected Pope Eugenius III, he wrote to congratulate him on the triumph of righteousness, saying (with singular disrespect for Innocent II) that the Church had 'confidence in him such as it had not had in his predecessors for a long time past'; and he made it clear that one of his first duties as pope would be to take action against Henry of Blois and the man whom he and his brother had made archbishop of York. 'When you have time, deal with them according to their works, so that they may know a prophet has arisen in Israel.'[1]

1 *Letters of St Bernard*, trans. Bruno Scott James (London, 1953) no. 205 (Latin edition,

The York election had been watched with anxiety in many quarters because Archbishop Thurstan (1114–40) had been a man of wide sympathies and European reputation. He had received the see as a reward for loyal service in the household of Kings William II and Henry I, but had become a hero of the church of York for his refusal to make profession of obedience to Canterbury; he had won the friendship and respect of successive popes and received consecration from Pope Calixtus II in spite of the prohibition of the king, he had done much to further the growth of monasticism in his province, in particular having given to the secessionist monks of St Mary's York the land on which they had built the Cistercian abbey of Fountains (1132); and finally he had united the barons of Yorkshire against the Scottish invasion of 1138 (pp. 36–7). When he died, the chapter of York (who were the official electors) wanted a successor who would remain firm against Canterbury, the king wanted to nominate a man who would be loyal against the Scots, and the monks of the province were determined to exercise their right (reaffirmed by the Lateran Council of 1139) to assist in the election and promote a monastic reformer.[2]

The northern (or anti-Canterbury) interest allied itself naturally with the monastic reformers whose leader was William abbot of Rievaulx; and since Rievaulx was a daughter-house of St Bernard's abbey of Clairvaux, their views soon became those of the whole Cistercian order. Apparently their first candidate was Waltheof prior of Kirkham, but he was vetoed by Stephen's men as too friendly with the Scots, since he was King David's stepson and had been brought up in his household. The initiative then passed to Henry of Blois who, as papal legate, secured the election of his nephew Henry de Sully, son of his (and Stephen's) eldest brother, William, the black sheep of the family (p. 4). Earlier in the year Henry of Blois had put him forward for Salisbury, but having failed to get him elected (p. 44) had consoled him with the abbacy of Fécamp; and now the young man, having no more sense than his father, refused to resign the abbey, believing that he could retain it in plurality in the same way as his uncle held Glastonbury with the see of Winchester. As a result the pope ordered a new election at York, and Henry of Blois advanced another relative, William fitz Herbert, son of

---

ep. 238), Eugenius III, Bernardo Pignatelli, had become a monk at Clairvaux in 1135, and since 1140 had been abbot of S. Paolo alle-tre-Fontane, Clairvaux's daughter-house outside St Paul's Gate at Rome.

2 The following account is based on David Knowles. 'The Case of St William of York' in *The Cambridge Hist. Journ.* v (1936), 162–77 and 212–14, reprinted in David Knowles, *The Historian and Character* (Cambridge, 1963), 76–97; cf. C. H. Talbot in *Cambridge Hist. Journ.* x (1950), 1–15.

his half-sister and treasurer of the church of York. In January 1141, shortly before the battle of Lincoln, he was elected by a majority of the chapter in the presence of the earl of York and at the express command of the king. Although he was quite a good man—in 1226 he was actually canonized—a powerful minority refused to accept his election as valid and appealed to Rome where, thanks to the Cistercian connection, they received the impassioned support of St Bernard.

The resulting struggle lasted for the best part of six years. St Bernard appealed, in effect, to public opinion and grew more and more indignant as Henry of Blois outwitted him with legal and diplomatic manœuvres in the papal curia. Henry was the very type of man whom Bernard hated—a nepotist, pluralist and Cluniac monk who had deserted his cloister, who built castles, took part in war, made a display of his wealth, bought pagan statues as works of art, and assumed a splendid air of *gravitas*, while proving himself a past master of political finesse.

> Behold! [St. Bernard wrote to Pope Lucius II in 1144], here, here I say is the enemy, here is the man who walks before Satan, the son of perdition, the man who disrupts all rights and laws. This is the man who has 'set his face against heaven', who has repudiated, reprobated, rejected and renounced the just judgment of the apostle, confirmed, consolidated, promulgated and clearly defined in solemn conclave. . . . I leave it to your judgment to decide how far the prestige of Rome has suffered in this matter. Would that the song in which they sing that Winchester is greater than Rome could be silenced on their lips![3]

The reason for the song was that while Innocent II was pope, Henry of Blois, bishop of Winchester, was papal legate and carried all before him. Two days after Innocent had died and (though he did not know it) on the very day on which his legatine authority expired, he consecrated his nominee to York as bishop (26 September 1143). To have the authority of *arch*-bishop, however, it was still necessary for William to receive the *pallium* from the pope; and this St Bernard was determined that he should not get. During the pontificates of popes Celestine II (1143–4) and Lucius II (1144–5) he and Henry exerted every ounce of influence for their respective interests, but it was only with the election of his former monk as Pope Eugenius III (15 February 1145) that St Bernard saw victory in sight.

> I am importunate, but I have reason to be, and my reason is the apostolate of Eugenius! For they are saying that it is not you but I who am pope, and from all sides they flock to me with their suits. . . . And now I have another reason for importunity and one no less compelling, for it is in a very good cause. My pen is again directed against that idol of

3 *Letters of St Bernard*, trans. B. S. James, no. 204.

York, with all the more reason because my other attacks with this weapon have not gone home. . . . Let me speak more clearly: it belongs to the Roman pontiff to command the deposition of bishops, for although others may be called to share his cares, the fulness of power rests with him alone.[4]

St Bernard saw to it that events took a dramatic turn. With scant regard for the continuity of papal policy, previous decisions were reversed or circumvented, and early in 1147 Archbishop William was deposed. A new election was ordered, and when the electors were divided, Eugenius decided against the king's candidate and in favour of Henry Murdac abbot of Fountains, who had been his fellow monk under St Bernard at Clairvaux.[5] On 7 December 1147 he consecrated him himself and gave him the pallium. Though Stephen at first refused to let him enter his see, he was the first archbishop since the Norman Conquest to have been elected and consecrated without the approval of the king.

This was a major defeat for Stephen, but it was made doubly serious by the fact that the disputed election had concentrated St Bernard's attention on England for six years, during which his constant thunderings against the king's nominee and the king's brother could not fail to be damaging to the king himself. Bernard himself became convinced that Stephen was opposed to ecclesiastical reform and the rule of righteousness, and consequently he did not consider his duty ended with the consecration of his own candidate as archbishop of York. He continued to watch English affairs warily, and even intervened in the internal affairs of another monastic order when he thought it was being disrupted by Stephen.

The order in question was that of Savigny which in 1147 was merged into that of Cîteaux through filiation with Clairvaux. This merger has generally been attributed to the personal conversion of Abbot Serlo of Savigny, but Robert de Torigni, who was in a position to know the facts, stated specifically that the real reason was that the monasteries subject to Serlo would not conform to his will.[6] We know from a bull of Pope Lucius II that as early as December 1144 the Savignac order was divided against itself; and we can deduce from the terms of the final submission

4 *Ibid*. no. 266.

5 His rival, the king's candidate, was Hilary dean of Christchurch, Hants. Though not a relative, he had been trained in the household of Henry of Blois. As consolation for his failure at York he was given the see of Chichester. He played an important part as a king's man in the Becket controversy (see H. Mayr-Harting in *E.H.R.* lxxviii (1963), 209–24).

6 'De abbatibus et abbatiis Normannoram' in *Chronique de Robert de Torigni*, ed. L. Delisle (*Soc. del'Hist. de Normandie*, 1873), ii. 189.

that the root of the trouble lay in England, since without mentioning the continental houses it included a statement that the English houses were to be subject to Savigny in perpetuity and carefully named them all: Furness, Buckfast, Buildwas, Neath, Quarr, Stratford, Coggeshall, Basingwerk, Combermere, Byland, Swineshead, Calder and the abbey of the Isle of Man (Rushen).[7]

The matter was of particular concern to Stephen because he was the chief patron of the order. Savigny was only eleven miles from Mortain of which he had been count since about 1113, and it was he who had founded the first and most important of its daughter-houses at Furness (1126), which in its turn claimed to be the mother-house of Calder, Byland, Rushen and Swineshead. He had also founded houses at Longvilliers in his county of Boulogne (1135) and at Buckfast in Devon (1136), and his wife had founded yet another at Coggeshall in Essex (c. 1139–41). Savigny was his special charity, but inevitably his attitude to it changed when, with the conquest of Western Normandy, it fell into the hands of Geoffrey of Anjou.[8] This would have been in 1142, shortly before the election of Serlo as abbot, and by December 1144 news of a schism in the order had, as already mentioned, reached the pope. Suspicions that the schism had a political origin are confirmed by the *Historia Fundationis* of Byland which records that in 1147 the abbot of Byland, whose founder supported the Angevins, went to the chapter-general at Savigny in order to plead that his house ought not to rank as a daughter-house of Stephen's abbey of Furness but of Savigny itself.[9] We are told that the abbots of all the fifteen French and Norman houses were present at the chapter, but that the only English abbots present (apart from Byland) were those of Neath and Quarr, whose patrons, Robert Earl of Gloucester and Baldwin de Redvers Earl of Devon, were two of the most prominent supporters of the empress. It seems clear, therefore, that if the abbot of Savigny could not exercise his authority over the other English houses, it must have been because of opposition from Stephen; and in these circumstances it would have been natural for St Bernard to offer, and for Serlo to accept, the

7 The bull of Lucius II is in Migne, *P. L.* clxxv. 917. The final submission was confirmed by Eugenius III in a bull of 10 April 1148 given at the Council of Rheims; Martène, *Thesaurus Novus Anecdotorum* (1717), i. 405. See also Dom Claude Auvry, *Histoire de la Congrégation de Savigny* which was written early in the eighteenth century and published by A. Laveille for the *Société de l'Histoire de Normandie* (3 vols, 1896–8).

8 Robert de Torigni in *Chronicles* iv. 143.

9 *Monast.* v. 569–70. The history itself gives the date as 1146 or 1147, but its references to the consecration of Henry Murdac and (later) to the council of Rheims make it certain that 1147 is correct. The founder of Byland was Roger de Mowbray, and as he was residing in Normandy he must have been supporting Duke Geoffrey.

protection of the Cistercian Order. We know that for some three or four years Furness continued to resist the union with Cîteaux, that its abbot Peter appealed to Rome but was eventually deposed, and that it lost its claim to be the mother-house of Byland.[10] Thanks to St Bernard Savigny recovered its authority in England, but because of St Bernard Stephen lost interest in what had once been his special monastic order. In 1148 he and his wife founded a magnificent new abbey at Faversham in Kent, but it was Cluniac.

The affair of Savigny was much less important than that of York, but it helps to explain why Stephen became anti-papal in his policy. For what was the use of appealing from St Bernard to Pope Eugenius III? What was thought at Clairvaux would inevitably be endorsed at Rome, and there was no doubting that it would be hostile to Stephen. For Henry of Blois, who was still Stephen's chief ecclesiastical adviser, it was an unenviable situation. In the early years of the reign he had persuaded, and even forced, his brother to pursue a papalist policy, because it was his Cluniac conviction that the Church would cooperate with the king if the king cooperated with the Church. Now that the pope was opposing the king, the king had to oppose the pope, but it is to Henry's credit that he kept his brother's opposition restrained and within defensible limits. Thus, though Stephen refused to accept Henry Murdac as archbishop of York because Eugenius had appointed him in spite of his declared opposition, he did not dispute the deposition of Archbishop William because that had to be regarded as a judicial sentence. Similarly, when the pope summoned the English bishops and abbots to attend a council of the Church at Rheims on 21 March 1148, he refused them permission to attend but nominated three bishops, Chichester, Hereford and Norwich, to go and present apologies for the archbishop of Canterbury and the others.

The only sign of disobedience to this royal command came from Archbishop Theobald who, though previously considered a nonentity, was beginning to develop a policy of his own. It was common knowledge that he was opposed to Henry of Blois and had not supported him in the York election, and it had probably been noted that his visit to Eugenius III at Paris in May 1147 had coincided with one from Geoffrey of Anjou.[11] Stephen was determined to show him who was master in the kingdom, and when the date for the Council of Rheims drew near, he moved to Canterbury to keep an eye on him. For Theobald, however, it was essential to make public demonstration of

10 The documents are summarized in *C.D.F.* 813–5 and 819.
11 The coincidence was pointed out by Frank Barlow in *E.H.R.* lxxii (1957), 306.

the fact that his first duty was to the pope. Escaping observation, he hired a fishing smack in a remote bay and crossed the channel 'rather as a survivor from a shipwreck than in a ship'.[12] At Rheims he was given a hero's welcome, and the pope prepared to excommunicate Stephen; the candles had already been lit for the ceremony when Theobald astonished everyone by begging mercy for the king. The pope, at first dumbfounded by his intervention, eventually gave way and allowed Stephen three months in which to give satisfaction before the penalty should be imposed, but Stephen showed no gratitude to Theobald; when he attempted to return to Canterbury, he was ordered to leave the country.[13]

The truth of the matter was that Stephen thought himself strong enough to resist the pope, because he had the support or acquiescence of all the other bishops. The departure of the empress had left everyone so anxious for peace that no-one was prepared to risk the start of yet another civil war. It was probably the realization of this fact which had caused Theobald to prevent the pope from excommunicating Stephen, and now, even when driven into exile, he was careful to refrain from hasty action. At the invitation of William of Ypres and the queen he took up residence in the abbey of St Bertin at Saint-Omer, so that he could conveniently negotiate through messengers with the king, and it was only when negotiations again broke down that he put the kingdom under interdict (12 September). The interdict proved, as he had feared, a failure; it was observed in his own diocese but all the other bishops (as John of Salisbury put it) 'preferred peace to duty'. Theobald therefore turned to an alternative tactic, sailed from Gravelines to the Suffolk coast and took up residence ar Framlingham, where he received bishops and heard ecclesiastical causes under the protection of Earl Hugh Bigod, an adherent of the empress.[14] This move was far more effective than any interdict or excommunication, for it threatened to make the archbishop an open supporter of the Angevins. Stephen appreciated the danger and immediately became less intransigent.

A further reason for Stephen's more accommodating attitude was that he wanted to secure the succession for his son Eustace. The

---

12 John of Salisbury, *Historia Pontificalis*, ed. and trans. M. Chibnall (Nelson's Medieval Texts, London, 1956), 7.

13 For full details see Saltman, *Theobald*, 25–30. Theobald's sole companion was Thomas Becket, according to the latter's reminiscence, *Materials for the History of Thomas Becket*, ed. J. B. Robertson (R.S. 6 vols, 1875–85), vi. 57–8.

14 Gervase of Canterbury, ed. Stubbs (R.S.), i. 136 gives the port of his arrival as 'Goseford' 'in terra comitis Hugonis Bigod', and he proceeded from there to Framlingham. Goseford is to be identified with Bawdsey Haven at the mouth of the Deben (*V. C. H. Suffolk*, ii. 201).

normal way to do this would be to have his son anointed in his own lifetime, and this was certainly what he wanted. He had already (about the beginning of 1147) invested him with the County of Boulogne which was his mother's inheritance, and all that was now required was to take him into association as king. The difficulty was that in England the only person who could anoint a king was the archbishop of Canterbury, and since no other bishop would act without him, it was essential for Stephen to come to terms with him. In October or November he managed to restore the semblance of normal relations by restoring to the archbishop the temporalities of his see, but there was still no sign of agreement on the main points at issue. Stephen still refused to accept Henry Murdac as archbishop of York, presumably intending to give way on this matter for nothing less than the consecration of his son as king; and Theobald was adamant that because of the ban of Pope Celestine II (1143–4) on any 'innovation' concerning the English throne, it was impossible for him to consecrate Eustace without express instructions from Rome. Stephen knew that while Pope Eugenius III was alive, those instructions would never be forthcoming, but if he was to retain any bargaining power he had to remain firm in his exclusion of Henry Murdac from York.

This necessity led to considerable difficulties, for Stephen's control of Yorkshire was by no means complete, and Henry Murdac found it possible to establish himself in parts of it without the king's permission. He reached Yorkshire in 1148, probably by sailing direct to the Humber, and is known to have been received by the citizens of Beverley. At York the citizens refused him entry, but he was able to reside at Ripon, next door to Fountains, of which (in strange imitation of Henry of Blois) he retained the abbacy.[15] From there he laid an interdict on the city of York, but it was ineffectual because William Earl of York and Hugh du Puiset, treasurer of the cathedral chapter, forced the clergy to disregard it.[16] In consequence the archbishop excommunicated both Hugh and the earl. Hugh replied by excommunicating the archbishop, and the citizens laid heavy penalties on anyone who tried to visit him at Ripon. For three years (1148–51) the church of York was in a state of schism.

Unfortunately no ecclesiastical schism could remain non-political.

15 Maurice and Thorold were suffragan abbots under him. (C. T. Clay in *Yorks. Arch. Journ.* 149 (1952), 17.) Cf. Æthelwulf who did not resign the priory of Nostell when he became bishop of Carlisle in 1133.

16 Hugh du Puiset (who was to become bishop of Durham, 1153–95) was the leader of the cathedral chapter because the dean, Robert de Gant, was an absentee as the king's chancellor. Hugh du Puiset was another of the numerous relatives of Henry of Blois.

Since the king was opposed to the archbishop, all laymen who were against the king rallied to the archbishop; and since parts of the province of York were in the Scottish kingdom, King David had an excellent excuse for intervening in person. Naturally he recognized Murdac, and so did the bishops of Durham and Carlisle. To make matters worse, King David arranged that the reception of the archbishop in Carlisle should coincide with the knighting of Henry Plantagenet son of the empress.[17] Henry, who was now sixteen years old, could doubtless claim that the only reason why he had travelled from Normandy to Scotland was to be knighted by the one close relative who was a king, but it is likely that an equally urgent reason (as in his expedition of 1147) was his determination to assist at any place where trouble was brewing for Stephen. According to the *Gesta Stephani* he was accompanied by Roger Earl of Hereford (the son and successor of Earl Miles) who wished to receive knighthood at the same time. King David received them in Carlisle and knighted them on Whit Sunday (22 May) 1149, with the assistance of his son Prince Henry of Scotland and Ranulf Earl of Chester.

The importance of the occasion was underlined by the fact that King David had secured the attendance of Earl Ranulf. This could not have been easy because the two men were old enemies, and the reason for their hostility was that Carlisle had been given to David in spite of Ranulf's claim to hold it as his patrimony (pp. 46–7). Clearly Ranulf would not have consented to meet David in that city unless an agreement about their conflicting claims had been prepared, and in fact an important purpose of the assembly was to witness their final concord. Ranulf recognized David as lord of Carlisle and did him homage, and in return David gave him the honour of Lancaster, a handsome recompense, since it included, among other things, the whole of Lancashire north of the Ribble.[18] In addition a marriage was arranged between one of the earl's sons and one of King David's grand-daughters, so that neither side was forced to regard its concessions as entirely lost to the family. It was a genuine compromise and the only way in which the conflicting claims could be reconciled. By its means the Angevin cause at last secured the whole-hearted loyalty of Earl Ranulf.

It seems that Henry Plantagenet and King David hoped for quick results from this alliance, for they planned to advance from Lancaster, where Ranulf was to join them with forces from his earldom, and to

17 John of Hexham (in *Symeon of Durham* (R.S.) ii. 322) states that Bishop Æthelwulf received Murdac 'when he (Murdac) came to King David in Carlisle'.
18 *Ibid*. ii. 323.

capture York. In fact the plan proved too ambitious, for though the allies got as far as 'approaching the city of York as if to attack it', they had to abandon their intention because of the sudden arrival of Stephen with a strong force of knights.[19] Forced to retreat, Henry Plantagenet made for Bristol, King David for Carlisle, and Earl Ranulf for Cheshire. It may be assumed that each of the allies blamed the other for this failure—the Scots complaining that Earl Ranulf had 'fulfilled none of the things which he had promised'[20]—but the truth of the matter was that, like many others before them, they had underestimated King Stephen's capacity for speed. He had received an early warning from the citizens of York (who like their fellow traders of Lincoln and London were notably loyal), and having a mercenary army at his beck and call, he had been able to advance without delay. His difficulties only began when he found that, in order to ward off any further advance from Carlisle, it was necessary to stay in Yorkshire more or less inactive for the whole of August.[21] Without battles there would be no loot, and yet he had to have money for the army's pay. We do not know whether such a situation was normal or not, but we do know that in this case he asked the citizens of York to pay a large sum of money for the destruction of a little castle at Wheldrake, which had been impeding access to the city from the south-east; that at the suggestion of the citizens of York, he marched on Beverley and imposed a heavy fine on the town for having admitted Henry Murdac without his permission; and that on his return to York 'he demanded a quantity of money from his nobles, singly and according to the quality of each person'.[22] We also have reason to believe that in order to hold Earl Ranulf in check he appointed a new earl of Lincoln.[23]

More important to Stephen than any of these defensive measures was the whereabouts of Henry Plantagenet; for while the Church remained intransigent the only way in which Stephen could ensure the succession for his son was by capturing and eliminating his rival. He sent knights to waylay him on his way southwards, and when he discovered that Henry had evaded them and reached Hereford, he alerted his son Eustace whom he had left in charge of the southern part

19 *G. S.* 216.
20 The quotation from John of Hexham (in *Symeon of Durham* (R. S.) ii. 323) led J. H. Round to think that Ranulf deserted David and Henry, and returned to Stephen's allegiance (*E.H.R.* x (1895), 87–91). That he was mistaken is shown by the active part which Ranulf played on Henry's behalf later in the year, but this was not known until the discovery and publication (in 1955) of the final portion of GS (pp. 214–40); cf. *E.H.R.* lxxv (1960), 654–60.
21 Henry of Huntingdon (R.S.) 282.
22 John of Hexham in *Symeon of Durham* (R.S.) ii. 323–4; cf. *G.S.* 144.
23 Gilbert de Gant; see Appendix I, p. 135.

of the kingdom. Eustace discovered that Henry was staying a night at the castle of Dursley (Glos) with the intention of proceeding to Bristol on the following day, and before daybreak he had laid ambushes at three places on the road, possibly with the assistance of the garrison of Berkeley.[24] He had no success. Forewarned of the danger, Henry had left Dursley in the middle of the night and reached Bristol safely. From there he had no difficulty in proceeding to Devizes, his mother's old headquarters, where he hoped to prepare for a further campaign.

At first his chief antagonist was Eustace who, from his base at Oxford, sent forces to ravage parts of Gloucestershire and harass the garrisons of Marlborough, Devizes and Salisbury, but towards the end of September Stephen returned from Yorkshire, determined to corner Henry and defeat him decisively. He concentrated his forces, and together with Eustace embarked on a policy of 'scorched earth' in Wiltshire, starting at Salisbury, and then proceeding to Marlborough and Devizes.

> They took and fired everything they came upon, set fire to houses and churches, and, what was a more cruel and bestial sight, fired the crops that had been reaped and stacked all over the fields, consumed and brought to nothing everything edible they found.[25]

The aim of this policy was to starve out the enemy castles and force Henry to give battle, and if allowed to run its full course it might well have succeeded. But Henry's allies were alive to the danger and did not desert him. Ranulf Earl of Chester created a major diversion by attacking Lincoln in force; he did not succeed in capturing the city, but he did succeed in drawing Stephen back to Lincolnshire and kept him busy when he got there. Soon afterwards Payn de Beauchamp and Earl Hugh Bigod created further diversions at Bedford and in East Anglia so that Eustace also was forced to leave Wiltshire. As a result Henry Plantagenet was able to get away from Devizes and, assisted by the earls of Gloucester and Hereford, launched an offensive in Devon and Dorset. He captured Bridport, which was a useful harbour, but failed to win any real success over Stephen's principal lieutenant, Henry de Tracy, who refused to give battle but took refuge in his castles (which included Barnstaple and Castle Cary) and lured Henry further from his base. In the meantime Eustace returned from East Anglia, made a

24 *G.S.* 216–8. Berkeley may have been held for Stephen since 1146 (above p. 90).
25 *G.S.* 220. It is not known whether the harvest was early or late, but I am inclined to put these events early in October. We know that on returning from York Stephen held a court in London in order to decide his next move, and this could well have been his Michaelmas Court (29 Sept.). He passed through Woodstock some time in October (*Reg.* iii. 455).

lightning attack on Devizes and very nearly captured it, his troops having penetrated the outworks of the castle before Henry returned and forced them to withdraw.[26]

The attack on Devizes must have occurred near the end of 1149, and Henry's advisers soon afterwards recommended him to return to Normandy. It was clear that he had failed to break the military deadlock in England, and without a considerable accession of strength would have no hope of doing so. By remaining in England he would draw endless attacks upon himself, and the land round every castle which he occupied would be in danger of being reduced to scorched earth. In such circumstances he was likely to prove more of an embarrassment than a help to his supporters. By returning to Normandy, however, he would not only secure a respite for England, but would also be able to collect an army large enough for an invasion in force. It was the only way in which he could win a decisive victory, and he was wise enough to see it. He returned to Normandy, probably in January 1150. He may have felt disappointed that the results of his year's work were not greater, but he had emerged with credit. He had proved his worth as a leader of men, and when he got home his father recognized the fact by declaring him of age (a boy of sixteen could often be considered an adult in the Middle Ages), and handed over to him the duchy of Normandy, as if he himself had been no more than his guardian or regent.[27]

With Henry Duke of Normandy the formation of the new opposition was complete. It was far more dangerous than the opposition which Stephen had had to meet in 1135. In that year he had won the throne because he had had the help of the Church and because no one wanted a woman as ruler. Now St Bernard had turned the support of the Church into hostility, and Stephen's rival was no longer a woman but Henry Duke of Normandy, a worthy grandson of King Henry I. The reasons, which in 1135 had induced men to put hereditary right aside, were no longer in existence; and since the spirit of the age was strongly in favour of the hereditary system, it would need only a final blow to ensure the triumph of Duke Henry as the rightful heir of England.

26 G.S. 216–24 is the sole authority for Henry's autumn and winter campaign, which was consequently unknown to historians writing before 1955.

27 Z. N. and C. N. L. Brooke in *E.H.R.* lxi (1946), 81–6, agreed with Haskins (*Norman Institutions*, 130, n. 26) that the absolute limits of date for Henry's accession to the duchy were November 1149–March 1150, but themselves favoured December 1149 or January 1150. Since they wrote, the newly discovered portion of the *Gesta Stephani* has filled a gap in our knowledge about which there was previously no information, and has made a date in 1150 more likely than one in 1149.

CHAPTER TEN
The Magnates' Peace, 1150-1154

One of the most puzzling features of Stephen's reign is the way in which it came to an end. The obvious ending would have been a battle royal between him and Duke Henry, but though from 1150 onwards the stage seemed set, the battle never happened. In part this was due to the fact that, once back in Normandy, Duke Henry became so involved in continental affairs that it proved impossible for him to return to England till 1153, but even when he did return there was still no major battle. The truth of the matter was that no such battle could be fought without the magnates, and the magnates were determined that it should not be fought at all.

The influence of the magnates in these years has sometimes been underestimated. Because the chronicles record little or nothing about events in England during the years 1150-52, it has been thought that the magnates, exhausted by internecine war, were no longer in a position to challenge Stephen's government. But this was not so. If Stephen had considered his position strong, he would presumably have taken advantage of Duke Henry's absence in Normandy, in order to crush his remaining enemies in England, but all he did was to make two half-hearted attempts on Worcester and eventually (in 1152) to capture Newbury. He was inactive not because he was secure, but because he did not dare to upset the precarious balance of power. The whole of England was in a state of suspense, the supporters of Duke Henry thinking it pointless to launch an offensive before their leader returned in force, and those of the king being anxious to postpone the day of reckoning as long as possible.

The situation is best illustrated by the well-known treaty made between Robert Earl of Leicester and Ranulf Earl of Chester at some date between 1149 and 1153.[1] It was styled an 'agreement' (*conventio*) and 'final peace and concord' (*finalis pax et concordia*), but it was not so much an alliance as a disarmament treaty. It recognized that though the two earls did not want to fight each other, they would probably be obliged to do so, because their respective liege lords were at war (Earl Robert's liege lord being King Stephen and Earl Ranulf's Duke Henry), but it stipulated that neither earl should go against the other with more than twenty knights, and that any goods captured should be returned. Neither liege lord nor anyone else should be permitted to attack the land of one earl from the lands and castles of the other, and neither earl was to make any attempt against the other's person unless he 'defied' him fifteen days in advance. A limitation was put on the building of new castles on the north, east and western borders of Leicestershire, both earls agreeing not to build any more between Coventry, Castle Donnington, Gotham, Kinoulton, Oakham and Rockingham, or (in what was probably the area of greatest danger) between Coventry and Hinckley, and Hinckley and Hartshill.

A clause which has received surprisingly little attention is that in which each earl undertook to aid the other against all men except his liege lord and one named ally. In the earl of Leicester's case this was straightforward, because the ally whom he named, Simon de Senlis Earl of Northampton and Huntingdon, was his son-in-law and a staunch supporter of his liege lord King Stephen. The earl of Chester's named ally, however, is more puzzling. He was Robert de Ferrers II Earl of Derby, and apart from this treaty there is no evidence to suggest that he was ever a supporter of Duke Henry. When next we hear of him, in May 1153, he was resisting Duke Henry actively and in alliance with his father-in-law William Peverel of Nottingham who had just attempted, but failed, to murder the earl of Chester by poison. Any alliance that he had with the earl of Chester can have been nothing more than a temporary convenience, but this apparently was what the earl of Chester wanted. At this juncture he seems to have been making truces with all his neighbours, even with William Peverel of Nottingham, for we are specifically told that the attempted poisoning took place 'when the earl was a guest in his (Peverel's) house'.[2]

The earl of Leicester also had private treaties or arrangements with other magnates. Indeed the situation becomes so complicated that it can only be explained by means of a diagram in which the supposed

1 F. M. Stenton, *The First Century of English Feudalism* (2nd ed. Oxford, 1961), 250–6 and 286–8.
2 *G.S.* 236.

adherents of King Stephen and Duke Henry are listed in two columns, the alliances and pacts between them being denoted by connecting lines.[3]

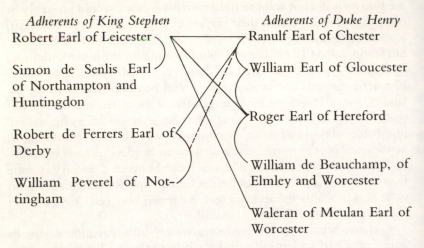

At first sight this elaborate patchwork of alliances might seem an effective way of preserving the peace, but its weakness lay in the fact that its inconsistencies could be exposed by the collapse of any one of its separate parts. This was demonstrated by a fierce quarrel which flared up between William de Beauchamp and Waleran of Meulan in 1151. The two men had rival claims to Worcester, but had sunk their differences in or after 1141 when, with Waleran's desertion from Stephen, they had been forced to regard each other as allis in support of the empress.[4] The compromise which they had reached was apparently that Waleran of Meulan should hold the city of Worcester

3 Simon de Senlis had married the daughter of Robert Earl of Leicester, Robert de Ferrers the daughter of William Peverel, and Ranulf Earl of Chester the daughter of Robert Earl of Gloucester. The 'treaty of love' between William Earl of Gloucester and Roger Earl of Hereford is printed in *Stenton Miscellany*, 144, and states specifically that William Earl of Gloucester had stood as guarantor for a treaty between the earls of Hereford and Leicester. For the earl of Hereford's alliance with William de Beauchamp and Waleran of Meulan's with the earl of Leicester who was his twin brother, see below notes 5 and 6.

4 For the rivalry between Waleran of Meulan and William de Beauchamp, see *Reg.* iii. 68. After he had joined the empress, Waleran evidently adopted William as his son; this is shown by the address of a writ 'G. comes Mell' Willelmo de Bellocampo filio suo' printed by H. W. C. Davis in *Essays presented to R. L. Poole*, 170. G. H. White (*T.R.H.S.*, 4th series, xiii (1930), 70) suggested amending 'filio' to 'fideli', but the evidence of the manuscripts is against him, and the probability is that Waleran had adopted William as his son and heir, as (in 1153) Stephen was to adopt Duke Henry. See David Crouch, *The Beaumond Twins* (Cambridge, 1986), 39, 52, and Supplement II below.

but William de Beauchamp the castle; and the reason for their quarrel in 1151 was that in the preceding year Stephen had attacked Worcester and captured the city but not the castle. The men of Waleran of Meulan (who himself was still in Normandy) found the resulting situation intolerable, seized the castle for themselves and held William de Beauchamp prisoner in it.

If the chart of alliances is consulted it will be seen how complicated the situation now became. Roger Earl of Hereford felt himself bound to recover Worcester castle for his close ally William de Beauchamp; King Stephen wanted to capture it for the crown; and Robert Earl of Leicester, who was one of Stephen's chief supporters, was determined to prevent anyone taking it from Waleran of Meulan who was his twin brother. The *Gesta Stephani* relates how Roger Earl of Hereford negotiated with Stephen for 'a pact of inviolable peace and friendship . . . on condition that he would besiege with him and hand over to him the castle of Worcester', but also sent messengers to Duke Henry urging him to return to England with all speed.[5] Henry of Huntingdon, on the other hand, tells us that it was 'by the guile (*arte*) of the earl of Leicester that the king's siege works were demolished and the castle of Worcester cunningly saved'.[6]

When loyalties were as confused as this, it was obviously impossible to think of strong government. Stephen could not trust the earl of Hereford's protestations of friendship any more than he could punish the earl of Leicester's duplicity. Though in theory a man's loyalty to the king or Duke Henry was liege-loyalty, which should override all other loyalties, there were several magnates who no longer gave it pride of place. They had become indifferent to the struggle for the throne, and were prepared to accept any solution which would leave them their hereditary lands in peace. They therefore pursued a policy of deliberate inertia and forced Stephen to remain inactive, while they waited to see if Duke Henry would prove as good as his word and launch an invasion of England from Normandy.

Duke Henry kept them waiting a long time. It was three years before he returned, not because he was idle, but because people and circumstances conspired against him. In the first place there was King Louis VII of France who returned from his crusade in November 1149. When he had set out, in June 1147, he had apparently not realized the potential danger of an Angevin empire which included England as well as Normandy. Now that he could not fail to see it, he recalled the

5 G.S. 228.
6 Henry of Huntingdon (R.S.) 282–3.

fact that his sister Constance was married to King Stephen's son Eustace, revived the alliance for which the marriage had been made (p. 45) and invited Eustace to France for a combined attack on Duke Henry. Eustace responded with alacrity: he was young and vigorous, and saw that his one real chance of securing the crown was to prevent an invasion of England by defeating Duke Henry in Normandy. But though he tried very hard, neither he nor Louis could win any victory worth the name. In spite of local successes at Arques and Séez in the early summer of 1151, no serious penetration of the Norman frontier was made, and eventually St Bernard, unfailingly prompt to advance good causes which were not in the interest of King Stephen, succeeded in reconciling Louis VII and the Angevins.[7] Peace was made at Paris in the last days of August 1151, and in return for the liberation of one of his vassals in Anjou, Louis VII formally invested Henry with the duchy of Normandy.

So far from having been weakened by the French war, Duke Henry had emerged from it with enhanced prestige, and he promptly summoned the magnates of Normandy to a council at Lisieux on 14 September in order to make preparations for the invasion of England. But before the council could be assembled, Henry received news that his father, Geoffrey, had died suddenly (7 September) on his way back from Paris to Angers. This provoked an immediate crisis, for though Geoffrey had designated Henry as heir to Anjou for the time being, he had made it clear that this was only a temporary measure. Before his death he had made the attendant bishops and nobles swear that they would not allow his body to be buried until Henry had taken an oath that, if ever he acquired England, he would hand over Anjou to his younger brother Geoffrey. Henry hesitated long, but eventually took the oath 'not without tears' before his father's funeral at Le Mans, though he took care to spend the autumn and winter in Anjou, making his control of the county sure.[8]

The delay made his English supporters restive, and in March 1152 they sent his uncle, Reginald Earl of Cornwall, to implore him to make more haste. Henry accordingly summoned another council at Lisieux. It met on 6 April and made detailed arrangements for the invasion of

7 For the details of the campaign see Robert de Torigni in *Chronicles* iv. 160–3. For St Bernard's part in the peace see the *Vita Prima* in Migne, P.L. clxxxv. 329, which dates the negotiations to a fortnight before Geoffrey's death, i.e. *c.* 24 August.

8 Newburgh Bkii, ch. 7. Robert de Torigni in *Chronicles* iv. 165 has nothing about Geoffrey's arrangement for his younger son to have Anjou eventually, nor does he name the castles of Chinon, Loudun and Mirebeau, which were the same three that John was to have in 1173. This is the sort of information which a contemporary writer might well have found it wise to suppress.

England, but once again news was received which caused him to delay. He learnt that on 21 March an ecclesiastical council under the presidency of the archbishops of Sens, Rheims, Rouen and Bordeaux had declared the marriage of King Louis VII and Eleanor of Aquitaine to be null and void. There had been rumours about the failure of this marriage for some years—Eleanor had not borne Louis a son, and during the Crusade her name had been freely linked with that of her uncle, Raymond Prince of Antioch—but until now everyone had imagined that Louis would hesitate to terminate the marriage for fear of losing Aquitaine, which was Eleanor's inheritance. The actual 'divorce' took most people by surprise, but Henry wasted no time in taking advantage of it. Some said that he had already courted Eleanor on his visit to Paris in the previous August, but whether that was so or not, he clearly did not intend to lose the chance of acquiring Aquitaine so easily. On about 18 May—that is to say less than two months after the 'divorce'—he married Eleanor, 'either suddenly or by premeditated design' (as Robert de Torigni put it), and thus won control of the whole of south-west France.[9]

Little more than a month later Henry was back at Barfleur and ready to sail for England, but once again he was delayed. Louis VII was enraged by his marriage and treated it as a cause for war, since quite apart from the provocative circumstances, it was an offence against feudal law to marry without one's overlord's consent. He renewed his alliance with Stephen's son Eustace, and once again invaded Normandy (16 July), but this time he had even less success than before. Though he captured Neufmarche-sur-Epte, he could not prevent Henry from devastating the Norman Vexin (which had belonged to Louis since 1144), or from forcing the French to retreat at all points. Though Henry's brother Geoffrey attempted a revolt in Anjou, Henry subdued it, and though Louis attacked in Normandy it was all to no avail.[10] Henry's position in Normandy was impregnable, and in the second week of January 1153 he sailed from Barfleur for England.

During the three years which Henry had spent in France the situation in England had changed little. The principal reason for this was the deliberate inertia of the magnates who, as we have already explained, had adopted a policy of 'wait and see' with private arrangements for limiting the scope of war. But considerable credit must also be given to the Church, which had developed its own policy of masterly inactivity. Pope Eugenius III and Archbishop Theobald

9 Robert de Torigni, in *Chronicles* iv. 165.
10 For details of the campaign see Robert de Torigni in *Chronicles* iv. 164–71.

adhered strictly to the view that there should be no innovation concerning the English throne; they continued to recognize Stephen as king, but refused to consecrate Eustace as his colleague and heir. In their view it was Duke Henry who was the lawful heir, and any consecration of Eustace would be an open defiance of the decrees of Pope Celestine II (p. 103). Stephen tried hard to make them change their mind. Towards the end of 1150 he recognized Henry Murdac as archbishop of York in the desperate hope that, as a fellow Cistercian, he would be able to persuade Eugenius to be more accommodating. When that failed he summoned Archbishop Theobald and the other bishops to London in 1152, and demanded that they should anoint his son king and confirm him with their blessing, only to be told that the pope had specifically forbidden the anointing of Eustace, on the grounds that his father (Stephen) had obtained the throne by perjury. Four years earlier few, if any, of the bishops would have dared to associate themselves with so bold a statement, but now they were solid in their support for Theobald. Stephen imprisoned them all, but once again Theobald escaped to the continent, and Stephen found it wise to release the others.[11]

Hard on the heels of this public rebuff came the death of Stephen's wife, Queen Matilda (3 May 1152). Everyone knew that in 1141 it had largely been due to her courage and determination that Stephen had been rescued from disaster, and most people would have supposed that without her influence Stephen would have shown even less determination. In the event, her death seems to have made him realize that if he continued inactive his whole position would soon be eroded. He spurred himself into action, besieged Newbury, and eventually captured it from John fitz Gilbert.[12] Then, hoping that the death of Brien fitz Count would have weakened the determination of the garrison, he proceeded to besiege Wallingford for the third time since 1139.[13] In previous sieges the main effort of the besiegers had apparently been directed against the landward defences of the town. Now Stephen built a castle at Crowmarsh on the opposite side of the river and succeeded in blocking all access to the bridge. Wallingford was thus completely hemmed in, and since the garrison could no longer

11 Henry of Huntingdon (R.S.) 283–4; Gervase of Canterbury (R.S.) i. 150–1.

12 Henry of Huntingdon (R.S.) 284; cf. *Histoire de Guillaume le Maréchal*, ed. Paul Meyer (Soc. de l'Histoire de France, 1891–1900), ll. 400–650.

13 The previous sieges had been in 1139 and 1146. It is a strange fact that we know nothing about the death of Brien fitz Count. He was still alive in 1147 (G.S. 210) but dead before September 1151 (see his wife's charter in *Docs. of the English Lands of the Abbey of Bec*, ed. M. Chibnall (Camden Third Series, lxxiii, 1951), p. 25, no. xlviii, which should be dated 1150–September 1151 while Henry was duke and his father still alive).

bring in supplies of food, a message was sent to Duke Henry (towards the end of 1152) saying that, unless he sent aid quickly, the castle would have to surrender.

Duke Henry's return to England was therefore timely. He probably landed at Wareham (mid-January 1153),[14] but since his force was considered small (we are told that it consisted of 140 knights and 3000 infantry and had been transported in 36 ships[15]) he did not march immediately to Wallingford, but (so far as can be seen) proceeded to Devizes in order to join forces with the earls of Chester, Cornwall, Hereford and Salisbury.[16] Then, aiming to divert Stephen from Wallingford, he attacked Malmesbury. His troops took the town by assault but failed to storm the castle and had to besiege it, and as a result Stephen set out to relieve it. He came by way of Cirencester, and on the evening of his arrival camped on the north side of the Avon, intending to cross the river and give battle in the morning. When the day came he decided to retreat instead, giving as his excuse that torrential rain had made the river impassable. The real reason was almost certainly the discovery that he could not trust his own army. Some of his leading barons were, as the *Gesta Stephani* put it, 'lax and exceedingly negligent in their service, and had already secretly sent envoys to make their peace with the duke'.[17] The most important of those involved was probably Robert Earl of Leicester, who is known to have been transferring his allegiance to Duke Henry at this time, but it looks as if quite a number of the magnates had adopted an attitude of neutrality, or suspended animation, on the lines suggested by the Church. They remained loyal to Stephen in that they obeyed his summons to the army, but they refused to fight against Duke Henry because he was the lawful heir to the kingdom. If Stephen had attempted a battle, these barons would probably have deserted him. As it was, they forced him to negotiate a truce. He agreed to retreat provided that he was allowed to demolish Malmesbury castle; and eventually he did retreat even though his castellan betrayed him and surrendered the castle to Duke Henry intact.

The agreement made at Malmesbury evidently provided for a withdrawal by both sides. To judge from subsequent events, it seems likely that the arrangement was that the king and the duke were to confine themselves to different parts of the kingdom and avoid a direct

14 Bristol would have been most unlikely as it would have been involved the dangerous voyage round Land's End in midwinter.
15 Newburgh Bki. ch. 29; Robert de Torigni in *Chronicles* iv. 171.
16 *Reg.* iii. 180.
17 G.S. 234; cf. Gervase of Canterbury (R.S.) i. 152, and *Reg.* iii. 438.

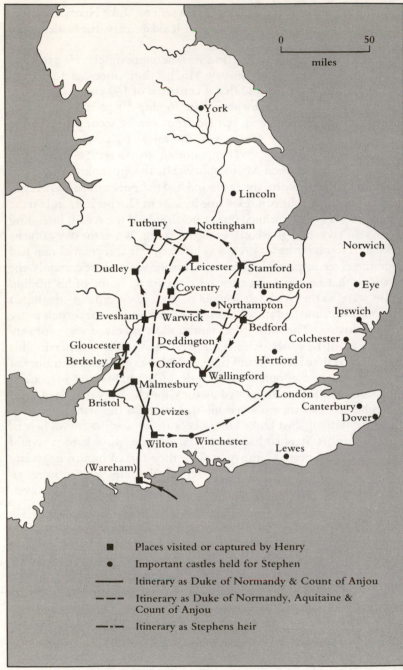

3. Duke Henry's Itinerary, 1153

confrontation for another six months. That at any rate would be the simplest explanation of Duke Henry's subsequent itinerary, for without any interference from Stephen he went to Bristol, Gloucester (where on 19 April he probably held his Easter court and took the additional title of duke of Aquitaine), Evesham, Tutbury (where he forced Earl Robert de Ferrers to submit), Leicester (where he spent Whitsun), Coventry, Warwick (where the countess of Warwick had outwitted the king's garrison and surrendered the castle, so that her husband, who was still in attendance on Stephen, died of shock when he heard the news), and Bedford (which had to be besieged and captured). [18]

After these activities it was probably the end of July or beginning of August before Henry advanced to the relief of Wallingford. His plan was to open up the bridge across the Thames, but to do this he had first to capture the king's siege-castle at Crowmarsh. He tried to take it by storm, but failed; and when he began to besiege it, Stephen seized his opportunity, gathered 'an inexpressibly large army from every part of his kingdom', and accompanied by his son Eustace with 'many earls and countless barons' arrived at Wallingford. The situation was almost identical with that at Malmesbury six months before. Once more there was only a river dividing the two armies. Once more Stephen was anxious to decide the issue in one great battle. And once more there were those who insisted that if the battle took place it could only be to the general prejudice of the kingdom.

> Wherefore [as the *Gesta Stephani* puts it] the leading men of each army, and those of deeper judgment, were greatly grieved and shrank, on both sides, from a conflict that was not merely between fellow-countrymen, but meant the desolation of the whole kingdom. [19]

Henry of Huntingdon says bluntly that Stephen and Henry were forced to make a truce against their will, and that both of them complained bitterly of the conduct of their nobles. [20] They had no option but to accept the terms which had been laid down for them; Stephen's siege-castle at Crowmarsh was to be destroyed, the two armies were to disengage, and negotiations were to be opened for peace.

18 For Henry's itinerary see Z. N. and C. N. L. Brooke in *E.H.R.* lxi (1946), 86–8, as revised by A. L. Poole in *G.S.* first ed., pp. xxiii–xxix.

19 *G.S.* 238.

20 Henry of Huntingdon (R.S.) 287, though he thought that the reason why the magnates insisted on peace was that 'they loved nothing more than discord' and did not want either side to win.

Though we are told that the king and the duke had a 'private' interview at Wallingford, addressing each other across the river, they took little part in the making of peace. Neither of them had wanted to compromise, and while others were advancing the cause of peace, they simply seized whatever military advantage they could get without attacking each other in person. Duke Henry captured Stamford (*c.* 31 August) and sacked Nottingham (though he failed to take the castle), while Stephen, ostentatiously keeping his distance, besieged and captured Earl Hugh Bigod's castle at Ipswich. To Stephen's son Eustace the arrangement seemed shameful. Realizing that a negotiated peace would inevitably exclude him from the throne he left his father's court in disgust and devastated Cambridgeshire and the lands of Bury St Edmunds. It may possibly have been his intention to provoke Duke Henry to break the truce and give battle, but before his purpose could be ascertained he died, quite suddenly, on 17 August. Some said that he had died of grief, others that he had been smitten by St Edmund in punishment for the damage which he had done to his abbey's lands.[21]

Meanwhile negotiations for the final peace were continuing under the direction of Archbishop Theobald and Henry of Blois bishop of Winchester. For this role Theobald was admirably suited, for though his sympathies were presumably with the Angevins, he had always acted with studied impartiality. In this respect he was in a better position than Henry of Blois, who was closely identified with his brother's cause. But Henry had other qualities. He was a realist, was known to have favoured a negotiated peace as early as 1140, and had a rare knowledge of the world. He had been one of the first to recognize that there could be no end to the hereditary claims and counter-claims unless all parties were prepared to compromise, and he had a grasp of detail which enabled him to formulate proposals which were practical. Earlier in the reign he had repeatedly failed, because neither side had been prepared to compromise on the central issue of the crown. Now that Eustace was dead the situation was easier, for those who might have hesitated to deprive Stephen's eldest son of the crown would feel no qualm in passing over his second son, William, who had never had the expectation of it. Peace was at last attainable, and on 6 November 1153 King Stephen and Duke Henry were persuaded to meet at Winchester for a final reconciliation. According to the account of Robert de Torigni,

21 *G.S.* 238; Robert de Torigni, in *Chronicles* iv. 176; Gervase of Canterbury (R.S.) i. 155.

In the assembly of bishops, earls and other magnates, the king first recognized the hereditary right which Duke Henry had in the kingdom of England; and the duke graciously conceded that the king should hold the kingdom all his life, if he wished, provided that the king himself, the bishops and other magnates should declare on oath, that after the death of the king, the duke should have the kingdom, if he survived him, peacefully and without contradiction. An oath was also taken that those landed possessions which had fallen into the hands of intruders (*quae direptae erant ab invasoribus*) should be restored to the ancient and lawful possessors who had them in the time of the excellent King Henry [I]. Also concerning those castles which had come into being since the death of the king; their number was said to be more than 1,115 and they were to be destroyed.[22]

Great difficulty must have been experienced in framing detailed terms which gave each side sufficient guarantees, and it is likely that the delay between the ceremony at Winchester and the promulgation of the treaty at Westminster (to which the king and duke proceeded before Christmas) was due to this cause. The document was in the form of a royal charter which described the agreements made and the oaths taken.[23] Stephen received the homage of Duke Henry together with explicit and detailed assurances that his second son, William, would be left in possession of all the lands which he or his wife had inherited in England or Normandy; judged by sheer wealth, therefore, William could expect to be the second man in the kingdom, for quite apart from his father's lands (p. 7), his wife, Isabel de Warenne, was one of the richest heiresses in the kingdom.[24] Duke Henry, on the other hand, was acknowledged as Stephen's successor and heir to the kingdom by hereditary right; and in order to stress the hereditary element, Stephen adopted Henry and took an oath to maintain him 'as his son and heir'. Then Stephen's second son, William, the earls, barons, citizens of cities and custodians of royal castles did Henry liege homage, saving only their fealty to the king while he lived. As a security, the most important of Stephen's castles were handed over to agreed castellans who took an oath to surrender them to Henry on Stephen's death, and gave him hostages; the castles of London and Windsor were entrusted to Richard de Lucy, Oxford to Roger de Buissi, Lincoln to Jordan de Buissi and Winchester and Southampton to Henry of Blois. Finally the archbishops, bishops and abbots took an oath to Duke Henry at the king's command, and undertook to punish infringements of the treaty by ecclesiastical law.

22 Robert de Torigni, in *Chronicles* iv. 177.
23 *Reg.* iii. 272.
24 J. H. Round, *Studies in Peerage and Family History* (London, 1901), 167–71.

In this way peace was assured between king and duke, but there was still the problem of their respective barons. As stated by Robert de Torigni, it was agreed in principle that all lands should be restored to those who had held them in the reign of Henry I, or, as the *Gesta Stephani* put it, that 'the disinherited should be restored to their own'.[25] This was no administrative detail. It was a formal admission that the barons held their lands, not by pleasure of the king, but by hereditary right; and as such it marked an important step in the creation of the English nobility. As we have seen at various points in this history, neither William I, William II nor Henry I had adhered strictly to the hereditary principle in regard to the fiefs of their vassals. By means of forfeitures and questionable escheats, they had stripped important families of their lands and given them to 'new' men who were bound by self-interest to the king and in doing so they had created a system which could only encourage civil war. Gilbert de Lacy had only needed a pretext to attempt to recover what he considered to be his rightful inheritance from Miles of Gloucester, and Simon de Senlis and Ranulf Earl of Chester had positively welcomed the opportunity of recovering 'their' earldoms or lordships from King David of Scotland. If peace was to be restored, all such disputes had to be settled. The only question was how.

The great difficulty was to decide which family was to receive which hereditary lands. On this point the oath taken at Winchester was deliberately vague, since it did not specify whether the lawful possessors were to be those who had held the lands at the beginning or end of Henry I's reign, though this was a matter of vital importance in view of the large number of forfeitures which Henry had made. No one could afford to be precise, and any systematic application of rigid principles would have been extremely dangerous. What had to be considered was not only the rights and wrongs of every situation but also the question of expediency, particularly when those who had profited from the war were supporters of Duke Henry. It was hardly to be expected that Roger Earl of Hereford would be forced to surrender the gains which he and his father had made in Herefordshire or the Marches, that Reginald Earl of Cornwall would not be allowed to enjoy the lands which he had won from Stephen in Cornwall, or that King David of Scotland would have willingly surrendered the grants made to him by either Stephen or the empress. In cases such as these it was necessary for both sides to turn a blind eye to the question of principle, in order to retain the good will of magnates who were too important to

25 *G.S.* 240, amending 'exheredati adpropriare vocarentur' to 'exheredati ad propria revocarentur'.

be offended; and it could only be hoped that time, and eventually death, would remedy all. In fact the peacemakers were remarkably fortunate in the death-roll of these years. Quite apart from Stephen's son Eustace, those who died in 1153 included King David of Scotland (24 May)—his son Prince Henry having died the year before—Simon de Senlis his rival in the earldom of Huntingdon (August), Roger Earl of Warwick (12 June), and Ranulf Earl of Chester (16 December); and in 1155 they were followed by Baldwin de Redvers Earl of Devon and Roger Earl of Hereford.

The general intention with regard to disputed inheritances was undoubtedly to compromise wherever compromise was possible. A striking example was the earldom of Huntingdon which, when the rival claimants were dead, was divided so that the son of Simon of Senlis could be earl of Northampton, while King David's grandson, Malcolm, was given the earldom of Huntingdon. There were some disputed inheritances, however, which could not be resolved as simply as this. Many lands had changed hands not once but several times in the course of the reign, and if in the end they were given to the Church—an economical form of charity for a baron who knew his claim to be weak—they were beyond all hope of recovery.[26] The only way in which individuals could make certain of the lands which they claimed as their own, was by making treaties or marriage alliances with their rivals, as in the well-known case of Robert fitz Harding and Roger de Berkeley,[27] or by getting their lands confirmed by Stephen and Duke Henry simultaneously.[28] Richard de Camville, who was one of Stephen's 'new' men, received a charter from Duke Henry 'at the request and command of King Stephen',[29] and William Chesney was given fresh lands by Stephen in order to compensate him for others which he was likely to lose to a pro-Angevin relative.[30] The aim was not so much that all the disinherited should be restored, as that conditions should be created in which the hereditary principle could become irreversible.

26 Thus Henry de Lacy gave Kirkstall abbey 420 acres of wood, moor and pasture which really belonged to Hugh Bigod (W. E. Wightman, *The Lacy Family in England and Normandy, 1066–1194* (Oxford, 1966, 109), and in 1148 Ernald de Bosco founded Biddlesden abbey on land which had been taken from Robert of Meppershall: 'Idem vero Ernaldus, praevidens in posterum quod forte terra illa sibi et haeredibus suis remanere non possit . . . fundavit ibi abbatiam' (*Monast.*, v. 366–7).

27 I. H. Jeayes, *Descriptive Catalogue of the Charters and Muniments at Berkeley Castle* (Bristol, 1892), 5; cf. *Reg.* iii. 309–11a.

28 For such informations see *Reg.* iii. 94–5, 96–7, 126–7, 215 and 239f., 457–8, 583–4 and 874–5.

29 *Reg.* iii. 140.

30 *Reg.* iii. 177.

There was to be an end to the old policy of setting up different families as rivals for particular honours and fiefs, for only the certainty of a strict hereditary system could bring peace.

In practice the difficulties were great because, in the last resort, there were more potential heirs than honours or fiefs. There were, for example, two rival earls of Lincoln, William de Roumare who supported the Angevins, and Gilbert de Gant, whom Stephen had set up against him in 1149. In the treaty of Westminster the difficulty of deciding which of them was the real earl had been circumvented by naming neither, but since William de Roumare had been appointed first and had the support of Duke Henry, Gilbert de Gant can have had little doubt that his own days as earl were numbered. It would not be surprising if he was aggrieved and felt that Stephen had not made sufficient effort to defend his interests, particularly as his brother, Robert de Gant, had also suffered losses in the peace. Robert's wealth had been due to the fact that Stephen had given him in marriage the daughter of William Paynel of Drax with all the English lands of her family, since William's sons had been disinherited for their support of the Angevin cause in Normandy. Now that peace was restored, the sons returned and forced Robert de Gant to give them a share of their father's inheritance.[31] The resultant upheaval seems to have caused the revolt of one of Robert's vassals at Drax in 1154, and to have led to an estrangement between Stephen and his chancellor, who was another member of the Gant family.[32] It was an affair which obviously caused bitterness, but the most remarkable thing about it was that as a revolt it was isolated. The barons must have been prepared to make considerable sacrifices in order to settle their disputes peacefully.

It is evident that many of the details of the baronial settlement were not elaborated either at Winchester or at Westminster, but were decided as occasion demanded in a series of meetings between king and duke. A third joint court was held at Oxford on 13 January 1154, so that all the principal men of England might do homage to the duke again, and it is likely that the opportunity was taken to enquire into the demolition of unauthorized or 'adulterine' castles. Now that the king and duke were acting in concert, it must have been difficult for barons to defy the authority of the sheriffs, and we are told that the castles 'melted away like wax before a flame'.[33] None the less, at a fourth

31 C. T. Clay in *E.Y.C.* vi. 33.

32 This was Robert's uncle, another Robert de Gant. He was also dean of York and had previously supported Stephen's archbishop, William fitz Herbert, against Henry Murdac. After Murdac's death (14 October 1153), when Eugenius III and St Bernard were dead also, a new pope restored William, but Robert de Gant appealed against him (May 1154) (Newburgh, BKi. ch. 26).

33 William of Newburgh, BKi. ch. 32.

meeting held at Dunstable, the duke complained that though most of the castles had been destroyed, the king had allowed some of his men to retain theirs.[34] The implication was that Stephen was trying to cheat him by disarming his opponents more thoroughly than his supporters, but Stephen denied the charge, and the two men met in apparent friendship again at Canterbury and Dover in late February or March. Henry still had his suspicions, however, and shortly before Easter (4 April 1154) he returned to Normandy in a hurry. According to one chronicler the reason for his haste was the discovery of a plot which, with the cognizance of Stephen's son William, the Flemish mercenaries had made to kill him.[35]

While Henry was absent from England, the only security he had for his kingdom lay in the good will of the magnates and the authority of the Church, which had undertaken to enforce the Treaty of Westminster with the sanction of ecclesiastic law. It might be thought that threats of excommunication would have meant little in a kingdom which had been wracked by civil war, but this was not so. In the course of the reign the Church had established a real ascendancy. At Stephen's accession it had demanded and obtained its liberty. When Stephen had violated that liberty by arresting the three bishops, it had put him on trial, forced him to appeal to Rome, and in 1141 in a legatine council it had proclaimed the empress 'Lady of the English'. In the latter part of the reign, the pope had deposed one archbishop of York and established another in the teeth of royal opposition, while the archbishop of Canterbury had attended a papal council in defiance of the king, and refused to anoint his son Eustace. There could be no doubt that the doctrines of high papalism had taken root in England, and that the authority of the Church was greater than it ever had been.

To a certain extent this ascendancy of the Church was a natural corollary of the weakness of the Crown, but it also reflected a personal disparity. The man who had effected the greatest extension of papal power was the king's brother, Henry of Blois, and he had succeeded because he displayed the very qualities which his brother most noticeably lacked. He had vision, personality and determination to the point of ruthlessness. Everything he did was on a grand scale; even his failings as a bishop—his military activities, the magnificence of his castles, and the nepotistical promotion of his relatives—were positively regal. He was a man of infinite capacity, and if his mother Adela had lived to see his full development, she must surely have repented of her decision

34 Henry of Huntingdon (R.S.) 290.
35 Gervase of Canterbury (R.S.) i. 157–8.

to make him a monk. He was the real grandson of the Conqueror.

Stephen, on the other hand, was cast in the image of his father, a man of great activity but little judgment. He had come to the throne at a time when civil war was almost inevitable, and the need was for a king of heroic proportions. Stephen was no hero. Although he was an excellent warrior and showed enterprise and speed in the beginning of campaigns and sieges, he too often failed to complete them; and though he seemed cheerful and gay, beneath the surface he was mistrustful and sly. He did not inspire the devotion which his grandfather or uncle had inspired; even his panegyrist, the author of the *Gesta Stephani*, found him colourless. On the other hand, like his father before him, he was easily pleased with the appearance of success; and now that, for the last seven months of his reign, he had no rival in England, he undertook a solemn progress through the northern parts of his kingdom 'encircling the bounds of England with regal pomp, and showing himself off as if he were a new king'.[36] One might almost have thought that he was ruling by the grace of God instead of by the favour of Duke Henry.

He died on 25 October 1154 and was buried beside his wife and son in the choir of the Cluniac abbey which he had founded at Faversham. Duke Henry did not attend the funeral, and did not even hurry to leave Normandy. He knew that there was no further danger of a disputed succession, and since Stephen had been able to govern the country for the previous seven months, he decided that it could govern itself for a few weeks more. He did not sail from Barfleur until 7 December, and was not anointed and crowned in Westminster Abbey until 19 December. It was the longest interval between the death of an English king and the coronation of his successor for more than a hundred years. In 1135 Stephen, like Henry I before him, had won the throne only because he had acted with speed. For Henry II delay was possible because a strict hereditary system was now accepted for the crown as well as for the nobles. The aim was no longer to choose the most eligible royal candidate, but to accept the man who was the lawful heir, that is to say the one with the best hereditary claim.[37] In the twentieth century a system which places such emphasis on the accident of birth may seem archaic and irrelevant, but in the twelfth century it was welcomed as a practical and progressive reform; and the fact which made it attractive was that to an age of turmoil and strife it brought stability and peace.

36 Newburgh, BK. i. ch. 32.
37 King John's succession to Richard I is the sort of exception which proves the rule, for in order to exclude Arthur, John eventually found it necessary to murder him.

Earls and Earldoms

J. H. Round in his appendix on 'Fiscal Earls' (*G.de M.*267–77) gave the general impression that in Stephen's reign an earldom was not an office but an almost empty honour, carrying with it only a few perquisites such as the earl's 'third penny'.

> . . .I will merely give it as my own conviction that while comital rank was at this period so far a personal dignity that men spoke of Earl Hugh, Earl Gilbert, or Earl Geoffrey, yet that an earl without a county was a conception that had not yet entered into the minds of men. In this of course we have a *relic* [my italics] of the earl's *official* character (*G. de M.* 273).

This view has continued to command general support, though some doubts have been expressed, notably by Sir Frank Stenton (*First Century of English Feudalism* (2nd ed.) 229–30). There are, however, powerful reasons for rejecting it entirely, at any rate for Stephen's reign and probably for the period preceding it also.

1. As shown in the detailed list, there were only five counties which had no earl in Stephen's reign—Kent, Hampshire, Berkshire, Middlesex and Shropshire. In Kent William of Ypres had everything but the title of earl, and was probably denied the title so as not to suggest that he was reviving his claim to the county of Flanders. It is likely that in Hampshire the earl's duties were performed by the bishop of Winchester. Berkshire would have been dependent on Windsor Castle and Middlesex on the Tower of London.

2. In a military capacity earls figure largely as the defenders of their counties in the chronicles of Stephen's reign. William d'Aumale was created earl of York because he defeated the Scots at the battle of the Standard (1138). Waleran of Meulan was very active, if not invariably

successful, in military operations round Worcester in 1140 (*John of Worcester*, 57, 60). Hervey Brito was created earl of Wiltshire and given Devizes castle so that he could defend his county the better; when he lost the castle he lost his county and earldom (*G.S.* 108, 116). When Hugh Pauper was made earl of Bedford (late 1137), the man who objected was Miles de Beauchamp who held Bedford castle, apparently as sheriff; and to give the new earl his earldom, it was necessary to capture the castle (*G.S* 46–8, 116). Finally there is the case of Geoffrey de Mandeville. Round thought it wicked of him to procure for himself the shrievalty and justiciarship as well as the earldom of Essex, but it would seem that this willingness and ability to do all the government jobs in the county made him the very ideal of the new style earls; he was an administrator as well as a military man, and of good family too.

3. In the cases of Cornwall, Wiltshire, Herefordshire, Lincolnshire and possibly Norfolk, there were rival earls appointed or recognized by Stephen and Matilda. This would have been natural if they were rival commanders in the shires concerned, but less easy to understand if their titles were merely ornamental.

4. Two earls were moved from one county to another, William de Roumare from Cambridgeshire to Lincolnshire, and William d'Aubigny from Lincolnshire to Sussex. If the titles were purely honorific, there would have been no point in such changes.

5. Some earls had more than one county. Quite apart from the normal couplings of Nottingham and Derby, Somerset and Dorset, Norfolk and Suffolk, Robert Earl of Leicester was given Herefordshire as an additional county, and Ranulf Earl of Chester Staffordshire. Stephen's son William was apparently given Norfolk as well as his earldom of Surrey (or Warenne). When such additional grants were made to an earl he was given 'totum comitatum de [Herefordiscira].'[1]

---

1 P. Latimer, 'Grants of the "totus comitatus" in twelfth-century England', *B.I.H.R.* 59 (1986), 137–46, claims that such grants conferred not earldoms but 'all the King's rights in a county'. He argues that the origin of such grants was in Normandy in the first quarter of the eleventh century. At that date the Duke of Normandy still styled himself *comes*, so that *comitatus* was what belonged to him. Latimer believes that when Duke William became king of England he continued to use the word *comitatus* in this sense even in England where his rights were in fact regal, but the evidence offered, a Domesday entry for Roger de Montgomery (D.B. i. 252) is not convincing. Henry I's gift of the *comitatus* of Shropshire to his Queen Adeliza (below p. 140) shows that the formula which applied to earls who were already earls of one county would apply also to kings and queens who would not wish to adopt an inferior title. In spite of this difference (which is mainly semantic) it is certainly true, as Latimer suggests, that the creation of such earldoms on a large scale could have led to the disintegration of the kingdom.

6. If earldoms were mainly honorific, it might have been expected that their titles would be systematically paraded, but in fact a man who was already an earl (or count) did not usually bother to change, or add to, the name of his county when given a new grant. Thus we more often find William Count of Warenne than William Earl of Surrey, Waleran Count of Meulan than Waleran Earl of Worcester and William Count of Aumale rather than William Earl of York. Robert de Ferrers is styled indiscriminately as 'Earl Ferrers' or 'Earl of Nottingham'.

7. There are writs in which the king addresses the earl and his whole county. In Henry I's reign there are seven cases each for the earls of Warwick and Northampton, five for Huntingdon, and one each for Gloucester and Surrey (*Reg.* ii. 654, 1044, 1151, 1415, 1445, 1446, 1845; 732, 743, 744, 770, 929, 966, 967; 1064, 1066, 1317, 1359, 1659; 1657; 639). In Stephen's reign we find similar cases for Essex (*Reg.* iii. 210, 533), Lincoln (*ibid.* 414), York (*ibid.* 101, 124, 991–2), Worcester (*ibid.* 966, 967), Huntingdon (*ibid.* 411, 884), Northampton (*ibid.* 611, 657, 671), Surrey (*ibid.* 692), Warwick (*ibid.* 597, 688–9), Gloucester (*ibid.* 344) and Richmond (*ibid.* 122), while the empress similarly addressed Hereford (*ibid.* 316 *a*) and Somerset (*ibid.* 190), and Duke Henry Norfolk (*ibid.* 364).

8. We also have charters addressed by earls to their own county and sheriff in the cases of Worcester, Warwick, Leicester, Hereford, Northumberland, Huntingdon and Northampton. Gloucester was an exception because Earl Robert had evidently come to a compromise with Miles of Gloucester who considered himself hereditary sheriff of Gloucester and retained the job even while he was earl of Hereford. Earl Robert of Gloucester, on the other hand, controlled Glamorgan. The following examples speak for themselves.

(*a*) G(ualeranus) comes Mell(enti) justiciariis et baronibus vicecomitibus et prepositis et ministris et omnibus fidelibus suis Francis et Anglis de Wirecestr(escira) et de Wiceo salutem. (*T.R.H.S.*, 4th series, xiii (1930), 69.)

(*b*) Rogerus comes de Warewica omnibus baronibus suis et vic(ecomiti) et baliis et ministris suis et collectoribus suis de Warewicasira salutem. *Worcester Cartulary*, ed. Darlington (P.R.S. 1962–3), no. 9.

(*c*) R(obertus) comes Legrecestrie Radulfo vicecomiti et omnibus baronibus et hominibus suis Francis et Anglis salutem. (*Reg. Antiq.* ii no. 324.)

(*d*) R(ogerus) comes de Herefordia vicecomitibus et prepositis et omnibus ministris suis de Gloecestresir(a) et Herefordscir(a) salutem. (1154–5) *Worcester Cartulary*, ed. Darlington, no. 47 cf. *Earldom of Herefored Charters*, nos. 33, 37.

(*e*) Ranulfus consul Cestrie Roberto dapifero, justicie, baronibus, vic(ecomiti), ministris, et ballidis, et omnibus servientibus de Cestriscira quicumque fuerint, Francis et Anglis salutem. (Stenton *Miscellany*, 29; cf. 28, 31, 32, 34, 36.)

(*f*) H(enricus) comes Northimbr(ie) Willelmo cancellario et Osberto vicecomiti et omnibus hominibus de Haliweresfolc et North-imberl(ande) salutem. (*Regesta. Reg. Scot.* i, no. 23; cf. nos. 24–8, 32, 43.)

(*g*) Henricus filius regis Scotie A(lexandro) episcopo et R(oberto) Foliot dapifero suo, et vicecomiti et omnibus amicis et ministris et hominibus suis de Hunted(one)scir(a) salutem. (*Ibid.* no. 16; cf. no. 15.)

(*h*) Robertus regis filius Gloucestriae consul, Wthredo Landavensi episcopo et Roberto Norr' vicecomiti de Glammorgan et omnibus baronibus suis et amicis et fidelibus et Francis et Anglis et Walensibus salutem. (*Glouc. Cart.* ii. 10; cf. ii. 135.)

(*i*) Simon comes de Norhantona omnibus hominibus suis tam Francis quam Anglis de Norhantonasir' salutem. (Farrer, *Honors and Knights' Fees*, ii. 297.)

9. Finally it should be noted that at the beginning of Henry II's reign eight counties were controlled directly by their earls. Earl Hugh (Bigod) accounted for Norfolk and Suffolk as if he were sheriff in 1155, Earl Richard (de Redvers) for Devon until 1157, and Earl Patrick for Wiltshire till 1160. Earl Roger seems to have controlled both Gloucestershire and Herefordshire till his fall in 1155 (see the address of (*d*) above). His earldom was then suppressed, but his brother Walter who inherited his lands and other possessions was sheriff of Gloucestershire (1155–7) and Herefordshire (1155–9). Earl Reginald retained Cornwall until his death in 1175 and did not account to the exchequer at all; nor did the earl of Chester whose earldom remained a palatine earldom for centuries. The obvious conclusion is that these earls had controlled their counties throughout the civil war, and having risked all for Henry's victory could not be stripped of the power which accrued to them as earls. If earldoms were to be reduced from official positions to ornamental titles, it had to be recognized that it could not be done at a moment when gratitude was the order of the day, but there can be little doubt that Henry II was only biding his time until suitable opportunities arose to transfer the earl's duties to humbler and less dangerous officials.

Notes to the list of earldoms and earls

1 BUCKINGHAM. Earl Walter Giffard is a nebulous figure who occurs in only one of Stephen's charters, and that a dubious one (*Reg*.iii. 284) in which he is styled *Walter comes de Buckingham*. His main estates were in Normandy, round Longueville, and he seems to have recognized the Angevins when they overran Normandy, and stayed there. He occurs in two of Duke Geoffrey's charters as *Comes Walterius Giffard* (*Reg*. iii. 734–5), and in one of Duke Henry's as *Waltero Giffart Comite de Longavilla* (*Reg*. iii. 600).

2 CHESTER. Earl Ranulf was the half-brother of William de Roumare Earl of Lincoln, and supported Stephen only in the years 1135–40 and 1146. For his career see H. A. Cronne, 'Ranulf de Gernons, Earl of Chester 1129–53' in *T.R.H.S.*, 4th series, xx (1937), 103–34, and R.H.C. Davis, 'King Stephen and the Earl of Chester revised', in *E.H.R.* lxxv (1960), 654–60. See Appendix VII below.

3 GLOUCESTER. Robert fitz Roy or Robert de Caen, so called because he was the illegitimate son of Henry I by (probably) Sibyl daughter of Robert Corbet burgess of Caen, was created earl of Gloucester between June and September 1120 (Round, *G. de M*. 420 ff). On Henry I's death he at first hoped to raise Theobald Count of Blois to the throne (p. 15), but eventually recognized Stephen as king in April 1136 (p. 21). After much hesitation he 'defied' Stephen after 22 May 1138, and from then until his death (31 October 1147) was the principal supporter of the empress Matilda. His grandson Robert (then aged 6) was granted the honour of Eudo Dapifer in England and Normandy by Duke Henry in 1153 or 1154, but if he ever received it, he had lost it by 1158. The whole incident raises question about Duke Henry's relations with the boy's father, Earl William. See David Crouch in *E.H.R.* 103 (1988), 69–75.

4 HUNTINGDON. This earldom came to King David by right of his wife, Maud daughter of Earl Waltheof, but he was her second husband and his claim was disputed by Simon de Senlis II who was Maud's son by her first marriage. Stephen was predisposed towards Simon (who supported him loyally) but anxious not to make an enemy of King David if he could help it, and he seems to have aimed at a compromise whereby Northampton would be detached from the earldom of Huntingdon and made a separate earldom for Simon. So far as Huntingdon was concerned, he granted it to King David's son Henry at the Treaty of Durham (5 February 1136) (see p. 19). Henry presumably forfeited it during the Scottish war of 1138, but held it again from the second Treaty of Durham (9 April 1139) till the end of 1141, when he

County	*Earl existing in 1135*	*Created by Stephen*	*Created by the Empress*
1. Buckingham	Walter Giffard		
2. Chester	Ranulf de Gernons		
3. Gloucester	Robert son of King Henry		
4. Huntingdon	King David of Scotland		
5. Leicester	Robert de Beaumont		
6. Warwick	Roger de Beaumont		
7. Surrey	William de Warenne		
8. Northampton		Simon de Senlis 1136/8	
9. Bedford		Hugh de Beaumont 1137	
10. York		William d'Aumale 1138	
11. Derby and Notts		Robert de Ferrers 1138	
12. Pembroke		Gilbert fitz Gilbert de Clare 1138	
13. Hertford		Gilbert fitz Richard de Clare 1138/41	
14. Worcester		Waleran of Meulan, c. 1138	
15. Northumbria		Henry son of King David 1139	
16. Lincoln		William d'Aubigny 1139	
16. "		William de Roumare 1140 (?)	
		Gilbert de Gant 1149	
17. Cambridge		William de Roumare 1139 only	
18. Sussex		William d'Aubigny 1140	
19. Essex		Geoffrey de Mandeville 1140	
20. Cornwall		Alan of Brittany 1140	Reginald fitz Roy 1140
21. Wiltshire		Hervey Brito 1140	Patrick of Salisbury, c. 1147
22. Hereford		Robert Earl of Leicester 1140	Miles of Gloucester 1141
23. Oxford			Aubrey de Vere 1141
24. Somerset and Dorset			William de Mohun 1141 only
25. Norfolk and Suffolk		William son of King Stephen 1148/9	Hugh Bigod 1141
26. Devon			Baldwin de Redvers 1141
27. Staffordshire			[Ranulf Earl of Chester 1153]
28. Kent		—	—
29. Berkshire		—	—
30. Hampshire		—	—
31. Middlesex		—	—
32. Shropshire		—	—
33. [Richmond]		Alan of Brittany 1136	—

finally lost it. It was subsequently held by Simon de Senlis II together with Northampton (G. W. S. Barrow, in *Regesta Regum Scottorum* i. 102).

5 LEICESTER. The earldom was held from 1118 by Robert de Beaumont II, the twin brother of Waleran of Meulan. On their father's death, Waleran (the elder) had received his Norman and French lands, and Robert his English lands. Robert did not rebel against Stephen until 1153, though his loyalty seems to have been lukewarm for some time before. He died in 1168. See Appendix V below.

6 WARWICK. Roger de Beaumont, first cousin of Waleran and Robert de Beaumont II, received the earldom soon after his father's death in 1119. He attacked Nottingham with partisans of the empress in 1140 (p. 43) and joined her formally in 1141 (*G.S.* 116–18 and *Reg.* iii. 597), but was with Stephen in 1146 (*Reg.* iii, 494) and in 1153 when he died (p. 116) See 'Geoffrey de Clinton and Roger Earl of Warwick: New Men and Magnates in the Reign of Henry I by David Crouch, *B.I.H.R* 55 (1982), 113–23.

7 SURREY. The earls of Warenne were also earls of Surrey, but almost invariably used the former style; the style *Willelmus comes de Sudreia* is found only in one dubious charter of King Stephen (*Reg.* iii. 284). There is endless confusion between the different generations of earls since they were all called William. William I died in 1088; William II, who married the widow of Robert de Beaumont I, died in 1138, William III, half-brother of Waleran and Robert de Beaumont II died in 1148 leaving only a daughter, Isabel, who married William (IV) the second son of King Stephen. All the earls concerned were loyal to Stephen. As explained below, William de Warenne IV was earl of Norfolk as well as Surrey.

8 NORTHAMPTON. See Huntingdon, no. 4 above. Simon de Senlis was styled earl soon after 1136, but his precise style is uncertain. Normally he was just *Comes Simon*, but two early charters of dubious value style him *Comes de Silvanecti* (*Reg.* iii. 132, 945), and three others (also dubious) as *Comes de Norhamtona* (*Reg.* iii. 284, 922, 964). In a charter of his own (*c.* 1141–48) he styled himself *Simon comes Northamton* (*Eynsham Cartulary*, ed. H. E. Salter, i. no. 98). He probably preferred the style *Comes Simon* because it left open his claim to the whole earldom of Huntingdon (including Northampton), which he seems to have held from 1141 till his death in 1153. He was consistently loyal to Stephen.

9 BEDFORD. According to *G.S.* 46–50, 116, Hugh de Beaumont, the younger brother of Waleran and Robert II de Beaumont, was given

the earldom in 1137 and lost it in 1141. G.H. White doubted whether the earldom was real (*T.R.H.S.*, 4th series, xiii (1930), 77–82), but the statements of *G.S.* are emphatic and repeated, and in view of the author's habitual accuracy they cannot be dismissed. Nor does it matter that Miles de Beauchamp was never earl; even as sheriff he might well have resented the instrusion of Hugh de Beaumont, particularly as it involved handing over Bedford castle to him. Hugh's appointment must have been a rebuff for King David of the Scots, since Bedfordshire was normally considered part of his earldom of Huntingdon (G. H. Fowler in *Beds. Hist. Rec. Soc.*, ix (1925), 33).

10 YORK. William d'Aumale was created Earl of York after he had helped to defeat the Scots at the Battle of the Standard (22 August 1138) (Richard of Hexham, in *Chronicles* iii. 165). He styled himself variously *Willelmus comes de Albemarla* and *Willelmus comes Eboraci*, the former being the more common. He was consistently loyal to Stephen, and played an active (and official) part in the election of William fitz Herbert as archbishop in 1141, as also in the exclusion of Henry Murdac from the city of York in 1148–51 (pp. 98, 103).

11 DERBY AND NOTTS. According to Richard of Hexham (in *Chronicles* iii, 165) and *OV* vi. 518, Robert de Ferrers was made Earl of Derby after the Battle of the Standard in 1138, but he died soon after, and in the only charter he issued as earl he styled himself 'of Nottingham' (Michael Jones, 'The Charters of Robert de Ferrers Earl of Nottingham, Derby and Ferrers', in *Nottingham Medieval Studies* xxiv (1980, 7–26, no. 14, in which he can be identified as Robert I because of the attestation of his brother William). Robert II used the title 'of Nottingham' in 5 of his charters, 'of Tutbury' in 1 and 'de Ferrers' in 13. He witnessed 7 times for Stephen (but never for the empress or Duke Henry), on 5 occasions as de Ferrers and on 2 as 'of Nottingham'. The indications are, as Jones suggests, that the title 'of Nottingham' was used *c*. 1138–45, though not to the exclusion of Ferrers. The variations in his title may have some connections with his relations with William Peverel of Nottingham whose daughter Robert II had married at any rate by 29 Sept. 1139. At first Robert seems to have got on well with his father-in-law, both being supporters of King Stephen. Later, however, relations became strained, because while William Peverel was the mortal enemy of Ranulf Earl of Chester, Robert Earl of Ferrers was singled out as the particular ally of Earl Ranulf in the latter's treaty with the earl of Leicester (1149–53, pp. 109–10 above). It may be that Ferrers was afraid that his wife might be disinherited in some way by her father, but if so he had chosen his ally unwisely, because early in 1153 Earl Ranulf got Duke

Henry to promise *him* the inheritance for himself (*Reg.* iii. 180). It is not surprising to find that in May 1153 the Earl Ferrers was in arms against Duke Henry, being forced to submit only after the Duke had besieged and captured his castle of Tutbury (about 1 June 1153). *G.S.* 234.

12 PEMBROKE. Stephen made Gilbert fitz Gilbert Earl of Pembroke in 1138 (*OV* vi. 520). His elder brother, Richard fitz Gilbert, had been killed during the Welsh rising of 1136, and another brother, Baldwin fitz Gilbert, who had subsequently been despatched to restore the situation, had failed to advance beyond Brecon (*G.S.* 16–20). Gilbert fitz Gilbert's promotion presumably indicates that he was now to take control of the Welsh in that part of Wales, and in fact he captured or built Carmarthen Castle *c.* 1144 (*Brut*(R.S.)144). He went over to the empress for a short while in the summer of 1141, but was otherwise loyal to Stephen till 1147 when he revolted (p. 93). He was reconciled to Stephen before his death in 1148 (Lees, *Records of the Templars*, 149–51). His son, Richard fitz Gilbert (Strongbow) supported Stephen and was not styled Earl by Henry II until 1172, and even then not 'of Pembroke'.

13 HERTFORD. Gilbert fitz Richard de Clare witnessed as *Comes Gisl' de Heorford* at Christmas 1141 (*Reg.* iii. 276), but it is generally believed that he got his earldom soon after 1138. This may well be correct, but it cannot be proved since it is often impossible to distinguish between the different Earl Gilberts. He revolted in 1147 (p. 93), but subsequently made his peace with Stephen, witnessing *Reg.* iii. 169–70 between 1148 and 1153. He does not seem to have witnessed for the empress ever. He died *c.* 1151–3.

14 WORCESTER. G.H.White (*art. cit.* 56–72) shows that Waleran of Meulan was styled earl of Worcester at any rate by the end of 1139, and suggests 1138 as the date of his creation. He went over to the empress before the end of 1141, and retired to his lands in Normandy, though he apparently considered himself earl of Worcester till the end of the reign, but Henry II never recognized his earldom or his right to the royal manors he had held in Worcestershire. This is one of the few cases in which Henry II did treat Stephen's grants as if they had never been made. See Appendix V below.

15 NORTHUMBRIA. By reviving this earldom for Henry son of King David, Stephen in effect surrendered it to the Scots. This was by the Treaty of Durham of 9 April 1139 (Richard of Hexham in *Chronicles* iii. 177, and G.W.S. Barrow in *Regesta Regum Scottorum* i. 102).

16 LINCOLN. Stephen recognized three successive earls of Lincoln, a fact which would be very puzzling if the earldom were merely a title, but which is understandable if the earl was an officer charged with defence of the county or earldom (*comitatum*).

(i) The first was William d'Aubigny *pincerna* who married Queen Adeliza, widow of King Henry I, and in her right became lord of the honour and castle of Arundel. He styles himself William Earl of Lincoln in three charters in which his identity is proved by references to his wife. They are in favour of Lewes Priory and the abbeys of Reading and Affligem—and in the case of Affligem there is also a charter by Adeliza refering to her husband as earl of Lincoln (*G. de M*. 324–5); Warner and Ellis, *Facsimiles*, no. 14; E. de Marneffe, *Cartulaire de l'abbaye d'Affligem* in *Analectes pour servir à l'histoire ecclésiastique de la Belgique*, 2ᵉ section, pp. 104, 106). In royal charters it is usually impossible to distinguish him from his successor, William de Roumare, since the normal style of both was *Willelmus comes de Lincolnia*; or (before he was an earl) from his father, William d'Aubigny *pincerna*, who died before June 1139 (*Reg*. iii. 973). If Robert de Torigny is right (*Chronicles* iv. 137) William had married Adeliza by September 1139, and it is tempting to assume that it was on his marriage that he was made earl of Lincoln, his connection with that county being that his mother, Maud Bigod, was a granddaughter, and possible co-heiress, of Robert de Tosny of Belvoir. We do not know precisely when he was transferred from Lincoln to Sussex, but it was certainly by Christmas 1141 when he attested a charter as *Comite Willelmo de Sudsexa* (*Reg*. iii. 276).

(ii) William de Roumare was in 1139 earl of Cambridge (see no. 17) and the date of his transfer to Lincoln is uncertain, though it seems to have been by 1142 which is apparently the date of his own charter marking the foundation of Revesby Abbey (Stenton, *Facsimiles of Early Charters from Northamptonshire Collections; Northants Rec. Soc.* iv (1930), 1–7). A charter by King Stephen in his favour as earl of Lincoln is *Reg* iii. 494, which may belong to either 1140 or 1146. If one were to guess when he was made earl of Lincoln, the most plausible date would be shortly before Christmas 1140 when Stephen visited him and his half-brother, Ranulf Earl of Chester, at Lincoln and (according to William of Malmesbury, *Hist. Nov.* para. 487) increased their honours. William is known to have supported the Angevins from soon after Christmas 1140, and there is nothing to suggest that he reverted to Stephen before 1146. Immediately before his return to England he had been on pilgrimage to Santiago de Compostela. This must have been after the foundation of Revesby abbey in 1143. For his return see G. Barrachlough, *The Charters of the Anglo Norman Earls of Chester* (1988), no

70. It is a curious fact that he did not witness any charters for the empress—the cause, as with his half-brother Earl Ranulf, may have been his opposition to King David of Scotland who was at her court—but he witnessed a charter for Duke Geoffrey at Rouen on 11 October 1147 (*Reg.* iii 599), gave charters of his own at Bolingbroke (Lincs) after 1148 (Stenton, *Danelaw Charters*, 515–16) and witnessed for Duke Henry at Rouen in 1151 and Devizes in 1153 (*Reg.* iii. 325, 179). In all these charters he is styled earl of Lincoln, but as is shown below, Stephen ceased to recognize him after *c.* 1149. Neither he nor the man whom Stephen appointed to succeed him witnessed, or was mentioned in, the Treaty of Westminster (December 1153), so that both parties were saved the embarrassment of deciding which was the rightful earl.

   (iii) Gilbert de Gant is usually stated to have been created earl of Lincoln *c.* 1147–8, but in a charter which he gave to Bardney Abbey and addressed to Robert Bishop of Lincoln (elected 13 December, consecrated 19 December 1148), he still styles himself plain *Gilbertus de Gaunt* (B.L., Cotton MS, Vespasian E. xx, f.54). In royal charters he may sometimes be confused with two other Earl Gilberts, of Pembroke and Hertford, but he is referred to as *Gilbertus comes Lincolnie* in a charter of Stephen's for Bridlington, and is addressed as *G. com Linc* in a writ of Stephen for William de Huntingfield (*Reg.* iii. 123, 414). It may be presumed that he was appointed during, or as a result of, Stephen's successful northern campaign in 1149.

17 CAMBRIDGE. There is only one reference to William de Roumare as earl of Cambridge, but it is in a charter of Alexander Bishop of Lincoln which belongs to 4 December 1139–24 March 1140 and is witnessed *testimonio Ranulfi comitis Cestriae et Willelmi comitis Cantabridgiae fratris ejus* (Round, *Feudal England*, 186–7, and *Monast.* vi. 949). Cambridgeshire normally formed part of the earldom of Huntingdon, which was presumably forfeited by its earl, Henry son of King David of Scotland, when the Scots army invaded England in January 1138. I would guess that it was as a result of this forfeiture that William de Roumare was given Cambridgeshire, and that he lost it when, by the Treaty of Durham (9 April 1139), Stephen restored to Henry all the lands he had previously held (G. W. S. Barrow, *Regesta Regum Scottorum*. i. 102). As a result, William would have been out of a job and in need of a new earldom. Hence his move to Lincoln (q.v.).

18 SUSSEX. William d'Aubigny *pincerna*, who had previously been earl of Lincoln, was earl of Sussex by Christmas 1141 (*Reg.* iii. 276). He witnessed a number of Stephen's charters, six as earl of Arundel, four as earl of Chichester, two as earl of Sussex, and one as count of Aubigny. As

Round has shown (*G. de M.*, 320–1) there is no particular significance in these various titles, since Arundel was in Sussex and his chief residence, and Chichester the county town; but there may be some significance in the one occasion in which he is styled by his family name, d'Aubigny, since the charter in question can be dated 1140 (*Reg.* iii. 399), and it could be that he had just given up Lincoln to William de Roumare, but not yet received Sussex instead. He is said to have received the empress on her landing at Arundel (September 1139), but was otherwise loyal to Stephen.

19 ESSEX. I have criticized Round's chronology in 'Geoffrey de Mandeville Reconsidered' (*E.H.R.* lxxix (1964), 299–307), but Round was almost certainly right to date Geoffrey's creation 1140. Within that year a likely date would be Whitsun, which Stephen spent at London with a poorly attended court. Unlike most of the other earls, Geoffrey had had previous administrative experience as sheriff of Essex (*Reg.* iii. 40, 543), so that if a noble administrator was what was required, Geoffrey would have been an ideal appointment. He went over to the empress in June—July 1141, but reverted to Stephen by September of the same year. He revolted again after his arrest in 1143 and died in 1144. See Appendix VI below.

20 CORNWALL. According to *G.S.* 102, 116, Earl Alan of Brittany was given Cornwall in 1140 and lost it to the empress's nominee in 1141. In a charter dated 1140 for St Michael's Mount he styled himself *A(lanus) dei gratia comes Bretann(ie) et Cornub(ie) et Richemontis* (*Monast.* vi. 990). (See also Richmond.) Earl Reginald, the empress's nominee, was an illegitimate son of King Henry I. In 1140 he married the daughter of William fitz Richard fitz Turold and was made earl of Cornwall not by the empress but by Robert Earl of Gloucester (*Hist. Nov.* para. 483, cf. *G.S.* 67). For the importance of Earl Robert's usurpation of his sister's rights in this matter see Karl Schnith, '*Regis et pacis inquietrix*: Zur Rolle der Kaiserin Mathilde in der Anarchie', (*Journal of Medieval History* 2 (1976), 135–58, esp. 144). The reason why Round thought he was not made earl until 1141 was *Reg.* iii. 400, but one should probably read R(oberto) instead of R(eginaldo) filio regis. As Reginald son of King Henry he witnessed one charter for Stephen at the Easter Court of 1136 (*Reg.* iii. 944). Otherwise his attestations are all for the Angevins and as earl.

21 WILTSHIRE. Hervey Brito was apparently Stephen's son-in-law, received Devizes castle from him in 1140, and lost it in 1141 (*G.S.* 108, 116). In a charter of 1140 (*Reg.* iii. 16) he is styled *H. comite de Wiltes-*

(*cira*). He was also lord of the honour of Eye in Suffolk, which Stephen himself had previously held (*C.Ch.R. v. 336–7*). The empress's nominee, Patrick Earl of Salisbury, was the son of Walter of Salisbury (d. 1147) who was possibly sheriff in the early years of Stephen's reign (*Reg.* iii. 684) and whose own father, Edward of Salisbury, had certainly been sheriff under William the Conqueror. Patrick was made earl at some date between 1141 and 1147. He was not an earl in *Reg.* iii. 839, but is so styled in a charter of Henry d'Oilly given before the death of Earl Robert of Gloucester (31 October 1147) (Salter, *Enysham Cartulary*, i. 75 (no. 71), Oxford Hist. Soc. xlix, 1906–7). His normal style was Earl of Salisbury, but in a charter of Henry fitz empress (1144–50) he was styled Earl of Wiltshire (*Reg.* iii. 704), and it may be assumed that, as in the case of Arundel—Chichester—Sussex, the titles were interchangeable.

22 HEREFORD. In a well-known charter of *c*. 1140 (*Reg.* iii. 437) Stephen granted to Robert Earl of Leicester *burgum Hereford et castellum et totum comitatum de Herefordscire praeter terram episcopatus et terram abbathiae de Rading' et aliarum ecclesiarum et abbathiarum que tenent de me in capite* H.W.C. Davis (*Essays to R.L. Poole* (Oxford, 1927, 172–6) thought this meant a grant of the earldom; G. H. White (*T.R.H.S.*, 4th series, xiii (1930), 72–7) thought it meant only a grant of the county. If we disregard the question of title, however, it is clear that the words used are the normal formula for the grant of a second county to a man who was already earl of one; cf. Norfolk and Staffs. The empress created Miles of Gloucester earl of Hereford on 25 July 1141 (*Reg.* iii. 393). Like his father before him he had previously been sheriff of Gloucester (which position he seems to have retained even while earl of Hereford), so he had administrative experience. He had supported Stephen until the empress landed in September 1139, but then went over to her and remained loyal to her until his death (24 December 1143).

23 OXFORD. The empress created Aubrey de Vere earl of Oxford, not in 1142 as Round maintained (*G. de M.* 180, 271) but in the last week of July 1141 (*Reg.* iii. 634, and *E.H.R.* lxxix(1964), 305). The terms of the charter were that he should be earl of Cambridge unless the King of Scots had that earldom (which he had). Failing Cambridge he was to choose (with the help of the earls of Gloucester, Essex and Pembroke) one of the four counties of Oxford, Berkshire, Wiltshire or Dorset. Round found it surprising that the empress did not know whether King David had Cambridgeshire or not, but the question was presumably one of legal rights which would have to be tested in a court. Aubrey had returned to Stephen's allegiance by 1145 and was recognized by him as count or earl, though not necessarily of Oxford, since he was only

styled *Comes Albericus* (*Reg.* iii. 460, 10, 118, 137, 272, 402) and he had been Count of Guisnes 1139–46 (*G. de M.*, 189). In Jan. 1156 King Henry II gave him the third penny of the pleas of Oxfordshire *ut sit inde comes* (*Book of Seals*, no. 40).

24 SOMERSET AND DORSET. William de Mohun was styled earl by the empress as early as June 1141 (*Reg.* iii. 274), and in *Reg.* iii. 190 she addressed him as *Comiti W. de Sumerseta*. Her charter to Aubrey de Vere, discussed above, also shows that in July 1141 she considered William to be earl of Somerset, not Dorset. G.S., (p. 128), however, says that William was made an earl not in June but in July, and that his county was Dorset and not Somerset. The two counties had a single sheriff, and it may well be that the author (if I have identified him rightly as the bishop of Bath) attributed William to Dorset, because he considered himself to be in control of Somerset. William de Mohun lost his earldom when he deserted the empress. This was certainly before 1144, for a letter of Brien fitz Count which cannot be later than that year, refers to him as a notorious turncoat (*E.H.R.* xxv (1910), 301). He can hardly have deserted her after the battle of Wilton (early 1143) because that battle and the resulting surrender of Sherborne castle put ⸱ Somerset and Dorset under her control (G.S. 148–50). It is therefore likely that the date of William's desertion was late 1141 or some time in 1142.

25 NORFOLK AND SUFFOLK. It is normally held that Hugh Bigod was created earl of Norfolk by Stephen after his revolt of 1140 and before the battle of Lincoln (2 Feb. 1141). The only evidence for this view is that in his account of Stephen's army at the battle, Henry of Huntingdon (*R.S.* p. 273) refers to Hugh as *consul de Estangle*. Henry was writing a few years later however, and he could well have used this title to identify his man without necessarily meaning that he was earl *by that date*. Like other chroniclers, Henry of Huntingdon could be casual about titles, and under 1141 (p. 278) he refers to Hugh as plain 'Hugonis Bigot'. On the other hand the evidence of the charters is plain. Hugh Bigod is a frequent witness for Stephen before 1141, but is never styled earl. After that he witnesses only three charters for Stephen, and though he is then styled Earl Hugh (though not of Norfolk), they are all subsequent to the Treaty of Westminster of December 1153 (*Reg.* iii. 27, 675, 896). Between 1141 and 1153 he only witnessed three royal or quasi-royal charters, two for the empress in July 1141 (*Reg.* iii. 275, 634) and one for Duke Henry in 1153/4 (*Reg.* iii. 364), and in all three he is styled Earl Hugh of Norfolk. The natural deduction is that the empress

made him earl of Norfolk, and that Stephen did not recognize him until he was forced to do so by the Treaty of Westminster. It is therefore interesting to find that in that treaty (*Reg.* iii. 272) Earl Hugh's status seems to have been left deliberately ambiguous. In the list of witnesses he is not styled earl, but his name is grouped with the other earls; and in the main text, though we find Hugh mentioned as earl, it is in a sentence attributing Norfolk to King Stephen's son, William.

> Incrementum etiam, quod ego Willelmo filio meo dedi, ipse dux [Henricus] ei concessit: castra scilicet et villas de Norwico cum septingentis libratis terrae, ita quod redditus de Norwico infra illas septingentas libratas computetur, et totum comitatum de Northfolk praeter illa quae pertinent ad ecclesias et praelatos et abbates et comites, et nominatim praeter tertium denarium unde Hugo Bygotus est comes, salva et reservata in omnibus regali justitia.

It will be noticed that the wording is very similar to that used in Stephen's grant of Herefordshire (q.v.) to the earl of Leicester and in Duke Henry's grant of Staffordshire to the earl of Chester. Stephen's son William was a great landowner in Norfolk by right of his wife, Isabel de Warenne, whom he married in 1148/9, thenceforward styling himself Earl William de Warenne as his father-in-law (d. 19 January 1148) had done. Since the general policy laid down in the treaty of Westminster was that Stephen's son was to have whatever was his lawful inheritance, it is tempting to think that his father-in-law, Earl Willam de Warenne III, might have had Norfolk also, but the treaty says specifically that this was not so; Norwich and Norfolk were the *incrementum* which Stephen had given his son, presumably on his marriage in 1148/9. William would then have been earl of two counties, Norfolk and Surrey, just as in 1140 Robert de Beaumont had Herefordshire as well as Leicestershire.

As for Hugh Bigod, Henry II thought it necessary to create him Earl of Norfolk *de Novo* in 1155: 'Sciatis me fecisse Hugonem Bigot comitem Norfolk'. *Cartae antiquae Rolls 11–20* (PRS, 1975) no. 553.

26 DEVON. Baldwin de Redvers is one of the few great men who did not attend Stephen's great Easter court of 1136. There is no evidence for the view that he had asked for Stephen for the earldom and been refused; what he had asked for was *quendam honorem* (i.e. a certain collection of fiefs) (Richard of Hexham in *Chronicles* iii. 146). According to *G.S.* 128 the empress made him earl of Exeter in July 1141, but he was an earl already in June (*Reg.* iii. 274) and in her charters he styled himself Earl of Devon. As with Arundel—Sussex there is no significance in these variations of titles. He was consistently loyal to the empress.

27 STAFFORDSHIRE. In 1153 Duke Henry granted Ranulf Earl of Chester:

> Stafordiam et Stafordiesir(am) et comitatum Stafordie totum quicquid ego ibi habui in foeudo et hereditate, excepto foeudo episcopi Cestrie et comitis Roberti de Ferrers et Hugonis de Mortuomare et Gervasii Paganel, et excepto foresto de Can(n)oc quod in manu mea retineo. (*Reg.* iii. 180)

As we have already seen in connection with Hereford and Norfolk this was the regular formula used when an earl was given a second county. It is quite possible that Ranulf had been in charge of Staffordshire before 1153, but there is no proof.

28 KENT. According to *The Chronicle of Battle Abbey*, ed. and trans. Eleanor Searle (Oxford Medieval Texts, 1980), 144, William of Ypres possessed the county of Kent (*Cantiae comitatum tunc possidebat*), and Gervase of Canterbury (R.S.) i. 121 says he abused it (*Cantia abutebatur*). The Pipe Roll for 2 Henry II, p. 65, shows that the revenues which he was still drawing from Kent in 1156 amounted to £261 *blanch* and £178 8*s* 7*d* *ad numerum*, or slightly more than three-quarters of the 'farm' of the county. It therefore seems certain that he was in charge of the county, but it is perfectly true, as Round stated in G. *de M*. 270, 275, that he was never styled earl. This was probably due to the fact that he had been a serious claimant to the county of Flanders in 1127, having at one point usurped the title, and being known by his enemies as *Willelmus ille adulterinus comes Iprensium*. If Stephen, whose county of Boulogne was a dependency of Flanders, had styled William *comes* even in England, the lawful count of Flanders might well have considered it an act of *lèse majesté*.

29 BERKSHIRE was presumably dependent on Windsor Castle.

30 HAMPSHIRE. The earl's functions may well have been performed by Henry of Blois bishop of Winchester.

31 MIDDLESEX presumably went with the Tower of London. Geoffrey de Mandeville Earl of Essex was sheriff of London and Middlesex while castellan of the Tower.

32 SHROPSHIRE. It is possible that the reason why no earl was created for this county, could have been that it was in the hands of Henry I's widow, Queen Adeliza, to whom it had been given on her marriage to the king—'uxori sue . . . comitatum Salopesberie dedit' (*Hist. Nov. para 451*). She did not die until 1151.

33 RICHMOND. The castelry or 'shire' of Richmond protected North Yorkshire from the Scots, and Earl Alan of Brittany was styled earl of Richmond as early as 1136 (*Reg.* iii. 204, 949). So far as can be seen, he was consistently loyal to Stephen until his death in 1146. Conan his successor does not appear under Stephen but was recognized by Henry II in 1156 and deposed in 1164. Conan's heiress, Constance, was married to King Henry II's son, Geoffrey. See also Cornwall (no. 20, above).

Appendix II

The chart below marks each participant's allegiance across the years. Years/periods run as column headers left to right:

Dec. 1135–Jan. 1136 | 1136 | 1137 | 1138 | 1139 | 1140 | Jan. 1141 | June 1141 | Sept. 1141 | Dec. 1141 | 1142 | 1143 | 1144 | 1145 | Early 1146 | Late 1146 | 1147 | 1148 | 1149 | 1150 | 1151 | 1152 | 1153

Principal participants in the Civil War 1136–53

Participant	Dec. 1135–Jan. 1136	1136	1137	1138	1139	1140	Jan. 1141	June 1141	Sept. 1141	Dec. 1141	1142	1143	1144	1145	Early 1146	Late 1146	1147	1148	1149	1150	1151	1152	1153
William Martel the King's steward	★	★	★	★	★	★	★	★	★	★	★	★	★	★	★	★	★	★	★	★	★	★	★
Robert de Vere the King's constable, d. *c.* 1151	★	★	★	★	★	★	★	★	★	★	★	★	★	★	★	★	★	★	★	★	★		
Richard de Lucy			★	★	★	★	★	★	★	★	★	★	★	★	★	★	★	★	★	★	★	★	★
William of Ypres			★	★	★	★	★	★	★	★	★	★	★	★	★	★	★	★	★	★	★	★	★
William de Warenne Earl of Surrey			★	★	★	★	★	★	★	★	★	★	★	★	★	★	★	★	★	★	★	★	★
William d'Aumale Earl of York			★	★	★	★	★	★	★	★	★	★	★	★	★	★	★	★	★	★	★	★	★
Robert de Ferrers Earl of Derby				★	★	★	★	★	★	★	★	★	★	★	★	★	★	★	★	★	★	★	★
Simon de Senlis Earl of Northampton				★	★	★	★	★	★	★	★	★	★	★	★	★	★	★	★	★	★	★	
Robert Earl of Leicester			★	★	★	★	★	★	★	★	★	★	★	★	★	★	★	★	★	★	★	—	
Roger Earl of Warwick, d. 1153		★	★	★	★	—	—	·	·	·	·	·	·	★	★	★	★	★	★	★	★		
HENRY OF BLOIS BISHOP OF WINCHESTER		★	★	★	★	★	★	—	—	·	·	·	★	★	★	★	★	★	★	★	★	★	★
Gilbert de Clare Earl of Pembroke, d. 1148			★	★	★	★	★	—	★	★	★	★	★	★	★	★	★	—	★	★	★		
Gilbert de Clare Earl of Hertford, d. 1152			★	★	★	★	·	·	★	★	★	★	★	★	★	—	★	★	★	★	★	★	
Geoffrey de Mandeville Earl of Essex, d. 1144			★	★	★	★	—	★	★	★	★	—											
Aubrey de Vere Earl of Oxford			★	★	★	★	—	·	·	·	·	★	★	★	★	★	★	★	★	★	★	★	★

NIGEL BISHOP OF ELY
Hugh Bigod Earl of Norfolk
Waleran of Meulan Earl of Worcester
Ranulf Earl of Chester
William de Roumare Earl of Lincoln
Reginald fitz Roy Earl of Cornwall
Miles of Gloucester Earl of Hereford, d. 1143
Roger Earl of Hereford, 1143–55
Brien fitz Count
Humphrey de Bohun the steward
John fitz Gilbert the marshal
KING DAVID OF THE SCOTS
Robert Earl of Gloucester, d. 1147
William Earl of Gloucester, 1147–83
Philip son of Robert Earl of Gloucester
Baldwin de Redvers Earl of Devon

Key: Supporting Stephen ★   Supporting the empress of Duke Henry ▬   Doubtful . . .

Table 3. Principal Participants in the Civil War, 1136–53

The Chronicle Sources

The most important source is the *Gesta Stephani* which was written by an admirer of King Stephen, who was close (and generally sympathetic) to Henry of Blois, and who had special knowledge of quite a wide district round Bath. In *E.H.R.* lxxvii (1962), 209–32, I have explained why I think that the author was Robert of Lewes who, after a brief period as deputy abbot for Henry of Blois at Glastonbury, became bishop of Bath and Wells (1136–66). In the same article I have also shown why I think that the bulk of the work (down to 1147) was written in 1148, and the rest after 1153. Though it gives no dates and is written in a literary form, it is by far the most comprehensive and detailed account of the reign. Unfortunately the text is incomplete with *lacunae* for the periods March–December 1137, February–May 1138, July 1138–June 1139, and *c.* May–December 1140. Historians who wrote before 1955 had to work from an even less perfect text which ended abruptly at 1148, but thanks to the discovery of a manuscript of the work in the Public Library at Valenciennes, the final portion of the work (to 1154) is now printed in the edition by K. R. Potter in Nelson's Medieval Texts (London, 1955), 2nd edition, revised by R. H. C. Davis, Oxford Medieval Texts, 1976.

The *Historia Novella* by William of Malmesbury, which has also been edited with a translation by K. R. Potter in Nelson's Medieval Texts (London, 1955) extends only to the end of 1142, when its author apparently died. It is a strictly contemporary document and is full of precise chronological details. Since William was a monk of Malmesbury, the district with which he was most familiar was much the same as that of the author of *Gesta Stephani*, but like him he travelled a certain amount; he was, for example, present at the council of Winchester in April 1141. The value of his work has recently been challenged by Robert B. Patterson in the *American Historical Review*, lxx (1965), 983–97, but in my opinion the fact that William dedicated his work to Robert Earl of Gloucester and generally reflected his point of view increases rather than decreases its value.[1] A detailed comparison of the *Historia Novella* with the other chronicles of the reign has left me with the greatest respect for William's accuracy.

Orderic Vitalis, though half English, was a monk of St Evroult in east Normandy. The last chapters of his *Ecclesiastical History* give a strictly contemporary account of the reign down to June 1141, with special emphasis on Normandy. Orderic was a supporter of King Stephen and an admirer of Waleran of Meulan and his brother, but at the end of his history he was convinced that Stephen's failure was total. He may not have lived to hear the news of the Rout of Winchester, but he leaves one in no doubt that he did not relish the prospect of Angevin rule in Normandy. His *History* is not well organized but is full of interesting details, especially about hereditary claims. While he is naturally better informed about Normandy than England, he is the only chronicler to tell the racy story of how Ranulf Earl of Chester captured Lincoln castle in 1140. The best edition (with translation) is that of Marjorie Chibnall in Oxford Medieval Texts (6 vols, Oxford, 1969–80).

The chronicle of Robert of Torigni is the main source of information for Norman affairs after the death of Orderic Vitalis. Robert became a monk of Bec (Archbishop Theobald's former monastery) probably in 1128. By 1139 he was known as a man of letters, for when Henry of Huntingdon visited Bec in that year, Robert showed him a copy of Geoffrey of Monmouth's *British History*. He was probably made claustral prior of Bec in 1149, and in 1154 he was elected abbot of Mont Saint-Michel—whence his designation as 'Robert de Monte' by Stubbs and others. Though he did not die until 1186, the manuscripts of his work show that his chronicle was already complete to 1154 when he moved to Mont Saint-Michel, and he is thought to have begun it *c.* 1150. It is an invaluable source, especially for the period when Henry was duke of Normandy. Since he lived in Normandy, he naturally favoured dukes Geoffrey and Henry more than Stephen. I have used the edition by Richard Howlett in *Chronicles of the Reigns of Stephen, Henry II and Richard I*, vol. iv (R.S., London 1889), but for Robert's complete works it is necessary to turn to the edition by Léopold Delisle in the Société de l'Histoire de Normandie (2 vols,

---

1 For an argued refutation of Patterson, see Joe. W. Leedom, 'William of Malmesbury and Robert Earl of Gloucester Reconsidered', *Albion* 6 (1974), 251–63.

Rouen, 1872). A translation of the relevant part of the text is to be found in Joseph Stevenson's *Church Historians of England*, vol. iv, part ii (London, 1856).

In the eighth book of his *Historia Anglorum* Henry of Huntingdon gives a complete but brief account of the reign (in 34 pages). Henry was a canon of Lincoln and archdeacon of Huntingdon, and consequently the district of which he had special knowledge was different from that of the *Gesta Stephani* and William of Malmesbury. He dedicated his *History* to Alexander Bishop of Lincoln, and presumably reflected his outlook. Though he thought that Stephen was untrustworthy, particularly in the way in which he arrested people at court, he shows no sympathy for the empress. He seems to have written his *History* almost year by year and to have died soon after its completion in 1154. I have used the edition by Thomas Arnold in the Rolls Series (London, 1879), but there is a translation by Thomas Forester in Bohn's Antiquarian Library (London, 1853). A new edition and translation is promised by Diana E. Greenway.

An English chronicle which covers only the opening years of the reign is the so-called *Chronicle of John of Worcester, 1118–40*, ed. J. R. H. Weaver (Oxford, 1908). This chronicle, formerly known as one version of 'Florence of Worcester', is itself composite, but its basis seems to be a genuine Worcester chronicle favourable to Stephen. In the printed edition of Florence (*Florentii Wigornensis Monachi Chronicon ex Chronicis*, ed. B. Thorpe, London, 1848–9) there are still further conflations, particularly with a Gloucester chronicle which derived its information from Miles of Gloucester who (from 1139) favoured the empress. The most detailed account of the empress's flight from Winchester in 1141 is supplied by this Gloucester Chronicle. A new edition of this whole complex of chronicles is badly needed, was promised by Professor R. R. Darlington, and is being completed by P. McGurk. There is a translation of Thorpe's text by Thomas Forester in Bohn's Antiquarian Library (London, 1854).

Hexham in Northumberland provided two chroniclers, though both of them were more interested in relations with the Scots than in the civil war between Stephen and Matilda. Richard of Hexham, who was prior from 1141 till at least 1154, wrote a detailed account of the reign down to April 1139 (in 40 pages). He was apparently writing before 1154. His history is entitled *De Gestis Regis Stephani et De Bello Standardii*, but it also has a marked interest in ecclesiastical affairs. His work contains the only known text of the bull by which Pope Innocent II recognized Stephen. I have used the edition by Richard Howlett in *Chronicles of the Reign of Stephen, Henry II and Richard I* (R.S., London,

1886), iii. 139–178. There is a translation by Joseph Stevenson in *Church Historians of England*, iv. (part i) 35–58.

John of Hexham wrote in less detail than Richard of Hexham, but covered almost the whole of Stephen's reign in 45 pages. In the form in which we have it, his work is apparently incomplete, since it ends abruptly towards the end of 1153. John seems to have written his work *c*. 1162–70. He is naturally interested in northern affairs and is a particularly valuable source for the disputed election to the archbishopric of York. He is usually identified with the Prior John who is found before 1178 and *c*. 1189–94. I have used the edition by Thomas Arnold in *Symeonis Monachi Opera Omnia* (R.S., London, 1885), ii. 284–332. There is a translation by Joseph Stevenson in *Church Historians in England*, vol. iv, part i.

Ailred Abbot of Rievaulx wrote an account of the Battle of the Standard (ed. Richard Howlett in *Chronicles of the Reigns of Stephen, Henry II and Richard I* (R.S., London, 1886), ii. 181–99). Ailred had been educated at the court of King David, but the *Relatio de Standardo* was intended, at any rate in part, as a glorification of Walter Espec the founder of Rievaulx. It is impossible to say with certainty when the tract was written, but Sir Maurice Powicke considered *c*. 1155–7 to be the most likely date. Ailred died in 1167.

The *Anglo-Saxon Chronicle* is unfortunately brief for Stephen's reign and its chronology confused. It was written at Peterborough in, or soon after, 1154. It records few facts of which we would not otherwise know, but has a memorable, if generalized, account of conditions during the 'anarchy' (see p. 80). I have used the translation by G. N. Garmonsway (Everyman's Library, London, 1953).

The *Historia Pontificalis* by John of Salisbury is really memoirs of the papal court and only of incidental interest for English affairs. But though John may not have written till 1164, he was present at the council of Reims in 1148 and himself witnessed the events he described. As he was subsequently a devoted servant of Archbishop Theobald, any failure of his memory is likely to have biased him towards the archbishop. I have used the edition by Marjorie Chibnall in Nelson's Medieval Texts (London, 1956).

The *Historia Rerum Anglicarum* by William of Newburgh (the relevant part of which is now translated by P. G. Walsh and M. J. Kennedy as *The History of English Affairs*, Book 1 (Aris and Phillips, Warminster, 1988)) was probably written in the last years of the twelfth century, but is not entirely without value for Stephen's reign. William was born near the Gipsy Race in the neighbourhood of Wold Newton, about 9 miles N.W. of Bridlington in 1136, and (according to his own statement) the priory of Newburgh (N. Yorks) which was founded in 1145 'nourished him from boyhood'. He seems to have died there not later than the spring of 1201, but most of his life is a mystery. He was the finest historian of his age and, as might be expected, contributes some useful facts about the North of England in the last years of Stephen's reign. More surprisingly he has preserved, from some unknown source, the most plausible account of the fall of Geoffrey de Mandeville. I have used the edition by Richard Howlett in *Chronicles of the Reigns of Stephen, Henry II and Richard I*, vol. i (R.S., London, 1884).

A late chronicle which occasionally has useful information is that of Gervase of Canterbury, edited by William Stubbs in *Gervasii Cantuariensis Opera Historica*, i. (R.S., London, 1897). He was not in any sense an eye-witness, since he was not professed a monk at Christ Church, Canterbury, until 1163, and did not begin to write his chronicle until *c.* 1188. His main sources were the continuation of Florence of Worcester and Henry of Huntingdon, but he was also well informed about Archbishop Theobald, and had some plausible traditions about the visit of Stephen and Duke Henry to Kent in 1154. He was very interested in chronology but did not always get it right; in particular his account of the early visits of Henry fitz empress to England was apparently based on incomplete or faulty information.

The following table summarizes most of the information given above, and may be useful for reference.

Name of source	Bias (S or M)	Locality of writer	Years covered (1135–1154)	Contemporary or later date of composition
Gesta Stephani	S	Bath (approx.)		contemporary
Robert of Torigni	M	Bec (Normandy)		c. 1150–4
Henry of Huntingdon	—	Lincoln and Huntingdon		contemporary
John of Hexham	—	Hexham		c. 1162–70
Anglo-Saxon Chronicle	—	Peterborough		after 1154
William of Newburgh	—	Newburgh		c. 1198 (?)
Historia Novella	M	Malmesbury		contemporary
Orderic Vitalis	S	St Evroult (Normandy)		contemporary
John of Worcester	S	Worcester		contemporary
Continuator of Florence of Worcester	M	Gloucester		contemporary
Richard of Hexham	—	Hexham		before 1154
Ailred of Rievaulx	—	Rievaulx		c. 1155–7?
Historia Pontificalis	M			c. 1164?
Gervase of Canterbury	—	Canterbury		c. 1188

Table 4. The Chronicle Sources

149

Appendix IV
Politics and Property

Since the first edition of this book a major debate on the hereditability of fiefs has been initiated by Professor J. C. Holt.[1] While agreeing that there was a tenurial crisis in twelfth-century England, he considered that it 'arose not because there was no law governing title and inheritance, or because kings flouted it, but because of the difficulties they encountered and created in applying it'. Pre-eminent among these difficulties was the distinction between patrimony, which was hereditary, and acquisition which was not. The estates won by those Normans who came over with the Conqueror were acquisitions (in theory not hereditable), but if in practice they passed from father to son they turned into patrimony and the next generation would hold them by hereditary right. If at a later date a particular baron acquired an additional estate (as Ranulf le Meschin acquired Carlisle) it would have been considered as quite distinct from his patrimony.

Holt's survey of the various laws and customs is masterly, but in some ways it can be read as a legal defence of the Norman kings' attitude to the hereditary rights and aspirations of their barons. He claims that circumstances were such that it was impossible for the king to follow the legal rules with consistency, discounting the contrary view that the

1 J. C. Holt, 'Politics and Property in Early Medieval England', *Past and Present* 57 (1972), 3–52; Stephen D. White, 'Succession to Fiefs in Early Medieval England', *Past and Present* 65 (1974), 118–27; Edmund King, 'The Tenurial Crisis of the Early Twelfth Century', *Past and Present* 65 (1974), 110–17, and 'King Stephen and the Anglo-Norman Aristocracy', *History* 59 (1974), 180–94. See also Holt's important presidential lectures in the fifth series of the *Transactions of the Royal Historical Society*: 'Feudal Society and the Family in Early Medieval England': 'i. The Revolution of 1066' (1982), 'ii. Notions of Patrimony' (1983), 'iii. Patronage and Politics' (1984) and 'iv. The Heiress and the Alien' (1985).

150

king was only too pleased when the intricacies of the law made it possible for him to use his own discretion and promote his own interests. In 'The place of Henry I's reign in English History'[2] Sir Richard Southern demonstrated how Henry I used the 'uncertainties which still hung over the right of hereditary succession' in order to distribute patronage to his own supporters and 'new men'. This did not mean that he denied or qualified the theory of feudal tenure; on the contrary, in his charters he emphasized it consistently. But when it came to practice he could often find a way round it by use of the recognized 'incidents' of wardship, marriage of heiresses and escheat, not to mention forfeiture. One has only to compare the solemn promises which he made in his coronation charter with the realities revealed in the one extant Pipe Roll of his reign (1130) to appreciate the gap between theory and practice. In the chronicles also we read of the disinherited (*exhereditati*). The most important of these were Henry's elder brother Robert, and nephew, William Clito, whom he deprived of the duchy of Normandy, but there was a large number of others who had been deprived, or felt cheated of, their rightful inheritance. They included the 'heirs' of William de Mandeville and Ivo de Grandmesnil (1102), Robert de Belleme, Roger of Poitou and Arnulf of Pembroke (1102), William son of Robert of Mortain, Robert de Stutville and Robert Malet (1106), Robert de Montfort (1107), Elias de Saint-Saëns (1111), Robert de Lacy (1114), William Count of Evreux (1118), Eudo Dapifer (1120), Ranulf Earl of Chester (1120/29) and/or his mother the Countess Lucy. A large part of their lands had been granted by Henry I to his closest friends or 'new men', and the fact that these new grants were made *in hereditate* did nothing to stabilize the situation, but led merely to conflicting hereditary claims by the old and the new owners.

I think it undeniable that these conflicting claims made the civil war of Stephen's reign virtually inevitable, fuelled it once it had begun and made the establishment of peace extremely difficult. I think also that once peace had been restored with the accession of Henry II, it was universally recognized that the continuation of peace depended on respect for hereditary right. That did not mean that there could be no more disputed successions. What it did mean was that since everyone recognized how dangerous such disputes could be, every effort was made to dampen them down rather than inflame them.

According to the Treaty of Westminster (1153) the disinherited were to be restored, but this bland statement was full of practical difficulties.

---

2 *Proc. Brit. Acad.* 48 (1962), 127–69, reprinted in slightly modified form in R. W. Southern, *Medieval Humanism and Other Studies* (Oxford, 1970), 206–33.

Any attempt to undo what had been done in the previous nineteen years, let alone the previous fifty-four, could only have led to a renewal of the civil war. Consequently compromise was essential. I have explained in Chapter X how Henry II encouraged marriage-treaties wherever possible, and how his task was made easier by the deaths of several important landowners, but his major problem must have been how to play for time without seeming weak and ineffectual.

His solution, whether by design or accident, was to alternate short bouts of decisive action in England with prolonged absences abroad. In 1155 he got rid of the Flemish mercenaries and forced William of Aumale (at Scarborough), Roger Earl of Hereford (at Gloucester and Hereford) and Hugh Mortimer (at Cleobury, Wigmore and Bridgnorth) into submission. But between January 1156 and January 1163 he spent only sixteen months in England. The rest of the time he was in Normandy, Anjou or Aquitaine (in July–September 1159 at Toulouse), and since litigants at his court had to seek him out wherever he might be, they could well have been discouraged by the distances involved. A knight called Richard d'Anstey who had a very complicated claim involving, among other things, the validity or invalidity of marriages which had to be referred to the ecclesiastical authorities, found it took him five years (1158–63) to win his claim, after incurring expenses totalling £344 7s. 4d.[3]

Such lengthy and costly procedures were obviously intolerable, and it was not surprising that some nobles looked back longingly to the days when a combination of self-help and royal indulgence could produce a quicker result. Robert III de Montfort recovered his father's Norman lands by kidnapping Waleran of Meulan, his wicked father-in-law, towards the end of 1153. Subsequently, when, with Henry II on the throne, such tactics were no longer permitted, he turned his attention to the English lands of his family, the Honour of Haughley (Suff.) to which was attached the constableship of England. This was then held by a cousin of his, Henry of Essex, whose title to it might well have proved good. But again Robert proved lucky. He found an opportunity to accuse his cousin of treason, having deserted the king in a battle against the Welsh. He challenged him to trial by battle, defeated him and was awarded his estates (April 1163).[4]

---

3 The essential document and commentary is in Patricia M. Barnes, 'The Anstey Case', in *A Medieval Miscellany for Doris Mary Stenton*, ed. Patricia M. Barnes and C. F. Slade (Pipe Roll Soc. lxxvi, for 1960), 1–24.
4 Robert de Torigni (R.S.) iv. 177–8; William of Newburgh (R.S.) i. 108; Gervase of Canterbury (R.S.) i. 165; *The Chronicle of Jocelin of Brakelond*, ed. and trans. H. E. Butler (Nelson's Medieval Classics, London, 1949), 68–71.

The cases of Richard d'Anstey and Robert de Montfort both came to a conclusion in 1163, after Henry II's long stay in France, but by then Henry II was already groping towards the doctrine of seisin which was to prove the key to the matter. The concept was not new (it is found several times in Stephen's reign and in Henry I's too) but the extent of its usefulness was not realized before 1153. The essential point of seisin was that it put one in possession of land by being installed as tenant by the requisite lord. It could be that the man given seisin did not really have a right to the land, but if he had been formally accepted as tenant, it was reasonable that he should be protected in that position until his right had been finally disproved in a court of law.

Henry II made it his business to give such protection. As time went on he realized that the essential point was to make it clear that this protection was limited to those who had been disseised within a specified period of time such as 'since the king last crossed to Normandy', usually no more than a year or so before. With such a formula the disinherited were not betrayed because their ultimate rights were not affected, but they were prevented from taking the law into their own hands. Their best hope was to wait for the deaths of their rivals in possession, and then present themselves to the relevant lord as the 'lawful heir'. But that took time, and time encouraged everyone to compromise if they possibly could.

The doctrine of seisin thus came to be the *sine qua non* of the pacification of England. It secured the hereditary system in spite of the hereditary disputes which in 1135 had made civil war inevitable. It could not satisfy everyone always, but it did satisfy most of the people most of the time, and gain the time necessary for the healing of old wounds and the establishment of a more stable society.

5 The whole of this subject has been put in a new light by S. F. C. Milsom, *The Legal Framework of English Feudalism* (Cambridge, 1976) which is a fundamental revision of Maitland's work and has opened up the possibility of yet further revisions. Of these the one which I have found most rewarding is Robert C. Palmer, 'The Feudal Framework of English Law', in *Michigan Law Review* 79 (1981) 1130–64.

Appendix V
The Beaumont Twins: Waleran of Meulan and Robert Earl of Leicester

The complexities of family, feudal and political loyalties have been admirably demonstrated by David Crouch in *The Beaumont Twins* (Cambridge, 1986) and it is important to highlight those of his findings which are most relevant to this book.

The twins' father, Robert de Beaumont I, held the earldom of Leicester in England, the honours of Beaumont, Brionne and Pontaudemer in Normandy and the County of Meulan in France. On his death the Norman and French lands went to Waleran, the elder twin, and the English lands to Robert, the younger, but neither of them was content with lands on one side of the Channel only. Robert acquired a large honour in Normandy by marrying the heiress of Breteuil (1121), and in 1138 King Stephen made Waleran Earl of Worcestershire, with large grants from the royal demesne in that county. When, in 1141, it became clear that the Anglo-Norman realm would be split, with Stephen remaining dominant in England and the Angevins taking over in Normandy, the Beaumont twins took prompt action to safeguard each other's interests. Waleran retreated to Normandy even though that meant deserting Stephen for the Empress (above, pp. 64–5), while Robert stayed in England, loyal to the King. Each protected the other's interests as best he could and juggled with his various loyalties. Robert made a success of it, transferring his allegiance to Duke Henry at the vital moment in 1153 and serving him as justiciar till his death in 1168. Waleran, on the other hand, was a clear loser by 1154. Excessive ambition may have played some part in his downfall, but the most important factor in it was that he had to contend not just with the rulers of England and Normandy, but also with the King of France from whom he held the County of Meulan. The French kings were habitually at war with the Normans, the most convenient route for their armies being through the County of Meulan. Sooner or later Waleran was bound to be placed in an impossible position, as he was in 1152 when he had to give Louis VII free passage across the bridge of Meulan so that he could attack Duke Henry (Waleran's liege lord) in Normandy. It was inevitable that Waleran should subsequently be mistrusted.

His position in England was hardly easier. One difficulty was inherent in the grant which Stephen made him (c. 1138) of the earldom of Worcestershire and lands from the forests and royal demesne of that county, for although the office and lands were genuinely within the gift of the crown, they had in practice been enjoyed by someone else. William de Beauchamp considered that the castle, sheriffdom and management of the forests and royal demesne of the county were virtually the perquisites of his family, acquisitions which had in practice become hereditary, having been held at some time or other by his father, uncle and grand-father. Stephen tried to overcome this difficulty by forcing William to become Waleran's tenant and vassal so that he continued to do the work of sheriff, though now under Waleran's authority. But naturally William attempted to escape Waleran's tutelage by deserting Stephen at the first opportunity. This he did in 1141, and he was rewarded by the Empress with a splendid charter which she gave him at Oxford between 25 July and 1 August (*Reg.* iii. 68). In it she granted him Worcester castle to be held of her in chief by hereditary right, and the sheriffdom and forests of Worcestershire to be held at the same rent (*firma*) as his father Walter had paid. 'And for this', continued the Empress,

> he became my liege man against all mortals, and specifically against Waleran Count of Meulan, in such a way that neither Count Waleran nor anyone else shall come to terms with me about these things, but that the said William shall always hold them from me in chief, unless he himself with good will and by voluntary concession should wish to hold them from the Count.

In other words, William de Beauchamp recognized that the Empress was likely to receive an approach from Waleran also, and was trying to ensure that she did not double-cross him by buying Waleran's support with exactly the same grants as had been made to him. In fact Waleran did succeed in making peace with the Empress within a very few weeks. As part of the bargain he allowed her to make herself the founder of 'his' abbey of

Bordesley (the endowments he had given it being manors of the royal demesne whose alienation by anyone but herself she was not prepared to recognize).

The relevant charters (*Reg.* iii. 115–16) were witnessed by both Waleran and William. We cannot be sure how they had settled their differences, but within a few years William de Beauchamp was once again holding the sheriffdom of Worcestershire from Waleran. As recompense Waleran had betrothed him to his own daughter (born in 1142 or 1143) and addressed him in the missives which he sent to him from France as 'his son', perhaps indicating adoption as his heir in the same way a Stephen was eventually to adopt Duke Henry (above, p. 119). Since Waleran could not easily come to England, it was understood that his twin brother, Robert Earl of Leicester, would co-operate with, or supervise, William de Beauchamp in Worcestershire, even though Robert was still supporting the King and William the Empress. Not surprisingly this arrangement had its difficulties and there was a crisis when Waleran's men, abandoning all pretence of friendship with William de Beauchamp, captured Worcester Castle and imprisoned William in it. Roger Earl of Hereford, a leading supporter of the Empress, was anxious to rescue William who was his ally, but what is astonishing is the fact that in order to do so he asked for, and got, assistance from King Stephen. Jointly they laid siege to Waleran's men in Worcester. The fact that they were unsuccessful was due, according to Henry of Huntingdon, to the guile of Robert Earl of Leicester who (more mindful of his duty to his twin-brother than to the king), managed to get the king's siege works destroyed. (Cf. above, p. 111.) No matter how the lawyers might define the concepts of liege-lord and liege-homage, it was clear that political and feudal obligations were not as enduring as family loyalty.

But family loyalty must not be exaggerated. The Beaumonts were a major clan. In addition to the twins, Waleran and Robert, there was a third brother, Hugh, whom Stephen made Earl of Bedford and who was a failure. Among their first cousins were Roger Earl of Warwick who played a lone hand in England, Robert de Neubourg who looked after Waleran's Norman lands in times of distress, Rotrou Bishop of Evreux and many relatives by marriage. Dr Crouch's conclusion after a thorough analysis of their resources is that 'kinship was convenient as a justification but might be discarded at need'. The Beaumont family never formed a power-bloc but only a loose and sporadic federation.

Appendix VI
Geoffrey de Mandeville

Two articles by Mr J. O. Prestwich in *E.H.R.* 103 (1988), 288–312 and 960–67 question my chronology of the charters granted by Geoffrey de Mandeville and consequently my account of his career, and urge a return to the dating and general interpretation proposed in 1892 by J. H. Round. Though I responded to these articles at the time, I give a summary of the matter here, because the interpretation of Stephen's reign which I have given in this book depends very largely on my interpretation of Geoffrey de Mandeville. He received two charters from Stephen (S1 and 2) and two from Matilda (M1 and 2), printed in G. *de M.* 51–3, 88–96, 140–4, 166–72 and in *Reg.* iii 273–6. Their dates and order as proposed by Round and Prestwich on the one hand and by me on the other are:

Prestwich/Round		Davis	
S1	1140	S1	1140
M1	Midsummer 1141	M1	Midsummer 1141
		M2	25 July–1 Aug. 1141
S2	Christmas 1141	S2	Christmas 1141
M2	Jan–June 1142		

What is at issue is the date of M2 which Prestwich and Round put after S2 (thus making Geoffrey change sides twice) while I put it before S2 (making Geoffrey change sides only once).

I first suspected that the date of M2 must have been 25 July–1 August 1141 (after Miles of Gloucester had been created Earl of Hereford and before the Empress left Oxford for the siege of Winchester) when I realized that two of the 'hostages', Wido de Sablé and Pagan de Clairvaux, were a couple of Angevins whose only other known attestations in England were all at Oxford in July 1141. Prestwich does not deny this but he claims that since in M2 , as in the twin charter for Aubrey de Vere, these two Angevins are not termed witnesses but 'hostages' they need not have been present. For my part I do not see what could have been the point of having hostages if they were not present to swear to their principals' loyalty or to surrender themselves as sureties, but I admit that nothing can (as yet) be proved about this. I therefore turn to the ten men named as *both* hostages *and* witnesses. Prestwich considers that they do not form an 'unusual combination, unlikely to have been with the empress at any other time', but in this he is mistaken. Though some of the witnesses are common, others are rare. Robert de Courcy attested no more than 5 charters for the Empress in England, all of them at Oxford within the period 1141–42, one of them dated 25 July 1141. Robert fitz Hildebrand witnessed no more than four charters for the Empress anywhere; one has no place-date, two are M2 and its de Vere twin both at Oxford, and the fourth is M1, the charter which the Empress gave Geoffrey de Mandeville at Westminster at midsummer 1141. Miles de Beauchamp only witnessed three charters for the Empress; all were given at Oxford, two being M2 and its de Vere twin, and the third for his relative William de Beauchamp given between 25 July and 1 August 1141. The witnesses point emphatically to the same date as the hostages.

Prestwich is impressed by Round's doctrine that it was essential to put the charters in order before attempting to date them. He recognizes that it is necessary to abandon Round's question-begging 'ascending scale' whereby each charter should 'represent an advance on its immediate predecessor', but remains convinced of Round's contention that S2 'expressly confirms' M1, and that S2 is 'expressly referred to' in M2. So far as our difference is concerned, it is only the second of these relationships that is at issue, and it is noticeable at once that here Round's language is less emphatic than in the other. He says only that S2 is 'expressly referred to' in M2. But is it? There are two references to lands which King Stephen and Queen Matilda gave Geoffrey, and another to a charter of the Queen. There is no reference to a *charter* of the King. Prestwich makes a good case for thinking that nonetheless the lands referred to as having been granted by King Stephen and his Queen are granted also in S2, but even that proves nothing about the respective dates of the two charters, because the simplest explanation of both is that both were confirmations of previous grants made by Stephen and his queen. Prestwich denies this, considering that all the items following the first general confirmation–clause in S2 must have been new grants. Here he is relying on an interpretation of charter formulae which is certainly too strict for this date. It has long been recognized that before 1150 the word *dare* (to give) could be used for renewals of grants as well as new gifts (Sir Frank Stenton, *The First Century of English Feudalism* (2nd ed. 1961), p. 162.. Cf. J. G. H. Hudson's Oxford D.Phil thesis, 'Legal Aspects of Seigneurial Control of Land in the century after the Norman Conquest', (1988), pp. 207ff.). Turning from the general to the particular, one of Prestwich's supposedly 'new' grants in S2 is the custody of the Tower of London (*et praeterea dedi ei et concessi custodiam turris Londonie*), but Geoffrey must have had it for the previous eleven months at least. He had it already when he detained Stephen's Queen and daughter-in-law in it, probably during (and certainly no later than) Stephen's captivity, so that Stephen must have given it to him before he was defeated at Lincoln on 2 February 1141 (see p. 58 above).

Finally it must be stressed that while the chronology which I have proposed fits well with the evidence of the chronicles, that of Prestwich and Round does not. William of Malmesbury (*Hist. Nov.* para. 499) mentions that though Geoffrey had sworn allegiance to the Empress (June 1141), he reverted to Stephen's Queen in order to assist her at the siege of Winchester (August–September 1141). The *Gesta Stephani* (p. 160) states that before his arrest in 1143 Geoffrey had brought the King's part of England so firmly under control that 'everywhere . . . he took the King's place and was listened to more eagerly than the King'. (Prestwich himself (p. 299) is prepared to place him 'in the line of succession to Ranulf Flambard, Robert Beaumont, Count of Meulan, and Roger of Salisbury'). How then can it be suggested that while Geoffrey was acting virtually as the King's chief justiciar, he was negotiating also with the Empress in what must have been a blaze of publicity (10 witnesses and 15 hostages) without any chronicler noticing the fact? Prestwich thinks that Stephen did know about the treaty, but seeing that it would not be binding until ratified by the Empress's husband and son (p. 293), thought it prudent not to arrest Geoffrey till matters had developed further, even though this involved a delay of several months. I have to admit that I find this interpretation of the *Gesta Stephani* far-fetched in the extreme. I prefer to take the straightforward meaning of the chronicles, and see no reason to alter the account of Geoffrey's arrest on pp. 78–9 above.

Appendix VII
Ranulf Earl of Chester and Coventry

In *E.H.R.* 86 (1971), 533–45 I published a charter of Ranulf Earl of Chester in which he granted Coventry to Robert Marmion. I dated it 1145–46 and noted that it stated that it was one of several agreements between Earl Ranulf and Robert Marmion. I linked it with an agreement between Earl Ranulf and Robert Earl of Leicester which was made 'in the fields between Leicester and Mountsorel'. In it Earl Ranulf granted Charley and all his woods next to the forest of Leicester to Earl Robert, without receiving anything in return. This transaction was, like the grant to Robert Marmion, datable to 1145–46, just at the time when Earl Ranulf was attempting to transfer his allegiance from the Empress to King Stephen (above, pp. 91–2), and I suggested that they could have been two of a whole series of agreements by which Earl Ranulf had attempted to buy his way back into favour with Stephen's supporters.

  J. H. Round had always assumed that in Stephen's reign barons could change sides at will. I believe that I have persuaded the vast majority of historians that in this matter he was wrong, and that neither Ranulf Earl of Chester nor Geoffrey de Mandeville had changed sides as often as he had supposed. But it still has to be emphasized that so far from being easy, changing sides was very difficult. Though the King or Empress might have been happy to purchase the support of a hostile baron, they were likely to meet opposition from their own supporters. This was because some of them, perhaps even many of them, would have lost lands to that particular baron in the course of the war, and it would have been only natural if they had not wished to receive him as a friend until he had made good their losses. Thus when Earl Ranulf, having defeated Stephen at Lincoln, attempted to rejoin his Queen at Winchester, it was not she but her army who rejected him (above, p. 59, n. 25). Similarly the *Gesta Stephani* tells us that after Earl Ranulf made peace with Stephen at Stamford in 1145, it was the King's barons and counsellors who reminded him of the crown estates which he still had to surrender, and harped on his untrustworthiness until he agreed to go back on his word and arrest the earl (above, pp. 91–2). In my opinion it is in this context that Earl Ranulf's grants to Robert Marmion and Robert Earl of Leicester should be seen. He was trying to purchase the support of those whose interests he had damaged. But there must have been many more than those two; those whom he is known to have despoiled included Earl Alan of Richmond, John Count of Eu, William Peverel of Nottingham, William d'Aubigny *Brito*, William Clerfaith and Gilbert de Gant. Were they all to receive grants as war reparation? And if not, how were they to be placated? Earl Ranulf would surely have laughed at the idea of changing sides being easy. He had tried it twice and had failed twice.

This general thesis has not been questioned in print, but doubts have been expressed about the two charters on which it was based.[1] Taking first the agreement with the Earl of Chester, Edmund King disagrees with my interpretation of it. He finds 'something implausible in the idea of two of the greatest men in England settling their differences over a piece of waste land in the Midlands by hard bargaining in the open fields',[2] but he was unable to offer an alternative explanation for the final words of the charter, written exactly where one would expect the place-date—*et agris deinter Legrecastram et Montsorel*—and apparently saw no parallel with the bargaining which took place between King John and his barons at Runnymede. Edmund King also finds it 'difficult to see what the Earl of Chester was up to' since 'in a period of five years he went from having a "secure castle" at Mountsorrel, to granting this castle to another earl, and then

---

1 Edmund King, 'Mountsorrel and its region in King Stephen's reign', *Huntington Library Quarterly* 44 (1980), 1–10; ed. Trevor John, *Medieval Coventry—a city divided?* (Coventry, 1981), itself a debate on the theme of R. H. C. Davis, *The Early History of Coventry* (Dugdale Soc., Occasional Papers, no. 24, 1976); ed. Geoffrey Barraclough, *The Charters of the Anglo-Norman Earls of Chester*, c. 1027–1237 (Record Soc. of Lancs and Cheshire, 1988) nos. 74–5.

2 King, *op.cit.* p. 3.

asking for lodging rights in it whenever he was in the district'.[3]
In my view such changes could easily occur in a civil war and can
be explained by the circumstances of the three charters involved.
If the first dated from 1145 when Ranulf was trying to make
peace with Stephen, the second could date from the time of his
arrest when Stephen ordered him to surrender his castle, and the
third (1149–53) when Earl Ranulf's fortunes had improved and
Stephen's were declining rapidly. Finally Edmund King considers that in the first charter 'the fields between Mountsorrel
and Leicester' could not have been neutral ground, since in his
view Earl Ranulf 'neither built Mountsorrel nor controlled it at
any time in Stephen's reign'[4]—and this in spite of the fact that one
of the charters under discussion was precisely a grant of
Mountsorrel by Ranulf Earl of Chester. It is also contradicted by
Edmund King's own demonstration that Mountsorrel was in the
parish of Rothley, for Rothley was granted or confirmed to Earl
Ranulf both by King Stephen in 1146 and by Duke Henry in
1153.[5]

Earl Ranulf's grant of Coventry to Robert Marmion is a more
difficult matter. It is written in a twelfth-century hand, but not (it
seems) by any of the earl's regular scribes. At one point the
original text has been erased and a phrase of nine words super-
imposed, and the seal is not Ranulf's but belongs to the late-
thirteenth century. As a result Joan Lancaster and (with some
hesitation) Geoffrey Barraclough have regarded it as a forgery.[6]
On the other hand it is hard to believe that the forger of a completely
new document would have produced it with such an obvious alter-
ation to the text. It is known that Robert Marmion had ambitions
on Coventry, and there is nothing wrong with the witness-list. An
endorsement of the charter is in the hand of Arthur Gregory who
in 1573 acquired the manor of Stivichal on his marriage to Jane
Ferrers of Tamworth; Tamworth being part of the former barony
of Marmion. Arthur Gregory then called Stivichal 'Marmion's
manor of Coventry', and embarked on a lengthy dispute with the

3 King, *op.cit.* p. 2

4 King, *op.cit.* p. 7

5 *Reg.* iii. 178 and 180. Graeme White, 'King Stephen, Duke Henry and Ranulf de
Gernons Earl of Chester', *E.H.R.* (1876), 555–65 shows (p. 556) that in these charters
Roelis is not Rowley Regis as stated in *Reg.* iii, but Rothley (Leics). It was probably
this error (mine) which caused Dr King to overlook these two charters.

6 Joan Lancaster in Trevor John, *op.cit.* pp. 33–5; Barraclough, *op.cit.* pp. 88–9.

Coventry corporation over his right to a court leet there, the corporation in its turn accusing him of forgery. 'Improving' a genuine charter would have been right in his line.[7]

The case for an authentic base to this charter is strengthened by Barraclough's rediscovery of another charter of Earl Ranulf's for Robert Marmion, very similar in style and with three of the same witnesses.[8] This time it is a grant of 'the fee of Robert of Arden' which was based on Kingsbury (Warwickshire) which, though fifteen miles away, was a dependency of what was later known as the Earl of Chester's manor of Cheylesmore in Coventry.[9] The original document is lost, but when Dugdale saw it in 1636 it was still in the possession of John Ferrers of Tamworth; in other words it had not fallen into the hands of Arthur Gregory. Barraclough considered it to be genuine, and the Coventry charter a forgery, but in my opinion the similarity of the two charters in content, formulae and provenance (till 1573) means that they must stand or fall together.

In that case it is probable that they are genuine. Their contents hang together neatly and it is hard to believe that they could have been invented by a forger. What is more there is no trace of any dispute between the Marmions and the Earls of Chester over Coventry except in 1144. William of Newburgh relates that then Robert II de Marmion turned the cathedral priory into a castle, and on the earl of Chester's approach went out to attack him, but fell into a ditch which he had dug as a trap for his enemies and was killed.[10] In the next year Earl Ranulf transferred his

7 Robert Bearman, 'Arthur Gregory and the Coventry Charter', *E.H.R.* 86 (1971), 545–7. I would further suggest that the reason for inserting the words *quod serviat mihi contra omnes homines et omnes mulieres* was to forestall arguments that Queen Isabella, who had inherited the Earl of Chester's residual rights in Coventry in 1330, had subsequently passed them on to the town.

8 Barraclough, *op.cit.*, no. 74 (p. 87) from Oxford, Bodleian Library, Dugdale MS. 13, p. 268. Dugdale's transcript is a facsimile in that it attempts to reproduce the script of the original (which is not like that of the Coventry charter but might be like that of the agreement with the Earl of Leicester), but does not give the outline of the parchment or show if there was any tongue, tag or seal.

9 Dugdale made the identification of Osbert's fee with Kingsbury and was clearly right, as shown by the charters which he transcribed next. See also *V. C. H. Warwickshire*, iv. 104. In Domesday Book, i. 239ᵛ, Kingsbury and Coventry are both shown as land of the Countess Godiva, held in farm from the king by one Nicholas. The manor of Cheylesmore makes its first appearance in 1249 as chief among the rights reserved to the Earls of Chester, *The Early Records of Medieval Coventry,*, ed. P. R. Coss (Records of Social and Economic History, N.S. xi, London, 1986) no. 22a (p. 33).

10 Newburgh, BK. i, ch. 12.

allegiance to the King, and it would not be surprising if, in doing so, he had had to buy off the hostility of Marmion's son (called Robert like his father) who was a minor, apparently in the custody of his widowed mother's second husband, Richard de Camville. He was one of Stephen's closest advisers (p. 67 above) with many lands in the South Midlands; Stephen would have found him a natural choice as constable of Coventry, and Earl Ranulf would have been glad to purchase his goodwill.

Appendix VIII
Regesta iii: Additions and Corrections

The following charters were missed by Professor Cronne and myself when we were editing *Regesta Regum Anglo-Normennorum 1066–1154, vol. iii, Regesta Regis Stephani ac Mathildis Imperatricis ac Gaufridi et Henrici Ducum Normanorum, 1135–1154* (Oxford, 1968). The first four, hitherto unpublished, were discovered by Dr David Crouch whose transcripts are printed here by his permission. The remaining seven have all been printed since 1968, and consequently I do not print the full texts here, but simply the necessary references.

207a Coggeshall Abbey (1147–52 at Coggeshall) Confirmation of the Queen's grant of the Abbey of Coggeshall

> S. rex Angl(orum) archiepiscopis, episcopis, abbatibus, comitibus, baronibus, iusticiis, vicecomitibus, et omnibus ministris et fidelibus suis Francis et Anglis totius Angl(ie), salutem. Sciatis quia prece et requisitione Matill(dis) regine vxoris mee et Eustach(ii) filii mei dedi et concessi et in perpetuam elemosinam confirmaui deo et ecclesie beate Marie de Coggeshala et abbati et monachis ibidem deo seruientibus manerium de Coggeshala totum cum omnibus pertinentiis suis. Quare volo et firmiter precipio quod ecclesia predicta et monachi teneant et habeant totam terram predictam bene et in pace et libere et quiete et honorifice in bosco et plano et pratis et pasturis et hominibus et aquis et stagnis et molendinis et viis et semitis et soca eṭ saca et tol et team et infangenetheof et omnibus aliis rebus et libertatibus et liberis consuetudinibus que ad terram illam pertinent cum quibus ego habebam illam in manu mea et dominio meo et sicut alie ecclesie melius vel liberius tenent alias elemosinas meas. Et vt hec donatio mea et confirmatio perdurent presentis sigilli mei impressione confirmo et subscriptorum attestatione corroboro. T(estibus) M. regina et Eustach(io) comite

Bolon(ie), et H. abbate Colecestr(ie), et Will(elm)o de Ipra, et
Will(elm)o de Mitrc' (*sic*) et Ric(ard)o de Luc(i), et Henr(ico) de Essexa,
et Ham(one) de sancto Claro, et Fulc(one) de Oilly, et Rog(er)o de
Fraxin(eto), et Henr(ico) [de] Nouo mercat(o), et Roberto de Valenc',
Apud Coggeshale.

MS. P.R.O. C56/52, m. 3 (Confirmation Roll, 7/8 Henry VIII)
Date: While the queen was alive, and Eustace was Count of
Boulogne.

207b Coggeshall Abbey (1135–46 at *Osinforth*) The Queen orders
her officials of Dover, Wissant and Boulogne that the monks are
to be free of toll and *transue*

M. dei gratia regina Angl(orum) ministris suis de Doure et de Wisant
et de Bolun(ia), salutem. Mando vobis et precipio quatenus abbas et
monachi de elemosina mea de Coggeshala sint quieti cum omnibus
rebus suis de tolneto et transue [sic] et omnibus consuetudinibus per
totam terram meam et Eust(achii) filii mei de Angl(ia) et Bolonia nec
quisquam super hoc eis disturbet vel inquietet. T(estibus) Rad(ulf)o (*sic*)
Luc', et Will(elm)o filio Gaut(eri), et Ric(ard)o de Monte acuto. Apud
Osinforth'.

MS. PRO C56/52 m. 3 (Confirmation Roll, 7/8 Henry VIII)
Date: While the queen was alive and before Eustace was count of
Boulogne. Though the name 'Osinforth' looks 'Oxenford', it is
hard to see why a Tudor scribe wrote it as he did unless that was
what was in his exemplar.

207c Coggeshall Abbey (1140–54 at London) Confirmation of the
grant by Geoffrey de Tregoz of land at Tolleshunt (Essex)

S. rex Angl(orum) episcopo London(ensi) et iusticiis et
vicecomitibus et baronibus et ministris et omnibus fidelibus suis de
Essex', salutem. Sciatis me concessisse et confirmasse donationem
illam quam Gaufr(idus) de Tresgoz fecit ecclesie sancte Marie de
Coggeshala et monachis in ea deo seruientibus de vna virgata terre
apud Toleshonta et de sexaginta acris terre iuxta illam et de
communi pasture ville eiusdem. Quare volo et precipio quod
ecclesia illa et monachi et terram et pasturam illam bene et in pace
et libere et quiete et honorifice teneant in perpetuam elemosinam
solutam et quietam de omni seculari seruitio et exactione sicut
predictus Gaufr(id)us eam illis dedit et concessit et carta sua
confirmauit. T(estibus) Warin(o) de Lusor', et H. de Essexc' et
Jord(ano) de Blossen(uilla). Apud London'.

MS. P.R.O. C56/52 m. 3 (Confirmation Roll of 7/8 Henry VIII)
Date: Henry of Essex and Warner de Lusors suggest a date no
earlier than 1140.

207d Coggeshall Abbey (1147–54 at Colchester). The abbey to have the lands of Adam de Beaunay as recognized by inquest.

S. rex Angl(orum) hominibus de Coggeshala salutem. Precipio quod omnes terre scilicet Gauelland er Cocland vel qualescumque sint que ante Adam de Belum[1] et alios ministros meos pro nostrum (*sic*) iusurand(o) fuerunt recognite et addite dominio per considerationem eiusdem Ade, et aliorum qui cum eo fuerunt, sint in dominio ecclesie. Et abbas et monachi bene et in pace eas teneant. Ne aliquis super hoc eos vexare vel inquietare presumat quod si fecerit minister comitis Eus(achii) filii[2] mei de Essex iustitiam eis modo faciant. T(este) H. de Essex'. Apud Colcestr'.

1 MS. Bolon(ia)
2 MS repeats filii.
MS. P.R.O. C56/52 m. 3 (Confirmation Roll 7/8 Henry VIII)
Date: While Eustace was Count of Boulogne.

340a Gisney (or Gigny), William de (1138–52 at Woodbridge). Confirmation of the grant by Gilbert Earl of Hertford of all his land in Haveringland (Norf.) and Whitwell (Norf.). Printed, *Stoke-by-Clare Cartulary*, ed. Christopher Harper-Bill and Richard Mortimer *Suff. Rec. Soc: Suffolk Charters* 4, (1982), no. 9.

342a Glastonbury Abbey (probably Nov. 1153, at Winchester). Duke Henry commands the Earl of Gloucester to reseise Bishop Henry (the abbot) and monks of Siston (Glos). Printed R. B. Patterson in *EHR* 87 (1972), 755; discussed and redated by David Crouch in *EHR* 102 (1988) 71–2. Mr N. E. Stacey tells me that there is a further MS. source for this charter in B.L., Add. MS. 22934, f. 42.

365b Gloucester, Robert son of the Earl of (Jan. 1154, at Dunstable). Duke Henry grants him the honour of Eudo Dapifer. Printed: David Crouch in *EHR* 102 (1988), 69–70.

463a Lincoln Cath. and See (1135–39, at Westminster). Roger of Salisbury orders the sheriff, constable and burghers of Lincoln to let the bishop have the 20*s* of land as commanded by the king. This is to be done according to the oath of 12 men of the city and 23 of the neighbourhood of Lincoln. Printed, *Reg. Antiq.* vii, no. 2050

837a Stixwould Priory (Nov./Dec. 1153–Oct. 1154 at St Albans). General Confirmation. Printed by Graeme White in *E.H.R.* 91 (1976), 565.

837b Stoke-by-Clare Priory (June 1143–49). Confirmation of the grant of the manor of Fornham (in Stoke) by Geoffrey son of Elinald. Printed, *Stoke-by-Clare Cartulary* (op. cit.), no. 8.

920a Warden Abbey (1146–54 and probably 1146). Confirmation of the grant of Sawtry (Huntingd.) to Warden Abbey (*beate Marie de Essartis*) by Earl Simon. Printed by Keith Stringer in *Journ of Soc. of Archivists* 6 (1980), 333. Cf. *Reg*. iii. 736.

CORRECTIONS

Introduction

pp. xvi–xvii.   The 'forged first seal' should now be regarded as a genuine seal in use from 1138 to June 1139. See p. 86 n.4.

p. xix l.22   for never *read* only once.

p. xix n.4 For v. 81 *read* v. 83, *and after* iv. 132. *add Cf.* **749**.

p. xxv   In list of sheriffs add for Lincs Hugh fitz Eudo *with ref. to* **463e**
 add for Oxon Atsur, c. 1150–3.

p. xxv n.7 *for* 1143 *read* 1138.

Charters

43   Re-date as 1146–47 during the young Henry's second visit to England (p. xlvi).

50   Original in London, College of Arms, Monastic Charters, Misc. 172.

116   Original charter now (since 1968) British Library, Add. Ch 75724.

178 and **180**   The following places are wrongly identified in the notes and index. Graham should be Grantham, not Greetham; Roeleia should be Rothley (Leics.) not Rowley; Derby should be the county borough, not West Derby (Lancs), Hecham (180) is Higham Ferrers (Northants). (Graeme White in *E.H.R.* xci (1976) 555–65.)

274   In the notes (p. 101, l.4) *for* Ashmole MS. 843 *read* Ashmole MS. 841 and in l.9. *after* IMPERATRIX *add* ROM'.

288   Original charter is now (since 1969), British Library, Add. Ch. 75727.

308 Note that Maurice fitz Geoffrey is identifiable as Maurice de Tiretot. (Graeme White, *E.H.R.* xci (1976), 555–65.)

626 The seal is no longer regarded a forgery.

631 In heading *for* at Oseney *read* at Oxford.

639 The date is probably 1150–52 (not c. 1138–39). See R. H. C. Davis in *Oxoniensia* xxxiii (1968), 60–1

679 The seal is no longer regarded a forgery. The date should be either Sept.–Dec. 1138 or April–Aug. 1139, while Waleran of Meulan was in England and before Henry Bishop of Winchester was papal legate.

718 The seal is no longer regarded a forgery.

749 The second witness should be R(oberto), not 'Roger' Earl of Gloucester.

820 Re-date as c. 1144 (M. Chibnall in *T.R.H.S*, 5th series 38 (1988), 111, n. 12).

836 The original charter is in the County Record Office, Trowbridge, Wilts, Accession 1213.

837 The original charter is now in the County Record Office, Trowbridge, Wilts, Accession 473/5

920 Re-date 1146–53, after the inauguration of Warden Abbey (K. Stringer, *Journ. Soc. Archivists* 6 (1980), 326.

922 Original charter now on loan to Shakespeare Birthday Trust, Stratford-upon-Avon.

963 and **964** The seals of these charters are no longer regarded as forgeries.

991 The second witness should be A(lgaro) episcopo Sancti Laudi as in n. 2.

In vol. iv (1969) the following charters should be added to the location list on pp. 27–31:

London, College of Arms; Monastic Charters, Misc. 172	? S **50**
Oxford, Oriel College Charter 416.	? S **636**
Wiltshire Record Office, Trowbridge, Acc.1213	? M **836**
Wiltshire Record Office, Trowbridge, Acc.473/5	? H **837**

In the same list the following changes of location should be noted:

(p. 29) London, Robinson Trust	**288**	now B.L. Add. Ch. 75727
(p. 31) Mr Edward Willes	**116**	now B.L. Add. Ch. 75724
(p. 31) Col. A. Gregory-Hood	**922**	now on loan to Shakespeare Birthday Trust, Stratford-upon-Avon

In the same list, p. 28:
l.24 (Ch. S 314) *for* xxii *read* xxi
l.37 (H 438) *for S read* H
l.38 (H 438 bis) *for S read* H

Genealogical Table

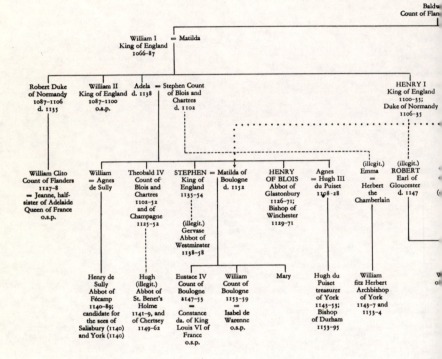

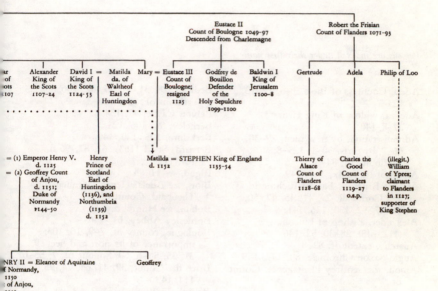

	Alexander King of the Scots 1107-24	David I King of the Scots 1124-53	= Matilda da. of Waltheof Earl of Huntingdon	Mary =	Eustace II Count of Boulogne 1049-97 Descended from Charlemagne			Robert the Frisian Count of Flanders 1071-93	
...107					Eustace III Count of Boulogne; resigned 1125	Godfrey de Bouillon Defender of the Holy Sepulchre 1099-1100	Baldwin I King of Jerusalem 1100-8	Gertrude	Adela	Philip of Loo

Eustace II
Count of Boulogne 1049-97
Descended from Charlemagne

Robert the Frisian
Count of Flanders 1071-93

= (1) Emperor Henry V. d. 1125
= (2) Geoffrey Count of Anjou, d. 1151; Duke of Normandy ?1144-50

Henry Prince of Scotland Earl of Huntingdon (1136), and Northumbria (1139) d. 1152

Matilda = STEPHEN King of England
d. 1152   1135-54

Thierry of Alsace Count of Flanders 1128-68

Charles the Good Count of Flanders 1119-27 o.s.p.

(illegit.) William of Ypres; claimant to Flanders in 1127; supporter of King Stephen

...NRY II = Eleanor of Aquitaine
of Normandy, 1150
: of Anjou, 1151
f Aquitaine, 1153
of England 154-89

Geoffrey

Index